Contents

	Introduction	4
	Dinky Toys History	5
	General Notes	6
	How to Use the Tables	7
Section 1	Army – *military vehicles, guns*	8
Section 2	Buses – *buses and coaches*	13
Section 3	Cars – *road and racing cars*	16
Section 4	Dublo Dinky – *range of small scale vehicles from the late 1950s*	30
Section 5	Farm Machinery – *tractors and farm implements*	31
	Colour Picture section	33
Section 6	Figures – *early lead figures, army personnel*	89
Section 7	Hong Kong Dinky – *1/42 scale American cars*	93
Section 8	Kits of Dinky Toys – *kit versions of some Dinky toys*	94
Section 9	Miscellaneous – *everything else!*	96
Section 10	Planes – *pre-war and post-war planes, the 1970s Big Planes*	102
Section 11	Plant (Construction) – *diggers, rollers, earthmoving equipment, cranes*	108
Section 12	Service Vehicles – *Police, ambulances, taxis, transporters*	110
Section 13	Ships – *waterline ships, the large wheeled boats*	115
Section 14	Tankers – *petrol tankers*	117
Section 15	Trains – *the small pre-war trains and signals*	119
Section 16	Trucks – *general commercial vehicles*	121
Section 17	TV Related Models	128
Section 18	Vans – *delivery vans with advertising*	130
Section 19	1/25 Scale Cars – *1/25 scale Ford Capri models*	136

6213476000

Introduction

"Dinky" Toys are undoubtedly the first name that springs to mind when we think of collectable models of road vehicles. This name has the same generic meanings as the "Hoover" with which we vacuum our floors, and "Black & Decker" our DIY efforts. The generic name of 'Dinky' is thoroughly justified, as the following pictures and tables will prove.

I had my first Dinky Toy, a 22c Motor Truck (which I still have), bought for me at the outbreak of World War II. At that time I was too young to appreciate it but further Dinkies were bought to ensure that I could have a continuous supply of birthday and Christmas presents during the war when toys were no longer produced. I started collecting seriously when I left my parents' home in 1960 and moved into my own flat. About 60 of my old Dinkies were found in the top of my old wardrobe. These had been overlooked in earlier trawls through childhood things in search for items to sell to raise money for real cars. These Dinkies, some 30, 36, 38, 39 and 40 series cars were put into a china cabinet in the new flat and admired by all visitors. It was then a very small step to go out and add the new cars to the collection even though the idea of adults 'playing with toys' was not generally acceptable. We collectors, and there were quite a few of us even then, used to buy them for fictitious younger brothers and nephews to avoid embarrassment in the local corner shop.

A significant milestone was the appearance of a magazine in England in late 1963, *Model Roads and Racing* soon to be renamed *Miniature Auto*. This had an introduction from no less a person than Stirling Moss, the hero of any car mad youth in those days. This was followed in 1966 by the original 'bible', *The History of British Dinky Toys, 1934–1964* by Dr Cecil Gibson. By this time we had come out of the closet. Our hobby was accepted in the adult world. This small book remained the only reference work until the production of Book 4 of the *Hornby Companion Series* in 1981. This covered the whole of the British production from 1934 to the end of the factory in 1979.

The swap meet scene was started by Cecil Gibson who bravely entertained a mob of collectors at his home in Leicester where toys, mostly Dinkies, were bought, sold, exchanged and admired. The start of club swap meets (open to anyone who turned up) was in 1971 when the Maidenhead Static Model Club held their first event on a dark, wet January Saturday in a badly lit bar of a hotel in Maidenhead.

The collecting population is so large today that there are meetings every weekend in many areas of the UK attended by greater or lesser numbers of dealers and collectors. These days it is possible, without having to travel too far, to visit a meet every Saturday and Sunday, with probably a weekday evening one as well.

Collecting
Dinky Toys

Mike Richardson

Francis Joseph
London
ISBN 1-870703-97-9

Acknowledgements

I would like to thank all collectors of Dinky Toys over the years who have each contributed some chunk of knowledge, however small it may have been, into the great volume of information which is now in the public domain. In particular, I would like to thank Michael Driver for the use of his collection for many of the photographs. The various auction houses have given us excellent illustrated catalogues and also the opportunity to see the many rare models which have passed through their hands. Particular mention must be made of Christies South Kensington in this area, although Phillips, Sotheby's and Vectis have also made considerable contributions in this field over the years.

© 2001 Francis Joseph Publications

ISBN 1-870703-97-9

Published by Francis Joseph,
5 Southbrook Mews, London SE12 8LG
Telephone 020 8318 9580

Photographs: Trevor Leek

Typesetting by
E J Folkard, 199 Station Road, Crayford, Kent DA1 3QF

Printed by Longo Group, Bolzano (Italy)

Front cover photographs: From top left: 237 Mercedes-Benz Racing Car; 30h Daimler Ambulance; 100 Lady Penelope's FAB 1; 29b Streamline Bus; 308 Leyland 308 Tractor.

Dinky Toy History

The Meccano factory in Liverpool started its life making the famous Meccano construction sets. These were made from sheet metal and tinplate and so a logical expansion was into the world of model, or rather toy, railways. Thus Hornby Trains appeared. Train layouts need accessories as effects which add to the realism. This necessitated cast figures for the various people needed on the stations and animals for the fields alongside the tracks. The lead figures were known as 'Modelled Miniatures' to differentiate them from the tinplate Hornby Accessories. When the first set of road vehicles was introduced the brand name was soon changed to 'Dinky Toys'. Hence our story begins in 1934.

An abundance of new introductions got the Dinky range off to an excellent start and it took on a life of its own. Very soon planes, ships and other non railway models were added and the advertising proudly announced 'now 150 varieties' by the end of 1934. These claims increased to 200, 250 and 300 over the years.

The first models were cast in lead but a change was made soon after, to a zinc-based alloy, still used today, called 'mazac'. By the end of 1934 all new models were made of mazac and only the old dies continued to use lead. By the end of 1935 lead was used only for the figures as all other continuing models had changed over. This of course means that some of the 1934/36 models can be found made from either material. The lead models did tend to bend if dropped and most seem to have damage to wing ends, where as the mazac ones survived with only a loss of paint. It is very unfortunate for us now that Meccano did not know the effects that a small contamination of lead would have on mazac models. This is the dreaded 'metal fatigue' which causes the model to expand and become distorted and brittle. The cause is not flexing as in the modern usage of the words but an internal reaction between the molecules. It is significant that the more impure the metal was the simpler the casting it was used for. This is due to the lowering of the flow properties proportional to the increase in impurities. Wheels are the parts most likely to succumb to fatigue expansion. The flat base of the 29c Double Deck Bus and similar chassis are also very often very warped, but the very deep, thin, intricate body of the bus is almost never fatigued.

Production and sale of all metal toys was prohibited by Government Order in 1942 and 1943 respectively to put all efforts into armaments manufacturing. Dinky put their dies into storage to wait for better times. These came in late 1945 when small quantities of metal were released to enable some toys to be on sale for Christmas that year. As the 1943 order caused any existing finished toys to be retained in the factory warehouse, not recycled, it is reasonable to assume that some, if not most, of the toys on sale in 1945 and early 1946 were either made pre-war and stacked, or were assembled in 1945 from mainly pre-war parts. This accounts for the difficulty in saying that a particular model was pre- or post-war. There is considerable overlap here but for convenience and simplicity the tables in this book treat the models in the era when they were manufactured rather than sold. From dated drawings it can be said that thick axles MUST be post-war.

From 1946 new models appeared thick and fast. The new post-war designs of cars were starting to appear on the roads and Dinky followed them in toy form. The colours used on the post-war reissues of the earlier models, the 30, 36, 38 and 39 series cars and similar trucks, were generally harsher in shade. Models also were limited to one or two colour schemes only. Gone were the multiplicity of the beautiful pre-war schemes.

By the early 1950s Dinky realized that their cataloguing system of main number with suffix letter had become unwieldy, and a dramatic change was needed. The original system had been convenient as it was Dinky's intention to sell the pre-war models in boxed sets rather than as loose models over the counter. In this way the buyer was expected to want a 22 Motor Vehicles set rather than a 22a Sports Car. By 1946 this idea had been totally abandoned and the toys reached the retailer in yellow boxes of six. By 1953 many of the models had their own individual yellow card box with the details of the model printed on it. During the period 1953 to 1954 all existing catalogue numbers with suffix letters were replaced by all figure numbers. There have been odd additional renumberings as the name of some models was changed from Dinky Supertoys to Dinky Toys.

As competition grew from other manufacturers both at home and overseas Dinky was forced to add new features to their toys. Windows, steering, suspension, opening doors, engine detail, electric lights, drivers, luggage and many other developments were steadily incorporated. Most of these new ideas were fitted to the new models but windows and drivers were sometimes added to existing models. This applies particularly to the 600 series of army vehicles. From the time when Corgi scooped them with their first advert 'The Ones with Windows' Dinky never quite got their place back in the market. They seemed to trail and were in financial difficulties by 1963. Subsequently they were bought over by Lines Bros, the Tri-ang Group in 1964. Lines had their own range of 1/42 scale Spot-On models but decided to drop them in favour of keeping the Dinky name going. Dinky had much better design and toolroom facilities at the time. Increasing market penetration from their competitors and changing fashions in the desires of children caused financial troubles to return in 1971, and the whole Lines organisation sent into liquidation. The Meccano and Dinky part of the business was sold to Airfix and reformed as Meccano Ltd. By 1977 panic had set in again with frantic attempts to revitalize the toy car market share. But it was all to no avail. The factory ceased production at the end of 1979 and was later pulled down and the site redeveloped.

A few models were assembled overseas in 1980 but these were often sold without printed boxes, and in fact some were even sold in bubble wrap. There was also an attempt to buy some models from their main French rival, Solido, with the Dinky name on the model and the packaging. These were listed as 500-508, but only the first six appeared in the shops.

The subsequent sale of the Dinky name to Matchbox has given collectors a new range of models to seek. They have nothing to do with the toys in this book. None of the old dies exist, or were sold to Matchbox, so production from 1981 onwards should be considered to be Matchbox, not Dinky Toys as we know them.

General Notes

Wheels and Tyres: Prewar the first wheels were lead castings. Next came plain mazac hubs with white, or sometimes bright coloured, rubber tyres. The tyres changed to black before 1939. Postwar the hubs gained a ridge like a hubcap, known as 'ridged' wheels to collectors, and the axles changed from thin to thick wire. Spun aluminium wheels, cast wire spoked and whizzwheels all followed in their time.

Boxes: The pre-war sets were in display boxes mainly with card cutout inserts to hold the models. Some sets were sold in simpler boxes where six models sat in two rows of three separated by vertical cardboard separators. This type of box was used after 1945 to send models to the shops. These boxes were usually surfaced in yellow with the model details printed on the ends of the lid. An austerity version of this box was made in plain brown card with a yellow labels glued to the lid ends. Some one the larger post-war planes had individual boxes of these two type also. Individual yellow cartons were the usual from 1954 to the early 1960s. Then there was a variety of packaging. Rigid clear plastic cases with yellow bases, window boxes, sleeve boxes with clear panels, back again to yellow card boxes, hanging display boxes. The most popular with collectors are the yellow boxes up to 1960.

Colours: Each assembly drawing for a model gives the specification for the paint colour, by internal Dinky reference number, type of tyres, type of wheels, the baseplate, glazing, driver and all other parts to enable consistency to be maintained over the months and years. Even the specification of how the axles are to be rivetted over is included. This is ideal in theory but causes problems in practice. The essence of an assembly line is that it keeps moving, stoppages cost money. For example, if the paint shop is set up to run casting for a van in red G30 and the supply of castings stops an hour or so before the end of the week, rather than clean down the equipment and change colour sometimes it is possible to paint some of the next job red G30 even though it is not specified. The main criterion at this point is, does painting this model, say a saloon car, look inappropriate in red? If the answer is no, then production goes ahead in the 'wrong' colour. This is how we collectors today have these exciting rare batches of odd colours to look for.

Fakes & Repaints: It is an unfortunate fact of life that when rare colour examples can command very much higher prices than the standard version there will be someone out there trying to turn one into the other with intent to deceive the buyer. Repainting and converting models is a perfectly respectable and indeed enjoyable pastime, the problem only occurs when the final intention is less than ethical. The first Foden and Guy trucks were held together by a small screw and nut at the rear making it very easy to switch bodies and cab/chassis units to make different colour combinations. The later ones, and most other Dinkies, were rivetted together making conversion more difficult to conceal, but by no means impossible. Odd decals appear on some models at swap meets and even in auctions and the vendor may suggest that these are rare, and therefore they want a lot of money for them. It is impossible to list all genuine variations in a book small enough to be carried in the pocket, so a general caveat has to be issued. If a model has a box, the colour chip on the box should match the model. If the model does not have a box when it should have, and is shiny mint, ask the question how has it survived in this excellent condition for so many years without protection? Look at axle ends, chassis rivets and any other areas for signs that the model has been taken apart at some point in its life. But, to avoid embarrassment to all concerned, always remember that the vendor did not necessarily do the work themselves, or even suspect that the model has been tampered with. Each collector must be his or her own judge and satisfy themselves of the authenticity of any item they are buying. There is no substitute for experience. The only way to get this expertise is to look at as many models as possible, making a few mistakes which are hopefully not too costly. The main thing to remember is that collecting is fun and that the vast majority of collectors and dealers enjoy what they are doing, are honest and trustworthy, and certainly in the case of dealers, want you to be pleased with your purchase so that they will see to you again.

How to use the tables

The models have been split into sections of like vehicles, except for Miscellaneous which contains all those which do not fit anywhere else. The type of models in each of the sections are listed in the contents page.

Ref No: This is the catalogue number of the model

Reno: This is a previous number (of 40a) or a subsequent renumbering (to 158)

Name: The name of the model given by Dinky

Production period: The year the model was introduced until the last year the model was in the catalogues

Colour: The most common, or specified, colours for the model

Market Value: The prices are, for pre-war and early post-war individual items, i.e. letter suffix catalogue numbers, in mint condition without boxes, except for Set boxes.

For post 1954 items, i.e. all-figure catalogue numbers, items must be mint with the correct mint box. In this context 'mint' means 'as it left the factory'. Models in poorer condition are worth considerably less, a chipped recent model having virtually no value. Where no price is quoted, but the letter "A" used, this indicates that the particular item is so rare that it can usually only be found at auctions. To give a value in these cases would be unrealistic.

Army

During the run up to the Second World War Dinky Toys launched their magnificent range of army vehicles. The Meccano Magazines of the times covered the full sized vehicles and then advertised the toys, which were becoming available in the shops. These models are generally much finer detailed than the contemporary cars and trucks from Dinky, it was almost as if the military toys came from a different factory. The scale was more consistent at 1/60, while the cars were roughly 1/43 and the buses and commercial vehicles were nearer to 1/76.

The pre-war army models were painted gloss green and fitted with green tinplate bases where appropriate. The wire tracks for the tanks and gun tractors were bright plated. The reissues from 1945 were mostly matt green with black bases and tracks. Some models also appeared in brown in the late 1940s.

All the early models were deleted from the British catalogues in1950 though some were still produced for the US market until 1954/55, but in green only.

The next generation of army vehicles was introduced from 1953, the 600 number range. These models were of contemporary vehicles, again very nicely detailed, and formed a very interesting group. These were in production for about ten years and so there are lots of them around today. The early versions were without driver and had no glazing, these were added to most, but not all, during their long run.

During the 1950s Dinky made some special models for the US market only, 139a Ford Staff Car, 30hm Daimler Ambulance and 25wm Bedford truck were some examples. These are strange subjects for sale to American children surely, how many ever saw a Daimler ambulance for real – they were not often seen in England for that matter. Later there was a special white UN version of 674 Austin Champ made only for sale in Germany. This is very rare now.

The last batch of military models appeared in the 1970s and were to a larger scale, sometimes even 1/32, and were very much aimed at the child, not the collector. They usually have working parts, firing shells and such things. They have never found favour with the collectors, the low prices they command now being a good indication of this lack of collectability.

Dinky also made a few special orders for the military command in England and South Africa. These were made by painting existing non-military models with matt green, or olive drab, paint. No accurate records exist on quantities produced and they are quite rare. However, there are certain people who are very clever at refinishing models in alternate liveries and great care must be taken when purchasing any of these odd models to ensure they are genuine, factory produced items. They have been omitted here as they were never on sale to the public, and are therefore outside the scope of this book.

10-TON ARMY WAGON
Tin tilt *Ref no:* 622 *Production Period:* 1954-1964 *Colour:* Olive drab *Market Value:* £70-£90/$100-$130

105MM HOWITZER WITH GUN CREW
With 3 plastic US soldier figures *Ref no:* 609 *Production Period:* 1974-1977 *Colour:* Olive drab *Market Value:* £25-£35/$35-$45

155MM MOBILE GUN
Ref no: 654 *Production Period:* 1973-1979 *Colour:* Olive drab *Market Value:* £20-£30/$30-$45

18-POUNDER GUN
Tinplate firing shield *Ref no:* 162c *Production Period:* 1939-1941 *Colour:* Gloss green *Market Value:* £40-£50/$60-$75

18-POUNDER GUN
US market only only from 1950 *Ref no:* 162c *Production Period:* 1948-1950 *Colour:* Matt green *Market Value:* £30-£40/$45-$60

18-POUNDER QUICK FIRING FIELD GUN UNIT
Contents: 162a, 162b, 162c *Ref no:* 162 *Production Period:* 1939-1941 *Market Value:* £180-£200/$270-$300

18-POUNDER QUICK FIRING FIELD GUN UNIT
Contents: 162a, 162b, 162c. US market only from 1950 *Ref no:* 162 *Reno:* to 691 *Production Period:* 1948-1955 *Market Value:* £120-£150/$180-$225

25-POUNDER FIELD GUN
Ref no: 686 *Production Period:* 1957-1970 *Colour:* Olive drab *Market Value:* £15-£25/$20-$35

25-POUNDER FIELD GUN SET
Contents: 686 25-pdr Field Gun, 687 Trailer, 688 Field Artillery Tractor *Ref no:* 697 *Production Period:* 1957-1964 *Market Value:* £130-£160/$200-$240

3-TON ARMY WAGON
Tin tilt *Ref no:* 621 *Production Period:* 1954-1963 *Colour:* Olive drab *Market Value:* £60-£80/$90-$120

5.5IN MEDIUM GUN
Ref no: 692 *Production Period:* 1955-1962 *Colour:* Olive drab *Market Value:* £30-£50/$45-$75

6-POUNDER ANTI TANK GUN
Ref no: 625 *Production Period:* 1975-1977 *Colour:* Olive drab *Market Value:* £20-£25/$30-$40

7.2IN HOWITZER
Ref no: 693 *Production Period:* 1958-1967 *Colour:* Olive drab *Market Value:* £30-£50/$45-$75

88MM GUN
Casting used for 662 *Ref no:* 656 *Production Period:* 1975-1979 *Colour:* Grey *Market Value:* £20-£30/$30-$45

AEC ARTICULATED TRANSPORTER WITH CHIEFTAIN TANK
974 Transporter without top deck with 683 Chieftain Tank *Ref no:* 616 *Production Period:* 1976-1977 *Colour:* Olive drab *Market Value:* £55-£70/$80-$110

AEC ARTICULATED TRANSPORTER WITH HELICOPTER
974 AEC Hoynor Car Transporter without top deck & 724 Sea King Helicopter *Ref no:* 618 *Production Period:* 1976-1979 *Colour:* Olive drab *Market Value:* £55-£80/$90-$120

ANTI-AIRCRAFT GUN ON TRAILER
Ref no: 161b *Production Period:* 1939-1940 *Colour:* Gloss green *Market Value:* £100-£125/$150-$190

ANTI-AIRCRAFT GUN ON TRAILER
From 1950 US market only *Ref no:* 161b *Reno:* to 690 *Production Period:* 1945-1955 *Colour:* Brown or matt green. From 1950 matt green *Market Value:* £80-£100/$120-$150

ARMOURED CAR
Casting used for 676 *Ref no:* 670 *Production Period:* 1954-1970 *Colour:* Olive drab *Market Value:* £25-£30/$35-$45

ARMOURED COMMAND VEHICLE
Ref no: 677 *Production Period:* 1957-1961 *Colour:* Olive drab *Market Value:* £50-£70/$75-$100

ARMOURED PATROL CAR
680 with turret from 676 *Ref no:* 667 *Production Period:* 1976-1977 *Colour:* Olive drab *Market Value:* £20-£30/$30-$45

ARMOURED PERSONNEL CARRIER
Ref no: 676 *Production Period:* 1955-1962 *Colour:* Olive drab *Market Value:* £40-£70/$60-$90

ARMY (PERSONNEL) PRIVATE SEATED (12)
Metal *Ref no:* 603 *Production Period:* 1957-1971 *Colour:* Tan with black beret *Market Value:* £40-£60/$30-$90

ARMY (PERSONNEL) PRIVATE SEATED (12)
Plastic *Ref no:* 603 *Market Value:* £30-£50/$45-$75

ARMY 1-TON CARGO TRUCK
Tin tilt *Ref no:* 641 *Production Period:* 1954-1962 *Colour:* Olive drab *Market Value:* £40-£60/$60-$90

ARMY COVERED WAGON
Tin tilt *Ref no:* 623 *Production Period:* 1954-1963 *Colour:* Olive drab *Market Value:* £45-£70/$65-$100

ARMY TANK
See under 'CARS' *Ref no:* 22f

ARMY WATER CARRIER
Ref no: 643 *Production Period:* 1958-1964 *Colour:* Olive drab *Market Value:* £70-£90/$100-$130

AUSTIN CHAMP
Ref no: 674 *Production Period:* 1954-1970 *Colour:* Olive drab *Market Value:* £40-£60/$60-$90

AUSTIN COVERED WAGON
Ref no: 625 *Reno:* of 30sm

AUSTIN COVERED WAGON (MILITARY)
Casting of 30s with tinplate tilt as 25b, US market only *Ref no:* 30sm *Reno:* to 625 *Production Period:* 1952-1954 *Colour:* Olive drab *Market Value:* £280-£350/$420-$500

AUSTIN PARA MOKE
342 Moke with plastic carrier & parachute *Ref no:* 601 *Production Period:* 1966-1977 *Colour:* Green *Market Value:* £60-£80/$90-$120

AUSTIN SEVEN CAR
As 35d but hole in seat for driver, wire screen surround *Ref no:* 152c *Production Period:* 1937-1941 *Colour:* Gloss green *Market Value:* £150-£180/$230-$270

BEDFORD MILITARY TRUCK
Casting of 25w, US market only *Ref no:* 25wm *Reno:* to 640 *Production Period:* 1952-1955 *Colour:* Olive drab *Market Value:* £180-£250/$270-$380

BEDFORD TRUCK
Ref no: 640 *Reno:* of 25wm

BERLIET MISSILE LAUNCHER
Casting of French Dinky 816 with English base *Ref no:* 620 *Production Period:* 1971-1973 *Colour:* Olive drab, white & red missile *Market Value:* £90-£120/$130-$180

BREN GUN CARRIER
With driver & gunner *Ref no:* 622 *Production Period:* 1975-1977 *Colour:* Olive drab *Market Value:* £20-£30/$30-$45

BREN GUN CARRIER AND ANTI TANK GUN
622 Bren Gun Carrier, 625 Anti Tank Gun *Ref no:* 619 *Production Period:* 1976-1977 *Colour:* Olive drab *Market Value:* £35-£45/$45-$60

CENTURION TANK
Rubber tracks *Ref no:* 651 *Production Period:* 1954-1970 *Colour:* Olive drab *Market Value:* £60-£80/$90-$120

CHIEFTAIN TANK
Ref no: 683 *Production Period:* 1972-1979 *Colour:* Olive drab *Market Value:* £20-£35/$30-$50

COMMANDO JEEP
Casting of 615 without screen *Ref no:* 612 *Production Period:* 1973-1979 *Colour:* Olive drab *Market Value:* £25-£35/$35-$45

COMMANDO SQUAD GIFT SET

Contents: 667 Armoured Patrol Car, 687 'Convoy' Army Truck, 732 Bell Police Helicopter *Ref no:* 303 *Production Period:* 1978-1979 *Colour:* Helicopter in olive drab *Market Value:* £70-£90/$100-$140

COOKER TRAILER

Wire stand *Ref no:* 151c *Production Period:* 1937-1941 *Colour:* Gloss green *Market Value:* £60-£90/$90-$135

'CONVOY' ARMY TRUCK

Ref no: 687 *Production Period:* 1978-1979 *Colour:* Green *Market Value:* £15-£20/$20-$30

DUKW

Ref no: 681 *Production Period:* 1972-1977 *Colour:* Olive drab *Market Value:* £10-£15/$15-$20

DAIMLER ARMOURED CAR (SPEEDWHEELS)

Reissue of 670 with extra detail *Ref no:* 676 *Production Period:* 1973-1975 *Colour:* Olive drab *Market Value:* £20-£25/$30-$40

DAIMLER MILITARY AMBULANCE

Casting of 30h, US market only *Ref no:* 30hm *Reno:* to 624 *Production Period:* 1952-1955 *Colour:* Olive drab *Market Value:* £120-£160/$180-$240

DAIMLER MILITARY AMBULANCE

Ref no: 624 *Reno:* of 30hm

FERRET ARMOURED CAR

Ref no: 680 *Production Period:* 1972-1977 *Colour:* Olive drab or tan *Market Value:* £10-£15/$15-$20

FIELD ARTILLERY TRACTOR

Ref no: 688 *Production Period:* 1957-1970 *Colour:* Olive drab *Market Value:* £30-£50/$45-$75

FIELD GUN UNIT

Ref no: 691 *Reno:* of 162

FODEN ARMY TRUCK

Casting of 432 Foden *Ref no:* 668 *Production Period:* 1976-1979 *Colour:* Olive drab *Market Value:* £30-£40/$45-$60

FORD FORDOR US ARMY STAFF CAR

Casting of 139a Ford Fordor Sedan, 1954 renumbered twice *Ref no:* 30hm *Reno:* to 170m, and 675 *Production Period:* 1952-1959 *Colour:* Olive drab with white stars on roof & doors *Market Value:* £200-£250/$300-$380

FORD FORDOR US ARMY STAFF CAR

Ref no: 170 *Reno:* of 139am

HANOMAG TANK DESTROYER

Ref no: 694 *Production Period:* 1975-1978 *Colour:* Grey *Market Value:* £30-£50/$45-$75

'HONEST JOHN' MISSILE LAUNCHER

Lorry as 667 *Ref no:* 665 *Production Period:* 1964-1976 *Colour:* Olive drab. White later grey missile *Market Value:* £100-£120/$150-$180

HOWITZER AND TRACTOR

Contents: 689 Medium Artillery Tractor, 693 7.2in Howitzer *Ref no:* 695 *Production Period:* 1962-1965 *Market Value:* £120-£160/$180-$240

JEEP

Casting as 25j. From 1950 US market only *Ref no:* 153a *Reno:* to 672 *Production Period:* 1946-1955 *Colour:* Matt green *Market Value:* £100-£125/$150-$190

LAND ROVER BOMB DISPOSAL UNIT

Ref no: 604 *Production Period:* 1976-1977 *Colour:* Green with orange panels grey plastic robot defuser *Market Value:* £45-£70/$70-$100

LEOPARD ANTI-AIRCRAFT TANK

Ref no: 696 *Production Period:* 1975-1979 *Colour:* Grey *Market Value:* £30-£50/$45-$75

LEOPARD RECOVERY TANK

Ref no: 699 *Production Period:* 1975-1977 *Colour:* Grey-green *Market Value:* £30-£50/$45-$75

LEOPARD TANK

Ref no: 692 *Production Period:* 1974-1979 *Colour:* Grey *Market Value:* £30-£50/$45-$75

LIGHT DRAGON MOTOR TRACTOR

Wire tracks *Ref no:* 162a *Production Period:* 1939-1941 *Colour:* Gloss green *Market Value:* £80-£110/$120-$160

LIGHT DRAGON MOTOR TRACTOR

US market only from 1950 *Ref no:* 162a *Production Period:* 1948-1955 *Colour:* Matt green *Market Value:* £70-£100/$100-$150

LIGHT TANK

Tinplate base *Ref no:* 152a *Production Period:* 1937-1941 *Colour:* Gloss green *Market Value:* £100-£140/$150-$200

LIGHT TANK

From 1950 US market only *Ref no:* 151a *Reno:* to 650 *Production Period:* 1945-1955 *Colour:* Brown or matt green from 1950 matt green *Market Value:* £100-£140/$150-$200

LIGHT TANK

Ref no: 650 *Reno:* of 152a

LORRY WITH SEARCHLIGHT

Casting of 151b, searchlight as 22s *Ref no:* 161a *Production Period:* 1939-1941 *Colour:* Gloss green *Market Value:* £275-£340/$400-$500

MECHANISED ARMY SET

Contents: sets 151, 152, 161, 162 *Ref no:* 156 *Production Period:* 1939-1941 *Market Value:* £2400-£3500/$3600-$5000

MEDIUM ARTILLERY TRACTOR

Ref no: 689 *Production Period:* 1957-1965 *Colour:* Olive drab *Market Value:* £80-£110/$120-$165

MEDIUM TANK

Ref no: 151a *Production Period:* 1937-1941 *Colour:* Gloss green, white triangle on turret bright wire tracks *Market Value:* £150-£200/$230-$300

MEDIUM TANK

US market only *Ref no:* 151a *Production Period:* 1945-1953 *Colour:* Matt green, no triangle black wire tracks *Market Value:* £130-£160/$200-$240

MILITARY AMBULANCE

Ref no: 626 *Production Period:* 1956-1965 *Colour:* Olive drab *Market Value:* £45-£70/$65-$100

MILITARY HOVERCRAFT
Ref no: 281 *Production Period:* 1973-1975 *Colour:* Olive drab *Market Value:* £25-£30/$35-$45

MILITARY VEHICLES
Contents: 621 3-ton Army Truck, 641 Army 1-ton Cargo Truck, 674 Austin Champ, 676 Armoured Personnel Carrier *Ref no:* 1 *Reno:* to 699 *Production Period:* 1955-1958 *Market Value:* £270-£370/$400-$550

MILITARY VEHICLES
Contents: 151a Medium Tank, 151b/620 Transport Wagon, 152b/671 Reconnaissance Car, 153a/672 US Army Jeep, 161b/690 Mobile AA Gun, for US market *Ref no:* 5 *Production Period:* c1953-c1954 *Market Value:* A

MILITARY VEHICLES GIFT SET
Ref no: 699 *Reno:* of 1

MISSILE ERECTOR WITH CORPORAL MISSILE AND LAUNCHER
Ref no: 666 *Production Period:* 1959-1964 *Colour:* Olive drab, white missile *Market Value:* £160-£220/$240-$330

MISSILE SERVICING PLATFORM VEHICLE
Casting used for 977 Servicing Platform Vehicle *Ref no:* 667 *Production Period:* 1960-1964 *Colour:* Olive drab *Market Value:* £120-£150/$180-$220

MOBILE A-A GUN
Ref no: 690 *Reno:* of 161b

MOBILE ANTI-AIRCRAFT UNIT
Contents: 161a, 161b *Ref no:* 161 *Production Period:* 1939-1941 *Market Value:* £450-£700/$650-$1000

RAF PRESSURE REFUELLER
Ref no: 642 *Production Period:* 1957-1960 *Colour:* Blue-grey *Market Value:* £90-£120/$130-$180

RECONNAISSANCE CAR
Ref no: 152b *Production Period:* 1937-1941 *Colour:* Gloss green *Market Value:* £110-£150/$165-$230

RECONNAISSANCE CAR
From 1950 US market only *Ref no:* 152b *Reno:* to 671 *Production Period:* 1945-1954 *Colour:* Brown or matt green. From 1950 matt green *Market Value:* £90-£110/$135-$165

RECONNAISSANCE CAR
Ref no: 671 *Reno:* of 152b

RECOVERY TRACTOR
Ref no: 661 *Production Period:* 1957-1965 *Colour:* Olive drab *Market Value:* £90-£120/$130-$180

ROYAL CORPS OF SIGNALS DESPATCH RIDER
Casting of 37b *Ref no:* 37c *Production Period:* 1937-1941 *Colour:* Khaki rider, green cycle white rubber wheels until 1939 then black *Market Value:* £150-£200/$225-$300

ROYAL TANK CORPS LIGHT TANK SET
Contents: 152a, 152b, 152c, 150d *Ref no:* 152 *Production Period:* 1937-1941 *Market Value:* £300-£450/$450-$650

ROYAL TANK CORPS MEDIUM TANK SET
Contents: 151a, 151b, 151c, 151d, 150d *Ref no:* 151 *Production Period:* 1937-1941 *Market Value:* £350-£500/$550-$750

SCORPION TANK
Ref no: 690 *Production Period:* 1974-1979 *Colour:* Olive drab *Market Value:* £20-£25/$30-$35

SCOUT CAR (DAIMLER)
Ref no: 673 *Production Period:* 1953-1962 *Colour:* Olive drab *Market Value:* £25-£30/$35-$45

SEARCHLIGHT LORRY
Basic casting as for 30e Breakdown Truck, searchlight as on 161a Lorry with Searchlight *Ref no:* 22s *Production Period:* 1939-1941 *Colour:* Matt green *Market Value:* £250-£350/$375-$525

STALWART LOAD CARRIER
Ref no: 682 *Production Period:* 1972-1977 *Colour:* Olive drab *Market Value:* £10-£15/$15-$20

STATIC 88MM GUN WITH CREW
Casting of 656 without wheels *Ref no:* 662 *Production Period:* 1975-1977 *Colour:* Grey *Market Value:* £20-£30/$30-$45

'STRIKER' ANTI-TANK VEHICLE
Ref no: 691 *Production Period:* 1974-1979 *Colour:* Olive drab *Market Value:* £30-£50/$45-$75

TANK TRANSPORTER
Casting used for 908 Mighty Antar *Ref no:* 660 *Production Period:* 1956-1964 *Colour:* Olive drab *Market Value:* £90-£120/$130-$180

TANK TRANSPORTER AND TANK
Contents: 651 Centurion Tank, 660 Tank Transporter *Ref no:* 698 *Production Period:* 1957-1964 *Market Value:* £130-£160/$200-$240

TASK FORCE SET
Contents: 680 Ferret Armoured Car, 681 DUKW, 682 Stalwart Load Carrier *Ref no:* 677 *Production Period:* 1972-1975 *Market Value:* £35-£45/$45-$60

TRAILER
Tinplate base *Ref no:* 162b *Production Period:* 1939-1941 *Colour:* Gloss green *Market Value:* £30-£40/$45-$60

TRAILER
US market only from 1950 *Ref no:* 161b *Production Period:* 1948-1955 *Colour:* matt green *Market Value:* £25-£30/$40-$50

TRAILER FOR 25-PDR FIELD GUN
Ref no: 687 *Production Period:* 1957-1970 *Colour:* Olive drab *Market Value:* £15-£20/$20-$30

TRANSPORT WAGON
Tinplate canopy and longitudinal seat inserts in back *Ref no:* 151b *Production Period:* 1937-1941 *Colour:* Gloss green *Market Value:* £140-£160/$200-$240

TRANSPORT WAGON
From 1950 US market only *Ref no:* 151b *Reno:* to 620 *Production Period:* 1945-1954 *Colour:* Brown or matt green, from 1950 matt green *Market Value:* £100-£130/$150-$200

TRANSPORT WAGON AND DRIVER
Ref no: 620 *Reno:* of 151b

US ARMY JEEP

Casting of 25y/405, US market only *Ref no:* 665 *Production Period:* 1955-1957 *Colour:* Olive drab *Market Value:* £200-£250/$300-$375

US ARMY JEEP

Ref no: 672 *Reno:* of 153a

US ARMY STAFF CAR

Ref no: 675 *Reno:* of 139am/170

US JEEP WITH 105MM HOWITZER

609 + 612 modified *Ref no:* 615 *Production Period:* 1968-1977 *Colour:* Olive drab *Market Value:* £35-£45/$45-$60

VOLKSWAGEN KDF WITH PAK ANTI-TANK GUN

Ref no: 617 *Production Period:* 1976-1977 *Colour:* Grey *Market Value:* £50-£75/$75-$110

WATER TANK TRAILER

Tin base *Ref no:* 151d *Production Period:* 1937-1941 *Colour:* Gloss green *Market Value:* £60-£90/$90-$135

Buses

People have had a fascination with buses and railways since they first appeared. In the early days they were the only way that many of us could visit interesting places. There have been bus collectors since the start of collecting, many people collect nothing but buses. It is a pity therefore that Dinky Toys, the world's leading manufacturer over the years, did not have a very imaginative attitude to them. Buses are a very small proportion of their output.

The first two offerings, in 1934, were a Tram and a Motor Bus, later more correctly called a Centre Entrance Bus. Both of these were to be replicas of typical transport of the time, except that the bus was an AEC Q-type with an offset engine of which only 23 were ever made. These were to a very small scale, 77 and 70mm long respectively.

The next introduction was a conversion of the die for 31 Holland Coachcraft Van into an imaginary streamlined coach. Pre-war this had some very attractive colours schemes, simplified after the war.

The first 'proper' bus was 29c Double Deck Bus of 1938. This started as an AEC with a plain radiator with a 'Y' pattern of bars on the front. This model also had cast stairs fixed to the chassis. After the war the same model reappeared but without the stairs. Later versions had more modern radiator grilles, and many other detail overlapping or concurrent differences. The number of different casting combinations during its production was almost limitless. It finally died out in 1963 to be replaced by the Routemaster, which remained in production until the end of Dinky in 1979.

The small series of four coaches introduced between 1948 and 1952 are very attractive. There are some authentic rare colour variations on some of these and the main ones are listed here. There are a few others and new ones are still coming to light even now as childhood accumulations of toys are being pulled out of attics.

The balance was made up by some Atlanteans and a few larger scale coaches based round only two castings.

There have been many 'special' versions of the Routemaster, not many of which were made in entirety by the factory, so some care has to be taken to establish authenticity.

ATLANTEAN BUS
Casting with single door *Ref no:* 292 *Production Period:* 1962-1965 *Colour:* Red & white 'Ribble', *Market Value:* £110-£130/$160-$190

ATLANTEAN BUS
Casting with single door *Ref no:* 292 *Production Period:* 1962-1965 *Colour:* Red & white 'Corporation Transport' *Market Value:* £90-£120/$130-$180

ATLANTEAN BUS
Casting of 292 Atlantean *Ref no:* 293 *Production Period:* 1963-1968 *Colour:* Green & white, 'Corporation Transport' *Market Value:* £90-£120/$130-$180

ATLANTEAN BUS (YELLOW PAGES)
At least 12 variations *Ref no:* 295 *Production Period:* 1973-1976 *Colour:* Yellow, 'Yellow Pages' *Market Value:* £40-£55/$60-$75

ATLANTEAN CITY BUS
Casting of 295 Atlantean *Ref no:* 291 *Production Period:* 1974-1978 *Colour:* Orange & white, 'Kenning Car, Van & Truck Hire' *Market Value:* £45-£55/$60-$75

ATLANTEAN CITY BUS
500 supplied to company *Ref no:* 291* *Colour:* White, 'London & Manchester Assurance' *Market Value:* A

ATLAS KENEBRAKE BUS
The first with windows & interior *Ref no:* 295 *Production Period:* 1960-1964 *Colour:* Light blue & grey *Market Value:* £45-£55/$60-$75

ATLAS KENEBRAKE BUS
The first with windows & interior *Ref no:* 295 *Production Period:* 1960-1964 *Colour:* All-over light blue *Market Value:* £70-£90/$100-$130

BOAC COACH
Ref no: 283 *Production Period:* 1956-1963 *Colour:* Dark blue with white roof, B.O.A.C., British Overseas Airways Corporation *Market Value:* £80-£100/$120-$150

CONTINENTAL TOURING COACH
In 1979 Catalogue but not issued *Ref no:* 248

CONTINENTAL TOURING COACH
Casting of 949 Wayne School Bus *Ref no:* 953 *Production Period:* 1963-1965 *Colour:* Turquoise with white roof, Dinky Continental Tours *Market Value:* £250-£300/$375-$450

DOUBLE DECK BUS
As prewar but no stairs, grille with Y *Ref no:* 29c *Production Period:* 1945-1948 *Colour:* Dark green with light green upper, red or green with cream or grey, *Market Value:* £120-£160/$180-$220

DOUBLE DECK BUS
Many casting variations, see Intro for more details *Ref no: 29c Reno: to 290 Production Period: 1948-1963 Colour:* Red or green lower, cream upper, after 1954 with 'Dunlop The World's, Master Tyre' transfer, from 1959, occasionally 'Exide' transfers from 291 *Market Value: £70-£100/$100-$150*

DOUBLE DECK BUS
Ref no: 290 Reno: of 29c

DOUBLE DECK BUS (EXIDE)
Ref no: 291 Production Period: 1959-1963 Colour: Red, 'Exide Batteries' *Market Value: £100-£140/$150-$210*

DOUBLE DECK MOTOR BUS
Cast stairs on chassis, grille with Y *Ref no: 29c Production Period: 1938-1941 Colour:* Various colours with cream upper & grey roof, later no grey roof, usually with 'Dunlop Tyres' transfers *Market Value: £250-£350/$380-$450*

DUPLE ROADMASTER COACH
Ref no: 282 Reno: of 29h

DUPLE ROADMASTER LEYLAND ROYAL TIGER COACH
Ref no: 29h Reno: to 282 Production Period: 1952-1960 Colour: Red or dark blue with silver flashes, wheels often match main colour; later *Market Value: £80-£100/$120-$150*

DUPLE ROADMASTER LEYLAND ROYAL TIGER COACH
Ref no: 29h Reno: to 282 Production Period: 1952-1960 Colour: Yellow with red flash and hubs, green lower with cream upper and hubs, has white treaded tyres. *Market Value: £150-£200/$220-$300*

DUPLE VICEROY 37 LUXURY COACH
Casting used for 293 Swiss Postal Bus *Ref no: 296 Production Period: 1972-1976 Colour:* Metallic blue *Market Value: £20-£25/$30-$45*

LONDON SCENE SOUVENIR SET
Contents: 289 routemaster 'esso', 284 london taxi *Ref no: 300 Production Period: 1979 Market Value: £60-£80/$90-$120*

LUXURY COACH
Ref no: 29g Reno: to 281 Production Period: 1951-1959 Colour: Blue or maroon with cream flash or cream or fawn with orange *Market Value: £60-£75/$90-$110*

LUXURY COACH
Ref no: 281 Reno: of 29g

MOTOR BUS (CENTRE ENTRANCE BUS)
Gold metal wheels, renumbered 29a *Ref no: 29 Reno: to 29a Production Period: 1934-1939 Colour:* Various colours with cream roof, later with 'Marmite Definitely Does You Good' decals *Market Value: £200-£225/$300-$340*

MOTOR BUS (CENTRE ENTRANCE BUS)
Ref no: 29a Reno: of 29

OBSERVATION COACH
Ref no: 29f Reno: to 280 Production Period: 1950-1960 Colour: Grey with red flash, cream with red *Market Value: £60-£90/$90-$140*

OBSERVATION COACH
Ref no: 280 Reno: of 29f

ROUTEMASTER BUS (DINKY TOYS)
Presented to press at launch of ad campaign *Ref no: 289* Production Period: 1973-1973 Colour:* Gold, 'Meccano Dinky Toys' / 'Multikit' *Market Value:* A

ROUTEMASTER BUS (ESSO...TYRES)
From 1973 dividing bar on upper window 5 deleted *Ref no: 289 Production Period: 1969-1979 Colour:* Red, 'Esso Safety Grip Tyres' *Market Value: £70-£90/$100-$140*

ROUTEMASTER BUS (LONDON STORES)
Made for participating London stores *Ref no: 289* Production Period: 1968-1968 Colour:* Red, 'Festival of London Stores 1968' *Market Value: £110-£140/$160-$200*

ROUTEMASTER BUS (MADAME TUSSAUD'S)
Casting as 'Esso', made for M. Tussaud's *Ref no: 289* Production Period: 1977-1979 Colour:* Red, 'Visit Madame Tussaud's' *Market Value: £80-£100/$120-$150*

ROUTEMASTER BUS (SCHWEPPES)
Ref no: 289 Production Period: 1965-1969 Colour: Red, 'Schweppes' *Market Value: £90-£110/$130-$160*

ROUTEMASTER BUS (TERN SHIRTS)
Ref no: 289 Production Period: 1964-1965 Colour: Red, 'Tern Shirts' *Market Value: £90-£110/$130-$160*

ROUTEMASTER BUS (THOLLENBEEK'S)
Belgian promotional *Ref no: 289* Production Period: 1979-1979 Colour:* Gold, 'Thollenbeek & Fils 1929 *Market Value:* A

SILVER JUBILEE BUS
Casting of 295, special silver box *Ref no: 297 Production Period: 1977 Colour:* Silver, 'National' and 'The Queen's Silver Jubilee 1977' *Market Value: £15-£20/$20-$30*

SILVER JUBILEE BUS (WOOLWORTHS)
Made for Woolworths, special box *Ref no: 297* Production Period: 1977 Colour:* Silver, 'Woolworths Welcomes the World' *Market Value: £25-£30/$25-$35*

SINGLE DECK BUS
Ref no: 29e Production Period: 1948-1952 Colour: Green with dark green flash, blue Colour with dark blue, cream with blue *Market Value: £60-£100/$90-$150*

SINGLE DECKER BUS
Opening white plastic doors *Ref no: 283 Production Period: 1971-1976 Colour:* Metallic red, later red, Red Arrow & logo on white side stickers *Market Value: £30-£50/$45-$75*

STREAMLINE BUS
Closed rear window *Ref no: 29b Production Period: 1945-1950 Colour:* Light green with dark green spats, grey with blue, grey with red, *Market Value: £60-£70/$90-$110*

STREAMLINED MOTOR BUS
Open rear window *Ref no: 29b Production Period: 1936-1941 Colour:* Various colours with cream above lower window line, *Market Value: £160-£200/$240-$300*

STREAMLINED MOTOR BUS
Open rear window *Ref no:* 29b *Production Period:* 1936-1941 *Colour:* Solid colours with darker shade on roof and wings *Market Value:* £100-£150/$150-$200

SWISS POSTAL BUS
Casting of 296, Swiss market only 1973-75 *Ref no:* 293 *Production Period:* 1973-1978 *Colour:* Yellow with white roof, PTT *Market Value:* £30-£40/$45-$65

TRAM CAR
Plastic rollers then gold metal wheels *Ref no:* 27 *Production Period:* 1934-1939 *Colour:* Various colours with cream upper half, later with 'Drink Delicious Ovaltine Every Day' decals *Market Value:* £150-£180/$220-$270

VEGA MAJOR LUXURY COACH
Casting of 952 without lights, replacing 952 *Ref no:* 954 *Production Period:* 1972-1976 *Colour:* Light grey, stickers: metallic maroon flashes *Market Value:* £70-£90/$100-$135

VEGA MAJOR LUXURY COACH (WITH ELECTRIC LIGHTS)
With flashing indicators *Ref no:* 952 *Production Period:* 1964-1971 *Colour:* Light grey, stickers: metallic maroon flashes *Market Value:* £70-£90/$100-$135

VEGA MAJOR LUXURY COACH PTT
Casting of 954 Vega Major for Swiss market *Ref no:* 961 *Production Period:* 1973-1977 *Colour:* Yellow with white plastic roof, decals: PTT *Market Value:* £150-£175/$225-$300

WAYNE SCHOOL BUS
Casting used for 953 Continental Coach *Ref no:* 949 *Production Period:* 1961-1964 *Colour:* Orange with red trim, School Bus *Market Value:* £150-£200/$225-$300

Cars

PRE-WAR and POST-WAR RE-ISSUES

22 Series: This was the first series of cars and general vehicles to be issued in the Dinky Toy range, appearing in late 1933. The set consists of two generic cars, a van and a truck on the same chassis, a farm tractor and a military tank. Originally introduced as 'Modelled Miniatures', a name used for the accessories for Hornby 'O' gauge trains, they were renamed 'Dinky Toys' in April 1934. From that point new dies were marked with the name Dinky Toys and existing dies were changed as they were returned to the toolroom for servicing or repair. These first six were virtually all made of lead. 22g and 22h, issued later and based on the Chrysler Airflow, were mainly mazak castings.

These toys were painted in a variety of bright, primary colours, but only the main colour schemes are listed here.

23 Series: The racing cars were given the base number 23. These were all modelled on specific cars unlike the 22 Series, although not all of them were so identified by Dinky. The first model, the 'Racing Car', later called the 'Small Open Racing Car' to differentiate it from no. 23c which was called 'Large Open Racing Car' after the war, was a quite good model of George Eyston's MG 'Magic Midget'. This was correctly made by Dinky with stub exhaust pipes and simple paintwork. The later version of the model, 23a, is the updated version of the MG, now a Magnette known as EX.135. This had a 6-cylinder engine, fishtail exhaust and horizontally striped 'Humbug' paint livery.

The 23m Thunderbolt Record Car of Eyston's was made in the correct livery of silver with Union Jack flags on the tailfin. It was supplied in a special box with the car's details printed on the lid. The same casting was used for 23s Streamlined Racing Car, painted in bright colours but without the flags and sold out of a trade box of six cars.

Later racing cars were all named by Dinky except for the small one in the 35 Series. 23a was issued in many, many different colours but only the main ones are listed. The other racers were usually only made in a very limited range of colours.

24 Series: This was a set of eight beautiful generic cars of the early 1930s style. Introduced in 1934 they all used the same chassis and radiator grille, basically a 'Bentley' type. There were minor chassis and grille variations during the 7 year production run. The names for this series were Limousine, Town Sedan and similar. The only one to give a pointer to its origin was 24d Vogue Saloon - Vogue being a name specific to the Humber Coupé of 1934.

The number of colours used for these cars is almost unlimited, certainly by Dinky practice before or after. Various shades of red, blue, green, yellow, lilac and others were used in almost any combination. Some colour schemes were more attractive than others and collectors will now pay a considerable premium for an exceptionally beautiful example. Unfortunately, this series suffers very badly from metal fatigue and so in spite of the long production run they are very rare in good to excellent condition.

30 Series: This was the first series of road vehicles to be given the names of the manufacturers of the prototypes. 30a, originally issued as 32 for a very short time, the Chrysler Airflow saloon was the first. Over the years Dinky sold many more of its Airflows than Chrysler did of the real thing, and it has remained an all time favourite with collectors. The next three cars were also given proper names and are quite good replicas of the Rolls, Daimler and Vauxhall. The radiator grilles were accurate, the one on the Vauxhall being changed from a 'criss cross' design to a 'shield' patterning the real car. The colours followed the line of the 24 Series but not quite so widely varied.

The next three models, 30e, 30f, 30g are also part of the 30 Series set and are listed here although they are not.

35 Series: Small 'OO' gauge train sets were becoming available and this series of small scale cars was designed to go with them. This was before the advent of Meccano's own Hornby Dublo. The colour range for the cars has always been quite wide. Many of the pre-war 35a and 35d models had the spare wheel cover on the rear picked out in a darker shade of the main body colour.

36 Series: This series consists models similar to six of the 24 Series but from new dies with individual radiator grilles as Humber, Rover, etc. They were in production at the same time as the 24 Series. The Town Sedan was not carried forward and the 24a Ambulance had become 30f Ambulance as well. The bodies were virtually the same as on the 24 Series but the front ends were modified to fit the new radiator grilles. The open Sports Tourers received cast-in spare wheels on their tails. There were also some other small changes to aid manufacture.

The main difference was to be the fitting of drivers and passengers to the cars. The closed cars were fitted with lithographed tinplate pairs of people, clipped into slots in the chassis, while the open cars had cast drivers rivetted into holes in the driver's seat. The colours followed the same pattern as for the previous series.

38 Series: This series of lovely sports cars was announced in 1940, after the outbreak of the war, but only three were issued before production stopped. 38e Triumph Dolomite was illustrated, a mould was at least started to be made, but no castings were ever manufactured. When the factory restarted after the war this mould was not used and the model was replaced by 38e Armstrong Siddeley Coupé, a new car in late 1945.

The pre-war cars were fitted with tin bases finished in a slightly yellowy silver lacquer, the post-war cars had black bases. The range of colours was quite large in 1940 but much reduced after 1945. The range was removed from sale in the UK in 1950 but kept on sale, and renumbered, in export catalogues until 1954/55. These later cars were also given some new colours and were available in the US, Canada, South Africa, and possibly a few other places.

39 Series: These six cars appeared in 1939 and showed how Dinky were really getting their act together. They were beautiful models then and are still justifiably extremely collectable today. There is a lovely range of colours both pre- and post-war. These were kept in production for the US market two years beyond their life in England. Some extra colours appeared during this time, often with coloured wheels, as well as the three duotone versions which were US market only at all times.

Post-War: When the war was over production restarted with the old dies. The 22 and 24 Series had been deleted by 1939 so only the 23, 30, 36, 38 and 39 Series cars reappeared, the 36 Series now without drivers. The colours were usually harsher, less in number and generally not quite so attractive. The chassis on the 30 and 36 Series were now only painted black. The tin bases on the 38 and 39 Series were also black.

POST-WAR NEW ISSUES

The first new models were the 40 series of British saloon cars. These were good models of the new cars slowly finding their way onto the roads of England as fast as the need for exports would allow. These models followed the pattern and quality set by the 38 and 39 Series cars. The 139 and 140 series followed covering US and UK quality cars. Colours started becoming more exciting as the years passed. 1953-54 saw the renumbering from 40a to 158 style and consequently all new releases after 1954 did not have suffix letters.

Production of the new models continued in much the same way until the late 1960s after which time there was much more emphasis on the toy aspect and thus the attractiveness to the collector was reduced. There were still some good models to come but the main thrust for the enthusiast was over by about 1970.

'SPEED OF THE WIND' RACING CAR
Ref no: 23e Production Period: 1936-1941 Colour: Red, green, yellow, blue or silver *Market Value:* £80-£100/$120-$150

'SPEED OF THE WIND' RACING CAR
Ref no: 23e Reno: to 221 Production Period: 1945-1956 Colour: Silver or red *Market Value:* £40-£50/$60-$75

'SPEED OF THE WIND' RACING CAR
Ref no: 221 Reno: of 23e

'THUNDERBOLT' SPEED CAR
Union Jack on tail, special box *Ref no: 23m Production Period: 1938-1941 Colour:* Silver with black detail *Market Value:* £150-£170/$220-$260

AC ACECA
Ref no: 167 Production Period: 1958-1963 Colour: Cream with brown or maroon roof grey with red, *Market Value:* £90-£120/$135-$180

ALFA ROMEO 1900 SUPER SPRINT
Ref no: 185 Production Period: 1961-1963 Colour: Yellow or red *Market Value:* £70-£90/$100-$140

ALFA ROMEO 33 TIPO LE MANS
Ref no: 210 Production Period: 1970-1973 Colour: Orangey-red, dark blue, both with black bonnet *Market Value:* £25-£35/$35-$50

ALFA ROMEO RACING CAR
Ref no: 232 Reno: of 23f /207

ALFA ROMEO SCARABEO OSI
Ref no: 217 Production Period: 1969-1974 Colour: Red, later dayglo orange *Market Value:* £25-£30/$35-$45

ALFA-ROMEO RACING CAR
In box *Ref no: 23f Reno: to 232 & 207 Production Period:* 1952 *Colour:* Red, '8' in white *Market Value:* £80-£100/$120-$150

ALFA-ROMEO RACING CAR
In bubblepack as 207 *Ref no: 23f Reno: to 207 Production Period:* 1952 *Colour:* Red, '8' in white *Market Value:* £160-£240/$240-$350

ALFASUD
Not issued *Ref no: 506*

ALFETTA GTV
From Solido - Cougar *Ref no:* 503 *Production Period:* 1981-1982 *Colour:* Yellow or red with clover sticker on bonnet *Market Value:* £14-£18/$20-$25

ALVIS
Renumbered 103 for US market *Ref no:* 38d *Reno:* to 103 *Production Period:* 1945-1955 *Colour:* Green or maroon *Market Value:* £100-£130/$150-$200

ALVIS SPORTS TOURER
Ref no: 38d *Production Period:* 1940-1941 *Colour:* Green *Market Value:* £140-£180/$210-$270

ALVIS SPORTS TOURER
Ref no: 103 *Reno:* of 38a

AMBULANCE
Similar to 30f *Ref no:* 24a *Production Period:* 1934-1941 *Colour:* Cream with red or grey chassis *Market Value:* £190-£250/$290-$375

AMBULANCE
Similar to 24a *Ref no:* 30f *Production Period:* 1935-1941 *Colour:* Grey with red chassis *Market Value:* £180-£225/$270-$340

AMBULANCE
Similar to 24a *Ref no:* 30f *Production Period:* 1946-1948 *Colour:* Cream or grey with black chassis *Market Value:* £100-£130/$150-$200

ARMSTRONG SIDDELEY
Ref no: 36a *Production Period:* 1945-1950 *Colour:* Blue, grey or dark blue *Market Value:* £90-£120/$135-$180

ARMSTRONG SIDDELEY
Ref no: 104 *Reno:* of 38e

ARMSTRONG SIDDELEY (LIMOUSINE) WITH DRIVER AND FOOTMAN
See introduction *Ref no:* 36a *Production Period:* 1937-1941 *Colour:* Various colours *Market Value:* £250-£350/$375-$525

ARMSTRONG-SIDDELEY (COUPÉ)
Renumbered 104 for US market *Ref no:* 38e *Reno:* to 104 *Production Period:* 1946-1956/7 *Colour:* Grey, green or red *Market Value:* £90-£120/$135-$180

ARMY TANK
Red, later green, rubber tracks *Ref no:* 22f *Production Period:* 1933-1939 *Colour:* Green with orange turret, *Market Value:* £200-£250/$300-$380

ARMY TANK
Red, later green, rubber tracks *Ref no:* 22f *Production Period:* 1933-1939 *Colour:* Grey *Market Value:* £180-£250/$270-$350

ASTON MARTIN DB3S (COMPETITION FINISH)
Casting as 104 *Ref no:* 110 *Production Period:* 1956-1959 *Colour:* Grey '20' or green '22' *Market Value:* £80-£110/$120-$165

ASTON MARTIN DB3S (TOURING FINISH)
Casting as 110 *Ref no:* 104 *Production Period:* 1957-1960 *Colour:* Light blue or pink *Market Value:* £130-£190/$200-$270

ASTON MARTIN DB5
Then used for 153 Aston *Ref no:* 110 *Production Period:* 1965-1970 *Colour:* Metallic red *Market Value:* £60-£80/$90-$120

ASTON MARTIN DB6
Wire wheels *Ref no:* 153 *Production Period:* 1967-1971 *Colour:* Metallic blue or metallic green *Market Value:* £60-£80/$90-$120

AUSTIN 1800
Casting used for 282 Austin 1800 Taxi *Ref no:* 171 *Production Period:* 1965-1967 *Colour:* Metallic blue or light blue *Market Value:* £45-£70/$65-$95

AUSTIN 7 CAR
Wire screen *Ref no:* 35d *Production Period:* 1938-1941 *Colour:* Blue, yellow, green, maroon, grey *Market Value:* £90-£130/$130-$200

AUSTIN 7 COUNTRYMAN
Ref no: 199 *Production Period:* 1961-1970 *Colour:* Blue with brown woodwork *Market Value:* £60-£90/$90-$135

AUSTIN A105
The first with windows *Ref no:* 176 *Production Period:* 1958-1963 *Colour:* Cream with blue flash or grey with red *Market Value:* £90-£110/$135-$165

AUSTIN A105
The first with windows *Ref no:* 176 *Production Period:* 1958-1963 *Colour:* Roof painted 2nd colour also *Market Value:* £120-£150/$180-$220

AUSTIN A30
Ref no: 160 *Production Period:* 1958-1962 *Colour:* Fawn or blue *Market Value:* £80-£100/$120-$150

AUSTIN ATLANTIC
Ref no: 106 *Reno:* of 140a

AUSTIN ATLANTIC CONVERTIBLE
Contrasting seat colour, white tyres on black car *Ref no:* 140a *Reno:* to 106 *Production Period:* 1951-1958 *Colour:* Black or blue *Market Value:* £120-£150/$180-$225

AUSTIN ATLANTIC CONVERTIBLE
Contrasting seat colour, white tyres on black car *Ref no:* 140a *Reno:* to 106 *Production Period:* 1951-1958 *Colour:* Pink, dark blue, some red *Market Value:* £180-£220/$270-$330

AUSTIN DEVON SALOON
From 1956: 2 colour scheme only *Ref no:* 40d *Reno:* to 152 *Production Period:* 1949-1960 *Colour:* Maroon, suede green, blue, red, dark blue, light blue, tan *Market Value:* £90-£120/$135-$180

AUSTIN DEVON SALOON
From 1956: 2 colour scheme only *Ref no:* 152 *Production Period:* 1956-1960 *Colour:* Pink with green upper or yellow with blue *Market Value:* £150-£220/$220-$330

AUSTIN DEVON SALOON
Ref no: 152 *Reno:* of 40d

AUSTIN HEALEY 100 (COMPETITION FINISH)
Casting as 103 *Ref no:* 109 *Production Period:* 1955-1959 *Colour:* Cream '23' or yellow '21' *Market Value:* £80-£110/$120-$165

AUSTIN HEALEY 100 (TOURING FINISH)
Casting as 109 *Ref no:* 103 *Production Period:* 1957-1960 *Colour:* Cream or red *Market Value:* £100-£130/$150-$200

AUSTIN HEALEY SPRITE MKII
Ref no: 112 *Production Period:* 1961-1965 *Colour:* Red *Market Value:* £80-£110/$120-$165

AUSTIN MINI-MOKE
Casting used for 106 'Prisoner', 305 Tiny's, 601 Para Moke *Ref no:* 342 *Production Period:* 1966-1974 *Colour:* Metallic green, later metallic green/blue *Market Value:* £35-£45/$50-$70

AUSTIN SOMERSET SALOON
From 1956: 2 colour scheme only *Ref no:* 40j *Reno:* to 161 *Production Period:* 1953-1960 *Colour:* Red, light blue *Market Value:* £90-£120/$120-$150

AUSTIN SOMERSET SALOON
From 1956: 2 colour scheme only *Ref no:* 161 *Production Period:* 1956-1960 *Colour:* Upper, red with yellow black with cream *Market Value:* £150-£200/$220-$300

AUSTIN SOMERSET SALOON
Ref no: 161 *Reno:* of 40j

AUTO-UNION RACING CAR
No driver, then from late 1936, with driver. *Ref no:* 23d *Production Period:* 1936-1941 *Colour:* Red, green, yellow, or silver *Market Value:* £100-£120/$150-$180

AUTO-UNION RACING CAR
Without driver *Ref no:* 23d *Production Period:* 1945-1950 *Colour:* Red, silver *Market Value:* £60-£80/$90-$120

BMW 530
From Solido - Cougar *Ref no:* 502 *Production Period:* 1981-1982 *Colour:* Metallic green or blue *Market Value:* £14-£18/$20-$25

BMW TILUX
Electric lights *Ref no:* 157 *Production Period:* 1968-1972 *Colour:* Blue & white *Market Value:* £50-£70/$75-$100

BRM RACING CAR
Ref no: 243 *Production Period:* 1964-1971 *Colour:* Green or metallic green, '7' *Market Value:* £50-£70/$75-$100

BEACH BUGGY
Ref no: 227 *Production Period:* 1975-1977 *Colour:* Yellow with white plastic hood *Market Value:* £20-£25/$30-$45

BENTLEY
Ref no: 36b *Production Period:* 1945-1950 *Colour:* Green or blue *Market Value:* £90-£120/$135-$180

BENTLEY (TWO-SEATER SPORTS COUPÉ) WITH DRIVER AND PASSENGER
See introduction *Ref no:* 36b *Production Period:* 1937-1941 *Colour:* Various colours *Market Value:* £250-£350/$375-$525

BENTLEY S SERIES COUPÉ
Ref no: 194 *Production Period:* 1961-1966 *Colour:* Grey or bronze *Market Value:* £80-£120/$120-$180

BREAKDOWN CAR (TRUCK)
Casting as 22c Truck, type 2 *Ref no:* 30e *Production Period:* 1935-1941 *Colour:* Red, yellow or grey with black wings *Market Value:* £80-£100/$120-$150

BREAKDOWN CAR (TRUCK)
Casting as 22c Truck, type 2 *Ref no:* 30e *Production Period:* 1945-1948 *Colour:* Grey, green or red *Market Value:* £50-£70/$75-$100

BRISTOL 450 COUPÉ
Ref no: 163 *Production Period:* 1956-1960 *Colour:* Green, '27' *Market Value:* £60-£80/$90-$120

BRITISH SALMSON (FOUR-SEATER SPORTS) WITH DRIVER
See introduction *Ref no:* 36f *Production Period:* 1937-1941 *Colour:* Various colours *Market Value:* £250-£350/$375-$525

BRITISH SALMSON (FOUR-SEATER SPORTS)
Ref no: 36f *Production Period:* 1945-1950 *Colour:* Green or grey *Market Value:* £100-£130/$150-$200

BRITISH SALMSON (TWO-SEATER SPORTS)
Ref no: 36e *Production Period:* 1945-1950 *Colour:* Red, blue or brown *Market Value:* £100-£130/$150-$200

BRITISH SALMSON (TWO-SEATER SPORTS) WITH DRIVER
See introduction *Ref no:* 36e *Production Period:* 1937-1941 *Colour:* Various colours *Market Value:* £250-£350/$375-$525

BUICK
From 1950 US only *Ref no:* 39d *Production Period:* 1945-1952 *Colour:* Maroon, beige or grey *Market Value:* £100-£130/$150-$200

BUICK VICEROY SALOON CAR
Separate headlamps *Ref no:* 39d *Production Period:* 1939-1941 *Colour:* Maroon, green or blue *Market Value:* £250-£350/$375-$525

CADILLAC 62
Ref no: 147 *Production Period:* 1962-1968 *Colour:* Metallic green *Market Value:* £70-£80/$100-$125

CADILLAC ELDORADO
Ref no: 131 *Production Period:* 1956-1963 *Colour:* Pink or yellow *Market Value:* £80-£120/$120-$180

CADILLAC ELDORADO
Ref no: 175 *Production Period:* 1969-1972 *Colour:* Metallic blue with black roof or metallic purple with black *Market Value:* £45-£55/$70-$85

CARAVAN TRAILER
Ref no: 30g *Production Period:* 1936-1941 *Colour:* Various 2-tone colour schemes *Market Value:* £90-£130/$135-$200

CHEVROLET EL CAMINO PICK-UP
Ref no: 449 *Production Period:* 1961-1968 *Colour:* Light green with white sides *Market Value:* £80-£100/$120-$150

CHEVROLET EL CAMINO PICK-UP WITH TRAILERS
449 + 2x2-wheeled trailers, 1 open, 1 closed *Ref no:* 448 *Production Period:* 1963-1967 *Colour:* Green & white with red trailers *Market Value:* £220-£280/$330-$420

CHRYSLER

From 1950 US only *Ref no:* 39e *Production Period:* 1945-1952 *Colour:* Blue, green, grey, cream *Market Value:* £100-£130/$150-$200

CHRYSLER

US market only *Ref no:* 39eu *Production Period:* 1950-1952 *Colour:* Yellow with red wings or light green with dark green wings *Market Value:* £450-£650/$700-$1000

CHRYSLER 'AIRFLOW' SALOON

Ref no: 30a *Reno:* from 32 *Production Period:* 1935-1941 *Colour:* Maroon, green, blue, red or turquoise *Market Value:* £225-£275/$340-$420

CHRYSLER 'AIRFLOW' SALOON

Ref no: 30a *Production Period:* 1946-1948 *Colour:* Green, blue or cream *Market Value:* £90-£120/$140-$180

CHRYSLER 'AIRFLOW' SALOON

Ref no: 32 *Reno:* to 30a

CHRYSLER ROYAL SEDAN

Ref no: 39e *Production Period:* 1939-1941 *Colour:* Green grey, blue *Market Value:* £250-£350/$375-$525

CITROEN DYANE

Ref no: 149 *Production Period:* 1971-1974 *Colour:* Bronze with black roof *Market Value:* £25-£30/$35-$50

CITROËN 2CV

From Solido - Cougar *Ref no:* 500 *Production Period:* 1981-1982 *Colour:* Green or red with duck stickers *Market Value:* £14-£18/$20-$25

CITROËN VISA

From Solido - Cougar *Ref no:* 504 *Production Period:* 1981-1982 *Colour:* Metallic maroon or green *Market Value:* £14-£18/$20-$25

CONNAUGHT RACING CAR

Ref no: 236 *Production Period:* 1956-1959 *Colour:* Light green, '32' *Market Value:* £70-£90/$100-$135

COOPER RACING CAR

Ref no: 240 *Production Period:* 1963-1969 *Colour:* Blue, white bonnet stripes, '20' *Market Value:* £50-£70/$75-$100

COOPER-BRISTOL RACING CAR

In box *Ref no:* 23g *Reno:* to 233 & 208 *Production Period:* 1953-1964 *Colour:* Green, '6' in white *Market Value:* £80-£100/$120-$150

COOPER-BRISTOL RACING CAR

In bubblepack as 208 *Ref no:* 23g *Reno:* to 208 *Production Period:* 1953-1964 *Colour:* Green, '6' in white *Market Value:* £160-£240/$240-$350

COOPER-BRISTOL RACING CAR

Ref no: 233 *Reno:* of 23g /208

CORVETTE STINGRAY

Ref no: 221 *Production Period:* 1969-1972 *Colour:* Bronze *Market Value:* £25-£35/$35-$50

CORVETTE STINGRAY

Casting used for 206 Customised Stingray *Ref no:* 221 *Production Period:* 1976-1978 *Colour:* White with black bonnet *Market Value:* £25-£35/$35-$50

CUNNINGHAM C-5R

Ref no: 133 *Production Period:* 1955-1960 *Colour:* White, blue stripes '31' *Market Value:* £70-£90/$100-$140

CUSTOMISED CORVETTE STINGRAY

Casting of 221 Corvette Stingray *Ref no:* 206 *Production Period:* 1979-1979 *Colour:* Red *Market Value:* £25-£30/$35-$45

CUSTOMISED LAND ROVER/OFF THE ROAD PICK-UP

Casting of 344 Land Rover with wide wheels, plastic roll-over cage, heavy bumpers *Ref no:* 202 *Production Period:* 1979-1979 *Colour:* Yellow *Market Value:* £20-£25/$30-$40

CUSTOMISED RANGE ROVER

Casting of 192 Range Rover with wide wheels, bumpers as 202 Land Rover *Ref no:* 203 *Production Period:* 1979-1979 *Colour:* Black *Market Value:* £20-£25/$30-$40

DAIMLER CAR

See introduction *Ref no:* 30c *Production Period:* 1935-1941 *Colour:* Various colours *Market Value:* £200-£250/$300-$375

DAIMLER CAR

Ref no: 30c *Production Period:* 1946-1950 *Colour:* Fawn or dark green *Market Value:* £90-£120/$140-$180

DAIMLER V8 2.5 LITRE

Ref no: 146 *Production Period:* 1963-1966 *Colour:* Metallic green *Market Value:* £60-£90/$90-$130

DE SOTO FIREFLITE

Casting used for 258 U.S.A. Police Car *Ref no:* 192 *Production Period:* 1958-1964 *Colour:* Grey with red flash & roof or green with fawn *Market Value:* £100-£140/$150-$210

DE TOMASO MANGUSTA 5000

Ref no: 187 *Production Period:* 1968-1976 *Colour:* Red & white, '7' *Market Value:* £35-£45/$50-$75

DELIVERY VAN

Cab/chassis as 22c *Ref no:* 22d *Production Period:* 1933-1935 *Colour:* Orange cab with blue back, blue with yellow *Market Value:* £300-£350/$450-$550

DINKY BEATS MORRIS OXFORD

Casting of 476 Morris Oxford with folded hood & 3 beat musicians *Ref no:* 486 *Production Period:* 1965-1969 *Colour:* Pink with green chassis *Market Value:* £90-£120/$140-$180

DINKY WAY GIFT SET

(Export cat. No.) *Ref no:* 237 *Reno:* of 240

DINKY WAY GIFT SET

Contents: 211 TR7, 255 Police Mini Clubman, 382 Convoy Dump Truck, 412 Bedford Van AA, 6 metres card roadway, 20 plastic road signs, decal sheet, export number 237: no decals on 412 *Ref no:* 240 *Reno:* to 237 *Production Period:* 1978-1979 *Market Value:* £60-£80/$90-$120

DINO FERRARI

Ref no: 216 *Production Period:* 1967-1974 *Colour:* Red, metallic blue *Market Value:* £40-£60/$60-$90

DODGE ROYAL SEDAN
Casting used for 258 U.S.A. Police Car *Ref no:* 191 *Production Period:* 1959-1966 *Colour:* Cream with brown flash, green with black *Market Value:* £90-£120/$140-$180

DODGE ROYAL SEDAN
Casting used for 258 U.S.A. Police Car *Ref no:* 191 *Production Period:* 1959-1966 *Colour:* White with blue *Market Value:* £160-£200/$240-$300

DRAGSTER SET
Ref no: 370 *Production Period:* 1969-1974 *Colour:* Yellow & red dragster, white then blue, then red launcher *Market Value:* £40-£50/$60-$75

ESTATE CAR
Ref no: 27f *Reno:* to 344 *Production Period:* 1950-1960 *Colour:* Fawn with brown panels *Market Value:* £65-£90/$95-$140

ESTATE CAR
Ref no: 27f *Reno:* to 344 *Production Period:* 1950-1960 *Colour:* Fawn or grey with red *Market Value:* £90-£120/$140-$190

ESTATE CAR
Ref no: 344 *Reno:* of 27f

FARM TRACTOR
Hornby to 1934, then Dinky Toys *Ref no:* 22e *Production Period:* 1933-1941 *Colour:* Yellow with blue wings, red or cream with blue or red wings *Market Value:* £250-£275/$375-$420

FERRARI 312/B2
Ref no: 226 *Production Period:* 1972-1974 *Colour:* Red *Market Value:* £20-£25/$30-$45

FERRARI 312/B2
Ref no: 226 *Production Period:* 1976-1979 *Colour:* Bronze with white or black interior & rear wing *Market Value:* £20-£25/$30-$45

FERRARI 312P
Ref no: 204 *Production Period:* 1971-1974 *Colour:* Metallic red with white doors, '60' or '24' *Market Value:* £25-£30/$40-$50

FERRARI P5
Ref no: 220 *Production Period:* 1970-1974 *Colour:* Metallic red *Market Value:* £25-£30/$35-$45

FERRARI RACING CAR
In box *Ref no:* 23h *Reno:* to 234 & 209 *Production Period:* 1953-1964 *Colour:* Blue with yellow nose, later yellow triangle *Market Value:* £80-£100/$120-$150

FERRARI RACING CAR
In bubblepack as 209 *Ref no:* 23h *Reno:* to 209 *Production Period:* 1953-1964 *Colour:* Blue with yellow nose, later yellow triangle *Market Value:* £160-£240/$240-$350

FERRARI RACING CAR
Ref no: 234 *Reno:* of 23h /209

FERRARI RACING CAR
Ref no: 242 *Production Period:* 1963-1971 *Colour:* Red, '24' *Market Value:* £50-£70/$75-$100

FIAT 2300 STATION WAGON
Casting used for 281 Fiat 2300 Pathé News *Ref no:* 172 *Production Period:* 1965-1968 *Colour:* 2-tone blue *Market Value:* £40-£60/$60-$90

FIAT 600
Ref no: 183 *Production Period:* 1958-1960 *Colour:* Light green or red *Market Value:* £60-£80/$90-$120

FIAT ABARTH 2000
Ref no: 202 *Production Period:* 1971-1974 *Colour:* Orange & white *Market Value:* £20-£25/$30-$40

FIAT STRADA
From Solido - Cougar *Ref no:* 501 *Production Period:* 1981-1982 *Colour:* Metallic blue or gold *Market Value:* £14-£18/$20-$25

FORD 40-RV
Ref no: 132 *Production Period:* 1967-1973 *Colour:* Silver, silver blue, some orange-red *Market Value:* £40-£70/$60-$100

FORD ANGLIA
Ref no: 155 *Production Period:* 1961-1964 *Colour:* Blue *Market Value:* £70-£100/$100-$150

FORD CAPRI
Ref no: 143 *Production Period:* 1962-1966 *Colour:* Green with white roof *Market Value:* £60-£80/$90-$120

FORD CAPRI
Casting used for 213 Ford Capri Rally *Ref no:* 165 *Production Period:* 1969-1975 *Colour:* Metallic green or metallic purple *Market Value:* £50-£70/$75-$100

FORD CAPRI RALLY
Casting of 165 Capri *Ref no:* 213 *Production Period:* 1970-1974 *Colour:* Metallic red or bronze *Market Value:* £35-£55/$50-$80

FORD CONSUL CORSAIR
Casting used for 169 Corsair 200E *Ref no:* 130 *Production Period:* 1964-1968 *Colour:* Metallic red or light blue *Market Value:* £60-£70/$90-$100

FORD CORSAIR 2000E
Casting of 130 with textured roof *Ref no:* 169 *Production Period:* 1967-1969 *Colour:* Silver with black roof *Market Value:* £60-£80/$90-$120

FORD CORTINA
Replaced by 133 *Ref no:* 139 *Production Period:* 1963-1964 *Colour:* Light blue or metallic blue *Market Value:* £80-£110/$120-$160

FORD CORTINA 1965
Casting used for 212 Ford Cortina Rally *Ref no:* 133 *Production Period:* 1964-1968 *Colour:* Metallic yellow with white roof or yellow *Market Value:* £60-£90/$90-$135

FORD CORTINA MK II
Casting used for 205 Lotus Cortina Rally *Ref no:* 159 *Production Period:* 1967-1969 *Colour:* White *Market Value:* £60-£80/$90-$120

FORD CORTINA RALLY
Casting of 133 Ford Cortina *Ref no:* 212 *Production Period:* 1965-1969 *Colour:* White with black bonnet, '8' *Market Value:* £70-£90/$100-$135

FORD ESCORT
Casting used for 270 Ford Panda Police Car *Ref no:* 168 *Production Period:* 1968-1976 *Colour:* Light blue *Market Value:* £45-£55/$65-$80

FORD ESCORT
Casting used for 270 Ford Panda Police Car *Ref no:* 168 *Production Period:* 1968-1976 *Colour:* Metallic red *Market Value:* £70-£90/$100-$135

FORD FAIRLANE
Ref no: 148 *Production Period:* 1962-1965 *Colour:* Light green or *Market Value:* £70-£80/$100-$120

FORD FAIRLANE
Ref no: 148 *Production Period:* 1962-1965 *Colour:* Metallic green (shades) *Market Value:* £120-£150/$180-$225

FORD FIESTA
Not issued *Ref no:* 508

FORD FORDOR
Ref no: 170 *Reno:* of 139a

FORD FORDOR SEDAN
Ref no: 139a *Reno:* to 170 *Production Period:* 1949-1956 *Colour:* Yellow, red, green or tan *Market Value:* £90-£125/$140-$190

FORD FORDOR SEDAN
1956 second colour on sides, 1958 second colour on lower sides only *Ref no:* 139a *Reno:* to 170 *Production Period:* 1956-1959 *Colour:* Cream with red sides or pink with blue *Market Value:* £170-£225/$250-$340

FORD GT RACING CAR
Ref no: 215 *Production Period:* 1965-1973 *Colour:* White *Market Value:* £30-£40/$45-$60

FORD GT RACING CAR
Ref no: 215 *Production Period:* 1965-1973 *Colour:* From 1970 green, '7' *Market Value:* £40-£50/$60-$75

FORD MODEL 'T' 1908
Casting used for 485, 109 Gabriel *Ref no:* 475 *Production Period:* 1964-1968 *Colour:* Blue body with red, brown or black chassis *Market Value:* £50-£70/$75-$100

FORD MODEL 'T' WITH SANTA CLAUS
Casting of 475 Model T with plastic Santa Claus, sack & Xmas tree *Ref no:* 485 *Production Period:* 1964-1967 *Colour:* Red & white *Market Value:* £90-£100/$130-$150

FORD MUSTANG FASTBACK 2+2
Ref no: 161 *Production Period:* 1965-1972 *Colour:* White or yellow *Market Value:* £40-£60/$60-$90

FORD TAUNUS 17M
Casting used for 261 Ford Taunus 'Polizei' *Ref no:* 154 *Production Period:* 1966-1968 *Colour:* Yellow with white roof *Market Value:* £40-£60/$60-$90

FORD ZEPHYR SALOON
Ref no: 162 *Production Period:* 1956-1960 *Colour:* Cream with green lower sides, duotone blue *Market Value:* £90-£120/$135-$180

FORD ZODIAC MK IV
Casting used for 255 Ford Zodiac Police Car *Ref no:* 164 *Production Period:* 1966-1971 *Colour:* Silver *Market Value:* £60-£65/$90-$100

FORD ZODIAC MK IV
Casting used for 255 Ford Zodiac Police Car *Ref no:* 164 *Production Period:* 1966-1971 *Colour:* Bronze *Market Value:* £90-£140/$125-$210

FRAZER NASH
Ref no: 100 *Reno:* of 38a

FRAZER-NASH
Renumbered 100 for US export *Ref no:* 38a *Reno:* to 100 *Production Period:* 1945-1955 *Colour:* Shades of blue or grey *Market Value:* £100-£130/$150-$200

FRAZER-NASH BMW SPORTS CAR
Ref no: 38a *Production Period:* 1941 *Colour:* Red with maroon seats, dark blue with putty *Market Value:* £150-£200/$220-$300

FUN A'HOY SET
Contents: 130 Ford Corsair with driver, 796 Healey Sports Boat with driver *Ref no:* 125 *Production Period:* 1964-1967 *Market Value:* £120-£160/$180-$240

GARDNER'S MG RECORD CAR
MG Magnette on base, special box *Ref no:* 23p *Production Period:* 1939-1941 *Colour:* Green with white flash, MG logo on nose, Union Jack on sides *Market Value:* £150-£180/$220-$270

GARDNER'S MG RECORD CAR
MG Record Car on base *Ref no:* 23p *Production Period:* 1945-1948 *Colour:* Green no flash *Market Value:* £80-£100/$120-$150

GOODWOOD SPORTS CARS
Contents: 112 Austin Healey Sprite, 113 MGB, 120 Jaguar E-type, 182 Porsche 356A + 9 plastic figures *Ref no:* 121 *Production Period:* 1963-1965 *Market Value:* £1000-£1200/$1500-$1800

HWM RACING CAR
Ref no: 23j *Reno:* to 235 *Production Period:* 1953-1960 *Colour:* Light green, '7' in yellow *Market Value:* £80-£100/$120-$150

HWM RACING CAR
Ref no: 235 *Reno:* of 23j

HESKETH RACING CAR 308E
1/32 scale *Ref no:* 222 *Production Period:* 1978-1979 *Colour:* Dark blue *Market Value:* £20-£25/$30-$45

HESKETH RACING CAR 308E
1/32 scale *Ref no:* 222 *Production Period:* 1978-1979 *Colour:* Olympus Special dark blue *Market Value:* £50-£80/$75-$120

HILLMAN IMP
Casting used for 214 Hillman Imp Rally *Ref no:* 138 *Production Period:* 1963-1972 *Colour:* Metallic green or metallic red *Market Value:* £60-£90/$90-$135

HILLMAN IMP RALLY
Casting of 138 Imp *Ref no:* 214 *Production Period:* 1966-1968 *Colour:* Blue, '35' *Market Value:* £60-£75/$90-$110

HILLMAN MINX
Ref no: 154 *Reno:* of 40f

HILLMAN MINX
Ref no: 175 *Production Period:* 1958-1961 *Colour:* Blue & grey or green upper & tan lower *Market Value:* £90-£110/$135-$170

HILLMAN MINX SALOON
From 1956: 2 colour scheme only *Ref no:* 40f *Reno:* to 154 *Production Period:* 1950-1958 *Colour:* Tan, shades of green; *Market Value:* £90-£120/$135-$180

HILLMAN MINX SALOON
From 1956: 2 colour scheme only *Ref no:* 154 *Production Period:* 1956-1958 *Colour:* Green with cream upper or blue with pink *Market Value:* £220-£270/$330-$400

HOLDEN SPECIAL SEDAN
The first with jewelled headlights & taillights *Ref no:* 196 *Production Period:* 1963-1969 *Colour:* Bronze with white roof *Market Value:* £50-£70/$75-$100

HOLIDAYS GIFT SET
Contents: 137 Plymouth Fury Convertible, 142 Jaguar Mk 10, 796 Healey Sports boat on trailer, 952 Vega Major Luxury Coach *Ref no:* 124 *Production Period:* 1964-1967 *Market Value:* £450-£650/$675-$1000

HOTCHKISS RACING CAR
Ref no: 23b *Production Period:* 1935-1941 *Colour:* Blue, yellow, orange or green with contrasting flash *Market Value:* £120-£150/$180-$220

HOTCHKISS RACING CAR
Ref no: 23b *Production Period:* 1946-1948 *Colour:* Silver with red flash, red with silver *Market Value:* £60-£80/$90-$120

HUDSON COMMODORE
Ref no: 171 *Reno:* of 139b

HUDSON COMMODORE SEDAN
Ref no: 139b *Reno:* to 171 *Production Period:* 1950-1956 *Colour:* Dark blue with tan or grey roof, cream with maroon *Market Value:* £110-£140/$170-$210

HUDSON COMMODORE SEDAN
1956 second colour on sides, 1958 second colour on lower sides only *Ref no:* 139b *Reno:* to 171 *Production Period:* 1956-1958 *Colour:* Red with light blue or blue with grey *Market Value:* £175-£225/$260-$340

HUDSON HORNET
Ref no: 174 *Production Period:* 1958-1963 *Colour:* Red & cream or yellow & grey *Market Value:* £90-£110/$140-$170

HUMBER (VOGUE SALOON) WITH DRIVER AND FOOTMAN
See introduction *Ref no:* 36c *Production Period:* 1937-1941 *Colour:* Various colours *Market Value:* £250-£350/$375-$525

HUMBER HAWK
Casting used for 256 Police Car *Ref no:* 165 *Production Period:* 1959-1963 *Colour:* Green with black roof & lower sides, green with black roof, cream with maroon roof & sides *Market Value:* £90-£120/$135-$180

HUMBER VOGUE
Ref no: 36c *Production Period:* 1945-1950 *Colour:* Brown or grey *Market Value:* £90-£120/$135-$180

INTERNATIONAL GT GIFT SET
Contents: 187 de tomaso, 215 ford gt, 216 dino ferrari *Ref no:* 246 *Production Period:* 1969-1972 *Market Value:* £90-£140/$135-$210

JAGUAR 'E'-TYPE 2+2
Ref no: 131 *Production Period:* 1968-1974 *Colour:* White, metallic purple, bronze or red *Market Value:* £90-£120/$140-$180

JAGUAR 3.4 LITRE MARK II
The first with steering *Ref no:* 195 *Production Period:* 1960-1964 *Colour:* Maroon, grey or cream *Market Value:* £80-£100/$120-$150

JAGUAR D-TYPE RACING CAR
Ref no: 238 *Production Period:* 1957-1964 *Colour:* Turquoise *Market Value:* £80-£120/$120-$150

JAGUAR E-TYPE
Interchangeable hardtop and folded hood *Ref no:* 120 *Production Period:* 1962-1967 *Colour:* Red *Market Value:* £60-£80/$90-$120

JAGUAR MARK 10
Suitcase & valise *Ref no:* 142 *Production Period:* 1962-1968 *Colour:* Metallic blue *Market Value:* £50-£70/$75-$100

JAGUAR SS (JAGUAR SPORTS CAR)
Renumbered 105 for US market *Ref no:* 38f *Reno:* to 105 *Production Period:* 1946-1956/7 *Colour:* Red, blue, grey or brown *Market Value:* £100-£150/$150-$220

JAGUAR SPORTS CAR
Ref no: 105 *Reno:* of 38f

JAGUAR XK120
Ref no: 157 *Production Period:* 1954-1956 *Colour:* Yellow, red *Market Value:* £110-£140/$165-$225

JAGUAR XK120
Ref no: 157 *Production Period:* 1954-1956 *Colour:* White, grey-green *Market Value:* £200-£250/$300-$375

JAGUAR XK120
Ref no: 157 *Production Period:* 1956-1962 *Colour:* Dark pink with turquoise sides, light grey with yellow sides *Market Value:* £200-£250/$300-$375

JEEP (SPARE ON REAR)
From 1948 US market only, as 153a (army) *Ref no:* 25j *Production Period:* 1947-1952 *Colour:* Red, green, blue *Market Value:* £80-£100/$120-$150

JEEP LATER UNIVERSAL JEEP (SPARE WHEEL ON SIDE)
Used for 669 US Army Jeep *Ref no:* 25y *Reno:* to 405 *Production Period:* 1952-1967 *Colour:* Green, red or orange *Market Value:* £60-£80/$90-$120

JENSEN FF
Ref no: 188 *Production Period:* 1968-1974 *Colour:* Yellow *Market Value:* £45-£70/$75-$100

LAGONDA
Ref no: 102 *Reno:* of 38a

LAGONDA (TOURER)
Renumbered 102 for US market *Ref no:* 38c *Reno:* to 102 *Production Period:* 1946-1955 *Colour:* Green, maroon or grey *Market Value:* £90-£120/$135-$180

LAMBORGHINI MARZAL
Ref no: 189 *Production Period:* 1969-1977 *Colour:* Green, yellow or blue, all with white *Market Value:* £30-£50/$45-$75

LAND ROVER
Ref no: 27d *Reno:* to 340 *Production Period:* 1949-1970 *Colour:* Orange or green, later red *Market Value:* £60-£70/$90-$110

LAND ROVER
Ref no: 340 *Reno:* of 27d

LAND ROVER
Casting used for 277, 282, 442, 604 Land Rovers *Ref no:* 344 *Production Period:* 1970-1978 *Colour:* Metallic red or metallic blue, white insert in back *Market Value:* £15-£20/$20-$30

LARGE OPEN RACING CAR
Ref no: 23c *Production Period:* 1945-1950 *Colour:* Silver, blue *Market Value:* £40-£60/$60-$90

LEYLAND JAGUAR XJ 5.3 COUPÉ / BIG CAT
Ref no: 219 *Production Period:* 1977-1979 *Colour:* White, blue & red Leyland decals *Market Value:* £40-£50/$60-$75

LIMOUSINE
See introduction *Ref no:* 24b *Production Period:* 1934-1940 *Colour:* Various colours *Market Value:* £250-£300/$375-$450

LINCOLN CONTINENTAL
Ref no: 170 *Production Period:* 1964-1969 *Colour:* Metallic orange with white roof or light blue with white *Market Value:* £90-£125/$140-$190

LINCOLN ZEPHYR
Ref no: 39c *Production Period:* 1945-1950 *Colour:* Brown or grey *Market Value:* £100-£130/$150-$200

LINCOLN ZEPHYR
US market only *Ref no:* 39cu *Production Period:* 1950-1952 *Colour:* Red with maroon wings or tan with brown *Market Value:* £450-£650/$700-$1

LINCOLN ZEPHYR COUPÉ
Ref no: 39c *Production Period:* 1939-1941 *Colour:* Grey, yellow, green *Market Value:* £250-£350/$375-$525

LOTUS CORTINA RALLY
Casting of 159 Ford Cortina Mk II *Ref no:* 205 *Production Period:* 1968-1972 *Colour:* White with red panels,'7' *Market Value:* £80-£100/$120-$150

LOTUS EUROPA
Ref no: 218 *Production Period:* 1970-1974 *Colour:* Yellow & blue, yellow & black *Market Value:* £30-£40/$45-$60

LOTUS FORMULA I RACING CAR
Ref no: 225 *Production Period:* 1970-1976 *Colour:* Metallic red, later metallic blue *Market Value:* £20-£25/$30-$45

LOTUS RACING CAR
Ref no: 241 *Production Period:* 1963-1969 *Colour:* Green, '36' *Market Value:* £50-£70/$75-$100

MG MIDGET (COMPETITION FINISH)
Casting as 102 & 129 *Ref no:* 108 *Production Period:* 1955-1959 *Colour:* Red '24' or white '28' *Market Value:* £110-£140/$165-$210

MG MIDGET (TOURING FINISH)
Casting as 108, 129 *Ref no:* 102 *Production Period:* 1957-1960 *Colour:* Light green or yellow *Market Value:* £130-£180/$200-$270

MG SPORTS CAR
Ref no: 35c *Production Period:* 1936-1941 *Colour:* Red, green, blue, maroon *Market Value:* £110-£140/$165-$210

MG SPORTS CAR
US market from 1949 *Ref no:* 35c *Production Period:* 1945-1952 *Colour:* Red or green *Market Value:* £60-£80/$90-$120

MG SPORTS CAR
102 without driver, US market only *Ref no:* 129 *Production Period:* 1955-1956 *Colour:* White with maroon seats or red with tan *Market Value:* £280-£330/$420-$500

MGB
First with opening doors *Ref no:* 113 *Production Period:* 1962-1968 *Colour:* Cream *Market Value:* £60-£80/$90-$120

MASERATI RACING CAR
In box *Ref no:* 23n *Reno:* to 231 & 206 *Production Period:* 1953-1964 *Colour:* Red with white nose flash,' 9' in white *Market Value:* £80-£100/$120-$150

MASERATI RACING CAR
In bubblepack as 206 *Ref no:* 23n *Reno:* to 206 *Production Period:* 1953-1964 *Colour:* Red with white nose flash,' 9' in white *Market Value:* £160-£240/$240-$350

MASERATI RACING CAR
Ref no: 231 *Reno:* of 23n /206

MATRA 630
Ref no: 200 *Production Period:* 1971-1974 *Colour:* Blue *Market Value:* £25-£35/$35-$50

MAYFAIR GIFT SET
Contents: 142 Jaguar Mk 10, 150 Rolls Royce Silver Wraith, 186 Mercedes 220SE, 194 Bentley S-type, 198 Rolls Royce Phantom V, 199 Austin Countryman, 4 plastic figures from 009 Service Station Personnel *Ref no:* 123 *Production Period:* 1963-1964 *Market Value:* £1500-£2000/$2200-$3300

MCLAREN M8A CANAM
Ref no: 223 *Production Period:* 1970-1974 *Colour:* White with metallic blue engine cover '5' *Market Value:* £20-£25/$30-$45

MCLAREN M8A CANAM
Ref no: 223 *Production Period:* 1976-1977 *Colour:* Metallic green *Market Value:* £20-£25/$30-$45

MERCEDES BENZ 220SE
Ref no: 186 *Production Period:* 1961-1966 *Colour:* Shades of blue *Market Value:* £35-£55/$50-$80

MERCEDES-BENZ 250SE
Stop lights *Ref no:* 160 *Production Period:* 1967-1973 *Colour:* Metallic blue *Market Value:* £40-£60/$60-$90

MERCEDES-BENZ 600
Ref no: 128 *Production Period:* 1964-1979 *Colour:* Metallic red, metallic blue *Market Value:* £50-£70/$75-$100

MERCEDES-BENZ C111
Ref no: 224 *Production Period:* 1970-1973 *Colour:* Metallic red, then (export) white, then red *Market Value:* £20-£25/$30-$45

MERCEDES-BENZ RACING CAR
Ref no: 23c *Production Period:* 1936-1941 *Colour:* Yellow, blue, green or red *Market Value:* £90-£110/$135-$170

MERCEDES-BENZ RACING CAR
Ref no: 237 *Production Period:* 1957-1968 *Colour:* White but 1960-62 cream, late matt white, '30' in red *Market Value:* £80-£100/$120-$150

MERCURY COUGAR
Ref no: 174 *Production Period:* 1969-1972 *Colour:* Metallic blue *Market Value:* £35-£45/$50-$70

MIDGET RACER
Ref no: 200 *Reno:* of 35b

MIDGET TOURER
No wire screen *Ref no:* 35d *Production Period:* 1945-1948 *Colour:* Blue, brown, yellow *Market Value:* £60-£80/$90-$120

MINI CLUBMAN
Casting used for 255 Police Mini Clubman *Ref no:* 178 *Production Period:* 1975-1979 *Colour:* Bronze or red *Market Value:* £30-£45/$45-$65

MONTEVERDI 375L
Ref no: 190 *Production Period:* 1970-1973 *Colour:* Metallic red *Market Value:* £35-£45/$50-$75

MORRIS MINI MINOR (AUTOMATIC)
Ref no: 183 *Production Period:* 1966-1974 *Colour:* Red with black roof, metallic red with black or all metallic blue *Market Value:* £70-£90/$100-$135

MORRIS MINI-TRAVELLER
Ref no: 197 *Production Period:* 1961-1970 *Colour:* White with brown wood or green with brown *Market Value:* £60-£90/$90-$135

MORRIS OXFORD
Ref no: 159 *Reno:* of 40g

MORRIS OXFORD (BULL NOSE) 1913
Casting used for 477 Parsley's Car & 486 *Ref no:* 476 *Production Period:* 1965-1969 *Colour:* Yellow body, blue chassis *Market Value:* £50-£70/$75-$100

MORRIS OXFORD SALOON
From 1956: 2 colour scheme only *Ref no:* 40g *Reno:* to 159 *Production Period:* 1950-1960 *Colour:* Green, grey *Market Value:* £80-£100/$120-$150

MORRIS OXFORD SALOON
From 1956: 2 colour scheme only *Ref no:* 159 *Production Period:* 1956-1960 *Colour:* Cream with green upper or pink with cream *Market Value:* £150-£200/$220-$300

MORRIS1100
Ref no: 140 *Production Period:* 1963-1968 *Colour:* Light blue *Market Value:* £40-£50/$60-$75

MOTOR CARS
Contents: 24a, 24b, 24c, 24d, 24e, 24f, 24g, 24h. *Ref no:* 24 *Production Period:* 1934-1940 *Market Value:* A

MOTOR CARS (WITH DRIVER, PASSENGERS, FOOTMEN)
Contents: 36a, 36b, 36c, 36d, 36e, 36f. *Ref no:* 36 *Production Period:* 1937-1941 *Market Value:* A

MOTOR SHOW SET
Contents: 127 Rolls Royce Silver Cloud, 133 Ford Cortina replaced in 1968 by 159 Ford Cortina, 151 Vauxhall Victor 101, 171 Austin 1800 *Ref no:* 126 *Production Period:* 1965-1969 *Market Value:* £900-£1200/$1350-$1800

MOTOR TRUCK
Cab/chassis as 22d *Ref no:* 22c *Production Period:* 1933-1935 *Colour:* Blue cab with red back, red with green, blue with cream, yellow with blue *Market Value:* £300-£350/$450-$550

MOTOR VEHICLES
Contents: 22a, 22b, 22c, 22d, 22e, 22f *Ref no:* 22 *Production Period:* 1933-1935 *Market Value:* £2000-£3000/$3000-$4500

MOTOR VEHICLES
Contents: 30a, 30b, 30c, 30d, 30e, 30f *Ref no:* 30 *Production Period:* 1935-1937 *Market Value:* A

MOTOR VEHICLES
Contents: 30a, 30b, 30c, 30d, 30e, 30g *Ref no:* 30 *Production Period:* 1937-1941 *Market Value:* A

NSU RO80
Ref no: 176 *Production Period:* 1969-1973 *Colour:* Metallic red *Market Value:* £35-£55/$50-$80

NSU RO80
Ref no: 176 *Production Period:* 1969-1973 *Colour:* Metallic blue *Market Value:* £100-£130/$150-$200

NASH RAMBLER
Casting used for 257 Canadian Fire Chief's Car *Ref no:* 173 *Production Period:* 1958-1962 *Colour:* Green with red flash or pink with blue *Market Value:* £60-£80/$90-$120

OLDSMOBILE
From 1950 US only *Ref no:* 39b *Production Period:* 1945-1952 *Colour:* Grey, cream, blue *Market Value:* £100-£130/$150-$200

OLDSMOBILE
US market only *Ref no:* 39bu *Production Period:* 1950-1952 *Colour:* Cream with tan wings or duotone blue *Market Value:* £450-£650/$700-$1000

OLDSMOBILE 6 SEDAN
Ref no: 39b *Production Period:* 1939-1941 *Colour:* Black or green *Market Value:* £250-£350/$375-$525

OPEL COMMODORE
French body casting of no.1420 *Ref no:* 179 *Production Period:* 1971-1974 *Colour:* Metallic blue with black roof *Market Value:* £30-£50/$45-$75

OPEL KAPITAN
Ref no: 177 *Production Period:* 1961-1967 *Colour:* Light blue *Market Value:* £60-£80/$90-$120

PACKARD
Ref no: 39a *Production Period:* 1945-1950 *Colour:* Brown, green or olive *Market Value:* £100-£130/$150-$200

PACKARD CLIPPER
Ref no: 180 *Production Period:* 1958-1963 *Colour:* Fawn with pink top, orange with grey top *Market Value:* £90-£120/$140-$180

PACKARD CONVERTIBLE
Ref no: 132 *Production Period:* 1955-1961 *Colour:* Green or tan *Market Value:* £80-£120/$120-$180

PACKARD SUPER 8 TOURING SEDAN CAR
Separate headlamps *Ref no:* 39a *Production Period:* 1939-1941 *Colour:* Green, grey, yellow, blue *Market Value:* £250-£350/$375-$525

PASSENGER CARS
Contents: 27f Estate Car, 30h Daimler Ambulance, 40e Standard Vanguard, 40g Morris Oxford, 40h Austin Taxi, 140b Rover 75 *Ref no:* 3 *Production Period:* 1952-1953 *Market Value:* £800-£1100/$1200-$1650

PEUGEOT 504
From Solido - Cougar *Ref no:* 505 *Production Period:* 1981-1982 *Colour:* Metallic blue or pale gold *Market Value:* £14-£18/$20-$25

PLYMOUTH FURY CONVERTIBLE
Casting as 115 Plymouth Fury Sports *Ref no:* 137 *Production Period:* 1963-1965 *Colour:* Metallic grey, green, blue or pink *Market Value:* £70-£90/$100-$140

PLYMOUTH FURY SPORTS
Casting as 137 *Ref no:* 115 *Production Period:* 1965-1968 *Colour:* White *Market Value:* £70-£90/$100-$140

PLYMOUTH PLAZA
Casting used for 265 & 266 Plymouth Taxi *Ref no:* 178 *Production Period:* 1959-1963 *Colour:* Pink with green, light blue with dark blue *Market Value:* £110-£140/$165-$210

PLYMOUTH PLAZA
Casting used for 265 & 266 Plymouth Taxi *Ref no:* 178 *Production Period:* 1959-1963 *Colour:* Light blue with white *Market Value:* £250-£300/$375-$450

PLYMOUTH STOCK CAR
Casting of 244 Police Car & 278 Yellow Cab with wide wheels *Ref no:* 201 *Production Period:* 1979-1979 *Colour:* Dark blue, stickers 34 on sides and boot, 426ci on bonnet *Market Value:* £40-£60/$60-$90

PONTIAC PARISIENNE
First with retractable aerials, casting used for 251 & 252 Police cars *Ref no:* 173 *Production Period:* 1969-1972 *Colour:* Metallic maroon *Market Value:* £45-£55/$70-$85

PORSCHE 356A COUPÉ
Ref no: 182 *Production Period:* 1958-1964 *Colour:* Cream, red, light blue *Market Value:* £90-£120/$140-$180

PORSCHE 356A COUPÉ
Ref no: 182 *Production Period:* 1958-1964 *Colour:* Pinkish maroon *Market Value:* £200-£250/$300-$375

PRINCESS 2200HL SALOON
1/35 scale *Ref no:* 123 *Production Period:* 1977-1979 *Colour:* Bronze, white with black roof, or all white *Market Value:* £25-£30/$35-$45

PRIVATE AUTOMOBILES
Contents: 39a Packard, 39b Oldsmobile, 39c Lincoln Zephyr, 39d Buick, 39e Chrysler, US, Canadian & SA markets *Ref no:* 2 *Production Period:* 1947-1949 *Market Value:* A

PRIVATE AUTOMOBILES
Contents: 30d Vauxhall, 36a Armstrong Siddeley, 36b Bentley, 38a Frazer-Nash, 39b Oldsmobile, US & SA markets, 30d, 36d Rover, 36b, 38a, 38c Lagonda, Canadian market *Ref no:* 3 *Production Period:* 1947-1949 *Market Value:* A

RACER
Early, no driver *Ref no:* 35b *Production Period:* 1936-1941 *Colour:* Red or silver *Market Value:* £110-£140/$165-$210

RACER (LATER MIDGET CAR RACER)
Ref no: 35b *Reno:* to 200 *Production Period:* 1945-1957 *Colour:* Red or silver *Market Value:* £50-£60/$75-$90

RACING CAR
Stub exhausts, no driver, then with driver & fishtail exhaust *Ref no:* 23 *Reno:* to 23a *Production Period:* 1934-1935 *Colour:* Cream, blue, white, yellow with contrasting flash *Market Value:* £140-£160/$210-$240

RACING CAR
With 'humbug' stripes *Ref no:* 23a *Reno:* of 23 *Production Period:* 1935-1941 *Colour:* Blue & white, brown & cream, orange & green, cream & orange *Market Value:* £300-£400/$450-$600

RACING CAR
With stripe or flash *Ref no:* 23a *Reno:* of 23 *Production Period:* 1935-1941 *Colour:* Various colours with contrasting stripe *Market Value:* £90-£120/$130-$180

RACING CAR SET
240 Cooper, 241 Lotus, 242 Ferrari, 243 BRM + 4 figures *Ref no:* 201 *Production Period:* 1965-1968 *Market Value:* £350-£400/$525-$600

RACING CARS
Contents: 23f/232 Alfa Romeo, 23g/233 Cooper-Bristol, 23h/234 Ferrari, 23j/235 HWM, 23n/231 Maserati *Ref no:* 4 *Reno:* to 249 *Production Period:* 1953-1958 *Market Value:* £900-£1200/$1300-$1750

RACING CARS
Contents: 23c, 23d, 23e *Ref no:* 23 *Production Period:* 1936-1941 *Market Value:* £400-£500/$600-$750

RACING CARS GIFT SET
Ref no: 249 *Reno:* of 4

RAMBLER CROSS-COUNTRY STATION WAGON
Black rear roof rack *Ref no:* 193 *Production Period:* 1961-1968 *Colour:* Yellow with white roof *Market Value:* £80-£100/$120-$150

RANGE ROVER
Casting used for 195, 203, 253, 254 *Ref no:* 192 *Production Period:* 1970-1979 *Colour:* Bronze or yellow *Market Value:* £25-£30/$35-$50

RENAULT 14
Not issued *Ref no:* 507

RENAULT R16
French body casting of 537 *Ref no:* 166 *Production Period:* 1967-1969 *Colour:* Dark blue *Market Value:* £40-£60/$60-$90

RILEY
Ref no: 158 *Reno:* of 40a

RILEY SALOON
Separate headlamps *Ref no:* 40a *Reno:* to 158 *Production Period:* 1947-1960 *Colour:* 40a: green, grey, dark blue, mid blue; 158: cream, green *Market Value:* £70-£110/$100-$165

ROLLS ROYCE CAR
See introduction *Ref no:* 30b *Production Period:* 1935-1941 *Colour:* Various colours *Market Value:* £200-£250/$300-$375

ROLLS ROYCE CAR
Ref no: 30b *Production Period:* 1946-1950 *Colour:* Fawn or dark blue *Market Value:* £90-£120/$140-$180

ROLLS ROYCE PHANTOM V
Ref no: 198 *Production Period:* 1962-1965 *Colour:* Metallic green & cream or 2-tone grey *Market Value:* £70-£90/$100-$135

ROLLS ROYCE PHANTOM V LIMOUSINE
Various versions of accessories *Ref no:* 152 *Production Period:* 1966-1976 *Colour:* Dark blue, later metallic blue *Market Value:* £35-£60/$50-$90

ROLLS ROYCE SILVER SHADOW
Ref no: 158 *Production Period:* 1967-1972 *Colour:* Metallic red, metallic blue *Market Value:* £40-£70/$60-$100

ROLLS-ROYCE PHANTOM V LIMOUSINE
Casting of 152 without opening bonnet *Ref no:* 124 *Production Period:* 1977-1979 *Colour:* Metallic blue *Market Value:* £40-£60/$60-$90

ROLLS-ROYCE SILVER CLOUD III
Ref no: 127 *Production Period:* 1964-1971 *Colour:* Metallic green, bronze *Market Value:* £60-£80/$90-$120

ROLLS-ROYCE SILVER WRAITH
First with suspension *Ref no:* 150 *Production Period:* 1959-1964 *Colour:* Light grey upper, dark grey lower *Market Value:* £60-£80/$90-$120

ROVER
Ref no: 36d *Production Period:* 1945-1950 *Colour:* Green or blue *Market Value:* £90-£120/$135-$180

ROVER (STREAMLINED SALOON) WITH DRIVER AND PASSENGER
See introduction *Ref no:* 36d *Production Period:* 1937-1941 *Colour:* Various colours *Market Value:* £250-£350/$375-$525

ROVER 3500 SALOON
Made in Hong Kong, issued after factory closure, 1/35 scale *Ref no:* 180 *Production Period:* 1979-1979 *Colour:* White *Market Value:* £15-£20/$20-$25

ROVER 75
Ref no: 140b *Reno:* to 156 *Production Period:* 1951-1956 *Colour:* Maroon, cream or red *Market Value:* £80-£100/$120-$150

ROVER 75
From 1956 two-colour finish (only) *Ref no:* 140b *Reno:* to 156 *Production Period:* 1956-1958 *Colour:* Light green upper with dark green lower, cream with blue *Market Value:* £100-£140/$150-$220

ROVER 75
Ref no: 156 *Reno:* of 140b

SAAB 96
Ref no: 156 *Production Period:* 1966-1970 *Colour:* Metallic red *Market Value:* £60-£80/$90-$120

SALOON CAR
Ref no: 35a *Production Period:* 1936-1941 *Colour:* Grey, blue, red, turquoise *Market Value:* £90-£130/$120-$190

SALOON CAR
US market from 1949 *Ref no:* 35a *Production Period:* 1945-1952 *Colour:* Grey or blue *Market Value:* £50-£70/$75-$100

SALOON CARS (LATER USA SALOON CARS)
Contents: 39a, 39b, 39c, 39d, 39e, 39f *Ref no:* 39 *Production Period:* 1939-1941 *Market Value:* £1750-£2500/$2500-$3800

SINGER GAZELLE
Ref no: 168 *Production Period:* 1959-1963 *Colour:* Cream & brown or grey & green *Market Value:* £90-£110/$135-$170

SINGER VOGUE
Ref no: 145 *Production Period:* 1962-1966 *Colour:* Metallic green *Market Value:* £60-£80/$90-$120

SMALL CARS
Contents: 35a, 35b, 35c *Ref no:* 35 *Production Period:* 1936-1941 *Market Value:* £400-£500/$600-$750

SMALL OPEN RACING CAR
Ref no: 23a *Reno:* to 220 *Production Period:* 1945-1956 *Colour:* Silver with red flash, red or blue with silver or cream *Market Value:* £40-£50/$60-$75

SMALL OPEN RACING CAR
Ref no: 220 *Reno:* of 23a

SPORTS CAR
Windscreen unit separate, grille surround shiny tinplate *Ref no:* 22a *Production Period:* 1933-1935 *Colour:* Red with cream wings & radiator, cream with red *Market Value:* £300-£350/$450-$525

SPORTS CARS GIFT SET
Contents: 107 Sunbeam Alpine, 108 MG midget, 109 Austin Healey 100, 110 Aston Martin DB3S, 111 Triumph TR2 *Ref no:* 149 *Production Period:* 1957-1959 *Market Value:* £1000-£1500/$1500-$2100

SPORTS COUPÉ
Grille surround shiny tinplate *Ref no:* 22b *Production Period:* 1933-1935 *Colour:* Yellow with green wings & roof, red with cream *Market Value:* £300-£350/$450-$525

SPORTS TOURER (2-SEATER)
See introduction *Ref no:* 24h *Production Period:* 1934-1941 *Colour:* Various colours *Market Value:* £250-£300/$375-$450

SPORTS TOURER (4-SEATER)

See introduction *Ref no:* 24g *Production Period:* 1934-1941 *Colour:* Various colours *Market Value:* £250-£300/$375-$450

SPORTSMAN'S COUPÉ

See introduction *Ref no:* 24f *Production Period:* 1934-1940 *Colour:* Various colours *Market Value:* £250-£300/$375-$450

STANDARD VANGUARD

Open wheel arches to 1950 *Ref no:* 40e *Reno:* to 153 *Production Period:* 1948-1960 *Colour:* Tan *Market Value:* £80-£130/$120-$200

STANDARD VANGUARD

Closed rear wheel arches *Ref no:* 40e *Reno:* to 153 *Production Period:* 1948-1960 *Colour:* Tan, light blue, cream *Market Value:* £80-£100/$120-$150

STANDARD VANGUARD

Closed rear wheel arches *Ref no:* 40e *Reno:* to 153 *Production Period:* 1948-1960 *Colour:* Dark blue, maroon *Market Value:* £300-£400/$450-$600

STANDARD VANGUARD SALOON

Ref no: 153 *Reno:* of 40e

STREAMLINED RACING CAR

Casting as 23m *Ref no:* 23s *Production Period:* 1939-1941 *Colour:* Light green or light blue *Market Value:* £80-£110/$120-$160

STREAMLINED RACING CAR

Casting as 23m *Ref no:* 23s *Reno:* to 222 *Production Period:* 1945-1957 *Colour:* Green, blue or silver *Market Value:* £40-£70/$60-$100

STREAMLINED RACING CAR

Ref no: 222 *Reno:* of 23s

STREAMLINED SALOON

Ref no: 22h *Production Period:* 1935-1941 *Colour:* Red, blue, cream *Market Value:* £180-£220/$270-$330

STREAMLINED TOURER

Ref no: 22g *Production Period:* 1935-1941 *Colour:* Red, dark blue, maroon *Market Value:* £180-£220/$270-$330

STUDEBAKER

Ref no: 39f *Production Period:* 1945-1950 *Colour:* Dark blue, grey or olive *Market Value:* £100-£130/$150-$200

STUDEBAKER GOLDEN HAWK

Ref no: 169 *Production Period:* 1958-1963 *Colour:* Green & cream or red & tan *Market Value:* £90-£120/$140-$180

STUDEBAKER LAND CRUISER

Comments as 139a *Ref no:* 172 *Production Period:* 1954-1958 *Colour:* Light blue or green *Market Value:* £100-£120/$150-$180

STUDEBAKER LAND CRUISER

Comments as 139a *Ref no:* 172 *Production Period:* 1954-1958 *Colour:* Maroon with cream, tan with cream *Market Value:* £150-£200/$225-$300

STUDEBAKER PRESIDENT

Ref no: 179 *Production Period:* 1958-1963 *Colour:* Yellow with blue flash or light blue with blue *Market Value:* £90-£120/$140-$180

STUDEBAKER STATE COMMANDER

Ref no: 39f *Production Period:* 1939-1941 *Colour:* Yellow, green or grey *Market Value:* £250-£350/$375-$525

SUNBEAM ALPINE (COMPETITION FINISH)

Casting as 101 *Ref no:* 107 *Production Period:* 1955-1959 *Colour:* Light blue '26' or pink '34' *Market Value:* £80-£100/$120-$150

SUNBEAM ALPINE (TOURING FINISH)

Casting as 107 *Ref no:* 101 *Production Period:* 1957-1960 *Colour:* Blue or pinkish-maroon *Market Value:* £90-£120/$135-$180

SUNBEAM RAPIER

Ref no: 166 *Production Period:* 1958-1963 *Colour:* Cream with orange sides, duotone blue *Market Value:* £85-£120/$130-$180

SUNBEAM TALBOT

Ref no: 101 *Reno:* of 38b

SUNBEAM-TALBOT

Renumbered 101 for US market *Ref no:* 38b *Reno:* to 101 *Production Period:* 1945-1954 *Colour:* Yellow, blue or brown *Market Value:* £100-£130/$150-$200

SUNBEAM-TALBOT SPORTS CAR

Ref no: 38b *Production Period:* 1940-1941 *Colour:* Red, maroon or royal blue *Market Value:* £150-£200/$220-$300

SUPER SPRINTER

Starter unit 754 *Ref no:* 228 *Production Period:* 1970-1972 *Colour:* Blue & orange *Market Value:* £20-£25/$30-$45

SUPER STREAMLINED SALOON

See introduction *Ref no:* 24e *Production Period:* 1934-1940 *Colour:* Various colours *Market Value:* £250-£300/$375-$450

SUPERFAST GIFT SET

Contents: 131 Jaguar E-type, 153 Aston Martin DB6, 188 Jensen FF *Ref no:* 245 *Production Period:* 1969-1972 *Market Value:* £130-£180/$200-$270

TALBOT LAGO RACING CAR

In box *Ref no:* 23k *Reno:* to 230 & 205 *Production Period:* 1953-1964 *Colour:* Blue, '4' in yellow *Market Value:* £80-£100/$120-$150

TALBOT LAGO RACING CAR

In bubblepack as 205 *Ref no:* 23k *Reno:* to 205 *Production Period:* 1953-1964 *Colour:* Blue, '4' in yellow *Market Value:* £160-£240/$240-$350

TALBOT-LAGO RACING CAR

Ref no: 230 *Reno:* of 23k /205

TOURING GIFT SET

Contents: 188 Caravan, 193 Rambler Station Wagon, 195 Jaguar 3.4, 270 AA Motorcycle patrol, 295 Atlas Kenebrake, 796 Healey sports boat on trailer *Ref no:* 122 *Production Period:* 1963-1964 *Market Value:* £700-£1000/$1000-$1500

TOW-AWAY GLIDER SET

135 Triumph 2000 with trailer & glider *Ref no:* 118 *Production Period:* 1965-1969 *Colour:* Car: cream with blue roof, trailer: cream with red *Market Value:* £90-£120/$135-$180

TOWN SEDAN

See introduction *Ref no: 24c Production Period: 1934-1941 Colour:* Various colours *Market Value:* £350-£400/$500-$600

TRIUMPH 'DOLOMITE'

Advertised in 1939/40 but never issued *Ref no:* 38e

TRIUMPH 1300

Ref no: 162 Production Period: 1966-1969 Colour: Light blue *Market Value:* £45-£70/$65-$95

TRIUMPH 1800 SALOON

Separate headlamps *Ref no:* 40b *Reno:* to 151 *Production Period: 1948-1960 Colour:* Grey, blue, fawn *Market Value:* £90-£120/$135-$180

TRIUMPH 1800 SALOON

Separate headlamps *Ref no:* 40b *Production Period:* 1948-1954 *Colour:* Black *Market Value:* £300-£400/$450-$600

TRIUMPH 1800 SALOON

Ref no: 151 *Reno:* of 40b

TRIUMPH 2000

2 suitcases *Ref no:* 135 *Production Period: 1963-1968 Colour:* Metallic green with white roof, see also 118 *Market Value:* £60-£80/$90-$120

TRIUMPH 2000

Provenance essential for these models *Ref no:* 135 *Production Period:* ? *Colour:* Various accurate Triumph colour schemes exist, not all are factory finished *Market Value:* A

TRIUMPH HERALD

Ref no: 189 *Production Period: 1959-1963 Colour:* Green roof & sides with white centre, or blue with white *Market Value:* £70-£90/$100-$140

TRIUMPH HERALD

Provenance essential for these models *Ref no:* 189 *Production Period:* ? *Colour:* Various authentic Triumph factory colours schemes *Market Value:* A

TRIUMPH SPITFIRE

Detachable seat belt *Ref no:* 114 *Production Period: 1963-1970 Colour:* Silver-grey, red, gold, purple *Market Value:* £80-£110/$120-$165

TRIUMPH TR2 (COMPETITION FINISH)

Casting as 105 *Ref no:* 111 *Production Period: 1956-1959 Colour:* Turquoise '25' or pink '29' *Market Value:* £80-£110/$120-$165

TRIUMPH TR2 (TOURING FINISH)

Casting as 111 *Ref no:* 105 *Production Period: 1957-1960 Colour:* Yellow or grey *Market Value:* £130-£160/$200-$240

TRIUMPH TR7 RALLY CAR

Casting of 211 TR7, 'Leyland' & '8' *Ref no:* 207 *Production Period: 1977-1979 Colour:* White with blue & red stripes *Market Value:* £25-£30/$35-$45

TRIUMPH TR7 SPORTS CAR

Casting used for 207 TR7 Rally Car *Ref no:* 211 *Production Period: 1976-1979 Colour:* Metallic blue-green, red, white (BL promotional) *Market Value:* £40-£60/$60-$90

TRIUMPH VITESSE

Replaced 189 Triumph Herald *Ref no:* 134 *Production Period: 1964-1967 Colour:* Metallic green with white flashes *Market Value:* £60-£80/$90-$120

UNIVERSAL JEEP

Ref no: 405 *Reno:* of 25y

VW PORSCHE 914

Ref no: 208 *Production Period: 1971-1974 Colour:* Yellow *Market Value:* £25-£30/$35-$45

VW PORSCHE 914

Whizzwheels *Ref no:* 208 *Production Period: 1976-1979 Colour:* Metallic blue with black bonnet *Market Value:* £20-£25/$30-$40

VANWALL

Ref no: 210 *Reno:* of 239

VANWALL RACING CAR

'Vanwall' decals *Ref no:* 239 *Reno:* to 210 *Production Period: 1958-1965 Colour:* Green *Market Value:* £45-£70/$65-$100

VAUXHALL CAR

See introduction *Ref no:* 30d *Production Period: 1935-1941 Colour:* Various colours *Market Value:* £200-£250/$300-$375

VAUXHALL CAR

Ref no: 30d *Production Period: 1946-1948 Colour:* Dark green or brown *Market Value:* £90-£120/$140-$180

VAUXHALL CRESTA

Ref no: 164 *Production Period: 1957-1960 Colour:* Grey & green or maroon & cream *Market Value:* £90-£120/$140-$180

VAUXHALL VICTOR 101

Self-adhesive chrome window surrounds *Ref no:* 151 *Production Period: 1965-1968 Colour:* Yellow, later metallic red *Market Value:* £60-£80/$90-$120

VAUXHALL VICTOR ESTATE CAR

Ref no: 141 *Production Period: 1963-1967 Colour:* Yellow *Market Value:* £40-£60/$60-$90

VAUXHALL VIVA

Ref no: 136 *Production Period: 1964-1972 Colour:* White, light metallic blue or blue *Market Value:* £60-£80/$90-$120

VOGUE SALOON

See introduction *Ref no:* 24d *Production Period: 1934-1940 Colour:* Various colours *Market Value:* £250-£300/$375-$450

VOLKSWAGEN (BEETLE)

Casting used for 1st issue 262 VW Swiss PTT Car *Ref no:* 181 *Production Period: 1956-1969 Colour:* Grey, green, dark blue, blue-grey, light blue *Market Value:* £60-£80/$90-$120

VOLKSWAGEN 1300 SEDAN/DE LUXE

Casting used for 260 'DB' & 262 'PTT'. *Ref no:* 129 *Production Period: 1965-1975 Colour:* Metallic blue *Market Value:* £45-£60/$70-$90

VOLKSWAGEN 1500
Suitcase, spare tyre *Ref no:* 144 *Production Period:* 1963-1966 *Colour:* Cream or gold *Market Value:* £40-£60/$60-$90

VOLKSWAGEN 1600TL FASTBACK
Ref no: 163 *Production Period:* 1966-1970 *Colour:* Red or dark metallic red *Market Value:* £35-£55/$55-$85

VOLKSWAGEN 1600TL FASTBACK
Ref no: 163 *Production Period:* 1966-1970 *Colour:* Metallic blue *Market Value:* £60-£90/$80-$135

VOLKSWAGEN KARMANN-GHIA COUPÉ
Ref no: 187 *Production Period:* 1959-1963 *Colour:* Red with black roof or green with cream *Market Value:* £70-£90/$100-$140

VOLVO 122S
Ref no: 184 *Production Period:* 1961-1964 *Colour:* Red *Market Value:* £80-£90/$120-$135

VOLVO 122S
Ref no: 184 *Production Period:* 1961-1964 *Colour:* White *Market Value:* £200-£250/$300-$375

VOLVO 1800S
Ref no: 116 *Production Period:* 1966-1971 *Colour:* Red or dark metallic red *Market Value:* £60-£80/$90-$120

VOLVO 265DL ESTATE CAR
1/35 scale, made in Italy *Ref no:* 122 *Production Period:* 1977-1979 *Colour:* Metallic blue or orange *Market Value:* £30-£40/$45-$60

WORLD FAMOUS RACING CARS
Contents: 230 talbot lago, 231 maserati, 232 alfa-romeo, 233 cooper-bristol, 234 ferrari, 239 vanwall *Ref no:* 249 *Production Period:* 1962-1963 *Market Value:* £800-£1/$1-$1

SECTION 4

Dublo Dinky

This small range was designed as accessories for the Hornby Dublo railway system. Most of the subjects were not modelled in the usual Dinky scale elsewhere in the range which is a pity as some of them are very interesting subjects. There was only 1 colour for each model, variations only involved the wheels: black or grey plastic, treaded or plain.

AEC MERCURY TANKER 'SHELL BP'
Ref no: 070 *Production Period:* 1959-1964 *Colour:* Green cab, red tank, Shell Petroleum Products BP *Market Value:* £75-£85/$100-$120

AUSTIN LORRY
Ref no: 064 *Production Period:* 1957-1962 *Colour:* Green *Market Value:* £45-£55/$65-$80

AUSTIN TAXI
Ref no: 067 *Production Period:* 1959-1966 *Colour:* Blue & cream *Market Value:* £65-£80/$90-$115

BEDFORD ARTICULATED FLAT TRUCK
Ref no: 072 *Production Period:* 1959-1965 *Colour:* Yellow tractor, red trailer *Market Value:* £60-£65/$85-$95

BEDFORD FLAT TRUCK
Ref no: 066 *Production Period:* 1957-1960 *Colour:* Grey *Market Value:* £50-£60/$70-$85

COMMER VAN
Ref no: 063 *Production Period:* 1958-1960 *Colour:* Blue *Market Value:* £45-£55/$65-$80

FORD PREFECT
Ref no: 061 *Production Period:* 1958-1960 *Colour:* Fawn *Market Value:* £60-£70/$85-$100

LANCING-BAGNAL TRACTOR & TRAILER
Ref no: 076 *Production Period:* 1960-1965 *Colour:* Maroon, blue driver *Market Value:* £60-£75/$85-$95

LAND ROVER, TRAILER & HORSE
Ref no: 073 *Production Period:* 1960-1967 *Colour:* Green Landrover, orange horsebox *Market Value:* £75-£85/$100-$120

LANSING-BAGNAL TRAILER (ONLY)
Ref no: 078 *Production Period:* 1960-1971 *Colour:* Maroon *Market Value:* £35-£40/$45-$55

MASSEY-HARRIS FERGUSON TRACTOR
Ref no: 069 *Production Period:* 1959-1965 *Colour:* Blue *Market Value:* £50-£60/$70-$85

MORRIS PICK-UP
Ref no: 065 *Production Period:* 1957-1960 *Colour:* Red *Market Value:* £34-£55/$65-$80

ROYAL MAIL VAN
Ref no: 068 *Production Period:* 1959-1964 *Colour:* Red *Market Value:* £75-£85/$100-$120

SINGER ROADSTER
Ref no: 062 *Production Period:* 1958-1960 *Colour:* Dark yellow, red seats *Market Value:* £60-£70/$85-$100

VOLKSWAGEN DELIVERY VAN 'HORNBY-DUBLO'
Ref no: 071 *Production Period:* 1959-1967 *Colour:* Yellow *Market Value:* £60-£70/$85-$100

Farm Machinery

Farm toys have been more popular in the US than Europe over the years but Dinky managed to produce a small but very interesting range. Starting in 1948 production of many items was kept up till 1970. The only pre-war tractor was in the first, 22 Series, selection. This was 22e, a Fordson type, which is covered in the CARS section of the book.

Most of the farm toys had only one colour scheme and there were few casting changes. In general they have not attracted high prices from collectors, the exceptions as always being the Gift Sets.

COW
1 of each colour in set *Ref no:* 2b *Production Period:* 1932-1941 *Colour:* Brown. Black & white *Market Value:* £20-£25/$30-$40

DAVID BROWN TRACTOR
Ref no: 305 *Production Period:* 1964-1975 *Colour:* Red & yellow, later white *Market Value:* £50-£80/$75-$120

DAVID BROWN TRACTOR AND DISC HARROW
Contents : 305 David Brown Tractor, 224 Disc Harrow *Ref no:* 325 *Production Period:* 1966-1972 *Market Value:* £70-£90/$100-$140

DISC HARROW
Ref no: 27h *Reno:* to 322 *Production Period:* 1951-1971 *Colour:* Red & yellow, later white & red *Market Value:* £15-£20/$20-$30

DISC HARROW
Ref no: 322 *Reno:* of 27h

FARM EQUIPMENT GIFT SET
Contents: as 1 Farmyard Equipment Gift Set *Ref no:* 398 *Reno:* of 1 *Production Period:* 1964-1965

FARM TRACTOR
See under 'CARS' *Ref no:* 22e *Production Period:* 1933-1941

FARM TRACTOR AND HAY RAKE
Contents : 27a/300 Massey-Harris Tractor, 27k/234 Hay Rake *Ref no:* 27ak *Reno:* to 310 *Production Period:* 1953-1966 *Market Value:* £150-£200/$230-$300

FARM TRACTOR AND HAY RAKE
Ref no: 310 *Reno:* of27ak

FARM TRACTOR AND TRAILER SET
Contents: 300 Massey-Ferguson Tractor, 428 Large Trailer *Ref no:* 399 *Production Period:* 1969-1973 *Market Value:* £100-£150/$150-$200

FARMYARD EQUIPMENT/FARM GEAR
Contents : 27a/300 Massey-Harris Tractor, 27b/320 Halesowen Harvest Trailer, 27c/321 Massey-Harris Manure Spreader, 27h/322 Disc Harrow, 27k/324 Hay Rake *Ref no:* 1 *Reno:* to 398 *Production Period:* 1952-1954 *Market Value:* £1000-£1400/$1500-$2000

FIELD MARSHALL FARM TRACTOR
Ref no: 27n *Reno:* to 301 *Production Period:* 1953-1966 *Colour:* Orange *Market Value:* £80-£100/$120-$150

FIELD MARSHALL TRACTOR
Ref no: 301 *Reno:* of 27n

FOUR-WHEEL HAND TRUCK
Ref no: 105c *Reno:* to 383 *Production Period:* 1949-1958 *Colour:* Blue or green *Market Value:* £15-£20/$20-$30

FOUR-WHEELED HAND TRUCK
Ref no: 383 *Reno:* of 105c

GARDEN ROLLER
No markings *Ref no:* 105a *Reno:* to 381 *Production Period:* 1948-1958 *Colour:* Green & red *Market Value:* £15-£20/$20-$30

GARDEN ROLLER
Ref no: 381 *Reno:* of 105a

GRASS CUTTER
Ref no: 105e *Reno:* to 384 *Production Period:* 1949-1958 *Colour:* Yellow with green *Market Value:* £15-£20/$20-$30

GRASS CUTTER
Ref no: 384 *Reno:* of 105e

HALESOWEN HARVEST TRAILER
Ref no: 27b *Reno:* to 320 *Production Period:* 1949-1970 *Colour:* Tan & red, later red & yellow *Market Value:* £25-£35/$40-$60

HALESOWEN HARVEST TRAILER
Ref no: 320 *Reno:* of 27b

HAY RAKE
Ref no: 27k *Reno:* to 324 *Production Period:* 1953-1970 *Colour:* Red & yellow *Market Value:* £25-£30/$40-$50

HAY RAKE
Ref no: 324 *Reno:* of 27k

HORSE
1 of each colour in set *Ref no:* 2a *Production Period:* 1932-1941 *Colour:* Brown. White *Market Value:* £20-£25/$30-$40

LAWN MOWER
Ref no: 386 *Reno:* of 751

LAWN MOWER
751 Dinky Supertoys, 386 Dinky Toys *Ref no:* 751 *Reno:* to 386 *Production Period:* 1949-1958 *Colour:* Green & red *Market Value:* £80-£100/$120-$150

LEYLAND 384 TRACTOR
Ref no: 308 *Production Period:* 1971-1979 *Colour:* Metallic red *Market Value:* £30-£45/$45-$60

LEYLAND 384 TRACTOR
Ref no: 308 *Production Period:* 1971-1979 *Colour:* Blue *Market Value:* £50-£80/$75-$120

MASSEY HARRIS/FERGUSON TRACTOR
Ref no: 300 *Reno:* of 27a

MASSEY-HARRIS MANURE SPREADER
Operated by a spring cord *Ref no:* 27c *Reno:* to 321 *Production Period:* 1949-1973 *Colour:* Red *Market Value:* £30-£40/$45-$60

MASSEY-HARRIS MANURE SPREADER
Ref no: 321 *Reno:* of 27c

MASSEY-HARRIS TRACTOR
From 1966 Massey-Ferguson *Ref no:* 27a *Reno:* to 300 *Production Period:* 1948-1971 *Colour:* Red with yellow wheels *Market Value:* £60-£80/$90-$120

MOTO-CART
Ref no: 27g *Reno:* to 342 *Production Period:* 1949-1961 *Colour:* Green & brown *Market Value:* £45-£50/$65-$75

MOTO-CART
Ref no: 342 *Reno:* of 27g

PIG
Ref no: 2c *Production Period:* 1932-1941 *Colour:* Pink *Market Value:* £15-£20/$20-$30

SACK TRUCK
Ref no: 107a *Reno:* to385 *Production Period:* 1949-1958 *Colour:* Blue *Market Value:* £15-£20/$20-$30

SACK TRUCK
Ref no: 385 *Reno:* of 107a

SHEEP
Ref no: 2d *Production Period:* 1932-1941 *Colour:* Cream *Market Value:* £15-£20/$20-$30

TRIPLE GANG MOWER
Ref no: 27j *Reno:* to 323 *Production Period:* 1952-1958 *Colour:* Red, yellow & green *Market Value:* £25-£30/$40-$50

TRIPLE GANG MOWER
Ref no: 323 *Reno:* of 27j

WEEK'S TIPPING FARM TRAILER
Ref no: 319 *Production Period:* 1961-1970 *Colour:* Red & yellow *Market Value:* £25-£30/$35-$45

WHEELBARROW
Ref no: 105b *Reno:* to 382 *Production Period:* 1949-1958 *Colour:* Brown & red *Market Value:* £15-£20/$20-$30

WHEELBARROW
Ref no: 382 *Reno:* of 105b

151a Medium Tank, pre-war issue. £150-£200/$230-$300.

151b Transport Wagon, post-war issue. £100-£130/$150-$200.

152a Light Tank, post-war issue. £100-£140/$150-$200.

152b Reconnaissance Car, post-war issue. £90-£110/$135-$165.

153a Jeep, the small one with the spare on the tail. £100-£125/$150-$190.

161b AntiAircraft Gun on Trailer, post-war issue. £80-£100/$120-$150.

162 18-Pounder Quick Firing Field Gun Unit. £150-£180/$220-$270.

601 Austin Para Moke, with parachute. £60-£80/$90-$120.

621 3-Ton Army Wagon. £60-£80/$90-$120.

5 models for America only: Top, l to r: 669 US Army Jeep (the large one with the spare on the side) £200-£250/$300-$375; 25WM/640 Bedford Military Truck £180-£250/$270-$380; Lower: l to r: 30hm/624 Daimler Military Ambulance £120-£160/$180-$240; 30sm/625 Austin Covered Wagon £280-£350/$420-$500; 139am/170m/675 Ford Fordor US Army Staff Car £200-£250/$300-$380.

623 Army Covered Wagon. £45-£70/$65-$100.

622 10-Ton Army Wagon. £70-£90/$100-$130.

626 Military Ambulance. £45-£70/$65-$100.

641 Army 1-Ton Cargo Truck,with driver. £40-£60/$60-$90.

642 RAF Pressure Refueller. £90-£120/$130-$180.

643 Army Water Carrier, with driver. £70-£90/$100-$130.

660 Tank Transporter. £90-£120/$130-$180.

651 Centurion Tank. £60-£80/$90-$120.

661 Recovery Tractor. £90-£120/$130-$180.

665 'Honest John' Missile Launcher. £100-£120/$150-$180.

667 Missile Servicing Platform Vehicle. £120-£150/$180-$220.

666 Missile Erector with Corporal Missile and Launching Platform. £160-£220/$240-$330.

670 Armoured Car. £25-£30/$35-$45.

673 Scout Car (Daimler). £25-£30/$35-$45.

674 Austin Champ in very rare UN livery. The production model was painted olive drab as the rest of the range.

676 Armoured Personnel Carrier. £40-£70/$60-$90.

677 Armoured Command Vehicle. £50-£70/$75-$100.

69 2 5.5in Medium Gun. £30-£50/$45-$75.

695 Howitzer and Tractor set (contents 689 and 693). £120-£160/$180-$240.

697 25-Pounder Field Gun Set (contents 686,687 and 688). £80-£110/$120-$165.

27 Tram Car, early issue without adverts. £150-£180/$220-$270.

29 Motor Bus, early issue without adverts. £200-£225/$300-$340.

29b Streamline Bus, post-war issue. £60-£70/$90-$110.

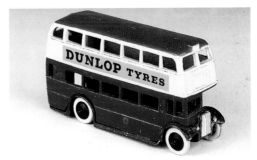

29c Double Deck Motor Bus, pre-war example in a particularly attractive colour scheme (note the grey roof). £250-£160/$180-$220.

29c/290: The 3 different radiators: Left: early post-war, same as pre-war; Centre: fine vertical bars in grille, with triangular badge at top; Right: the last type with fine vertical bars but oval badge at top. £00-£00/$00-$00.

29c First post-war type, 1945-48. £120-£160/$180-$220.

29c Second type bus with triangular badge. £70-£100/$100-$150.

29c Third type bus with oval badge. £70-£100/$100-$150.

290 The last of the Double Deck buses with spun alloy wheels. £70-£80/$100-$120.

291 The 'Exide' version of the Double Deck Bus. £100-£140/$150-$210.

29e Single Deck Bus. £60-£100/$90-$150.

29f Observation Coach. £60-£90/$90-$140.

29g Luxury Coach. £60-£75/$90-$110.

29h Duple Roadmaster Leyland Royal Tiger Coach. £80-£100/$120-$150.

282 a rarer version in the yellow and red livery. £150-£200/$220-$300.

283 BOAC Coach with super decals. £80-£100/$120-$150.

292 Atlantean Bus with 'Ribble' livery. £90-£120/$130-$180.

293 Atlantean Bus with 'Corporation Transport' decals. £90-£120/$130-$180.

295 Atlas Kenebrake Minibus. £70-£90/$100-$130.

289 The 1st Routemaster, in 'Tern Shirts' livery. £90-£110/$130-$160.

949 Wayne School Bus. £150-£200/$225-$300.

952 Vega Major Luxury Coach. £70-£90/$100-$135.

953 Continental Touring Coach. £250-£300/$375-$450.

961 Vega Major Coach in 'PTT' livery for Swiss market only. £150-£175/$225-$300.

23m 'Thunderbolt' Speed Car, note the flags on the fin and the special box. £150-£170/$220-$260.

27d Landrover, with a 27m/341 Trailer in special olive drab paint for a military order. Very rare.

35 Series Cars: 35b Racer, 35a Saloon Car and 35d Midget Tourer. £50-£80/$75-$120 each.

36a Armstrong Siddley saloon (tyres replaced). £90-£120/$135-$180.

36b Bentley Sports Coupé. £90-£120/$135-$180.

36f British Salmson 4-Seater Sports. £100-£130/$150-$200.

38a Frazer-Nash BMW Sports Car. £100-£130/$150-$200.

39b Sunbeam-Talbot Sports Car. £100-£130/$150-$200.

38c Lagonda Tourer. £90-£120/$135-$180.

38d Alvis Sports Tourer, a pre-war example. £140-£180/$210-$270.

38e Armstrong-Siddeley Coupé. £90-£120/$135-$180.

38f SS Jaguar Sports Car. £100-£150/$150-$220.

39a Packard Sedan. £100-£130/$150-$200.

39b Oldsmobile Sedan. £100-£130/$150-$200.

39c Lincoln Zephyr. £100-£130/$150-$200.

39d Buick Sedan. £100-£130/$150-$200.

39e Chrysler. £100-£130/$150-$200.

39f Studebaker. £100-£130/$150-$200.

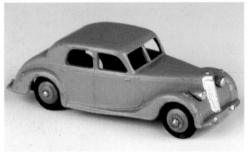

40a Riley Saloon. £70-£110/$100-$165.

40b Triumph 1800 Saloon. £90-£120/$135-$180.

40d Austin Devon Saloon (actually a 152 as it is in green). £90-£120/$135-$180.

40e Standard Vanguard Saloon, with open rear wheels. £80-£130/$120-$200.

40e Standard Vanguard Saloon with covered rear wheels. £80-£100/$120-$150.

40f Hillman Minx Saloon. £90-£120/$135-$180.

154 Duotone version of 40f Hillman Minx. £220-£270/$330-$400.

40g Morris Oxford Saloon. £80-£100/$120-$150.

40j Austin Somerset Saloon. £90-£120/$120-$150.

139b Hudson Commodore Sedan, 1st version with colour split at window level. £110-£140/$170-$210.

139b/117 Hudson. The duotone version is the 'highline' split. The colour change on the 'lowline' version changes at the ridge at the top of the front wheelarch. Right: £175-£225/$260-$340.

23f Alfa Romeo Racing Car. £80-£100/$120-$150.

23g Cooper Bristol Racing Car. £80-£100/$120-$150.

23h Ferrari Racing Car, full yellow nose version. £80-£100/$120-$100.

23j H.W.M. Racing Car. £80-£100/$120-$150.

23k Talbot Lago Racing Car. £80-£100/$120-$150.

23n Maserati Racing car. £80-£100/$120-$150.

236 Connaught Streamlined Racing Car. £70-£90/$100-$135.

237 Mercedes-Benz Racing Car. £80-£100/$120-$150.

238 Jaguar D-type Racing Car. £80-£120/$120-$180.

239 Vanwall Racing Car. £45-£70/$65-$100.

240 Cooper Racing Car. £50-£70/$75-$100.

241 Lotus Racing Car. £50-£70/$75-$100.

242 Ferrari Racing Car. £50-£70/$75-$100.

243 BRM Racing Car. £50-£70/$75-$100.

101 Sunbeam Alpine (Touring). £90-£120/$135-$180.

102 MG Midget (Touring). £130-£180/$200-$270.

103 Austin Healey 100 (Touring). £100-£130/$150-$200.

104 Aston Martin DB3S (Touring). £130-£190/$200-$270.

105 Triumph TR2 (Touring). £130-£160/$200-$240.

106 Austin Atlantic Convertible. £180-£220/$270-$330.

107 Sunbeam Alpine (Competition). £80-£100/$120-$150.

108 MG Midget (Competition). £110-£140/$165-$210.

109 Austin Healey 100 (Competition). £80-£110/$120-$165.

111 Triumph TR2 (Competition). £80-£110/$120-$165.

112 Austin Healey Sprite Mark II. £80-£110/$120-$165.

113 MGB. £60-£80/$90-$120.

114 Triumph Spitfire. £80-£110/$120-$165.

116 Volvo 1800S. £60-£80/$90-$120.

120 Jaguar E-type with removable hardtop. £60-£80/$90-$120.

125 Fun A'Hoy Set (contents: 130 Ford Corsair and 796 Healey Sports Boat and Trailer). £120-£160/$180-$240.

129 Volkswagen 1300 Sedan. £45-£60/$70-$90.

130 Ford Consul Corsair. £60-£70/$90-$100.

131 Cadillac Eldorado. £80-£120/$120-$180.

131 Jaguar E-type 2+2 Coupé. £90-£120/$140-$180.

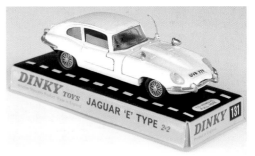

131 Jaguar E-type 2+2 Coupé. £90-£120/$140-$180.

132 Packard Convertible. £80-£120/$120-$180.

132 Ford 40-RV. £40-£70/$60-$100.

132 Ford 40-RV in the rare red/yellow finish.

133 Cunningham C-5R Racing Car. £70-£90/$100-$140.

133 Ford Cortina (1965 model). £60-£90/$90-$135.

134 Triumph Vitesse. £60-£80/$90-$120.

135 Triumph 2000 Saloon, standard colour. £60-£80/$90-$120.

135 one of the special prototypical colour schemes.

136 Vauxhall Viva saloon. £60-£80/$90-$120.

138 Hillman Imp Saloon. £60-£90/$90-$135.

139 Ford Cortina (1963 model). £60-£90/$90-$135.

140 Morris 1100 Saloon. £40-£50/$60-$75.

141 Vauxhall Victor Estate Car. £40-£60/$60-$90.

142 Jaguar Mark 10 Saloon. £50-£70/$75-$100.

143 Ford Capri Coupé. £60-£80/$90-$120.

144 Volkswagen 1500 Saloon. £40-£60/$60-$90.

145 Singer Vogue Saloon. £60-£80/$90-$120.

146 Daimler V8 2.5 litre. £60-£90/$90-$130.

147 Cadillac 62. £70-£80/$100-$125.

150 Rolls-Royce Silver Wraith. £60-£80/$90-$120.

152 Rolls-Royce Phantom V Limousine. £35-£60/$50-$90.

153 Aston Martin DB6 Coupé. £60-£80/$90-$120.

154 Ford Taunus 17M. £40-£60/$60-$90.

155 Forrd Anglia Saloon. £70-£100/$100-$150.

156 Rover 75 Saloon, a late duotone version. £100-£140/$150-$230.

156 SAAB 96 Saloon. £60-£80/$90-$120.

157 Jaguar XK 120 Coupé, an early single colour example. £100-£140/$165-$225.

157 Jaguar XK 120 Coupé, a late duotone version. £220-£250/$300-$375.

158 Rolls-Royce Silver Shadow. £40-£70/$60-$100.

159 Ford Cortina Mark II Saloon. £60-£80/$90-$120.

160 Austin A30 Saloon. £80-£100/$120-$150.

161 Ford Mustang Fastback 2+2. £40-£60/$60-$90.

162 Ford Zephyr Saloon. £90-£130/$135-$180.

162 Triumph 1300 Saloon. £45-£70/$65-$95.

163 Bristol 450 Coupé. £60-£80/$90-$120.

163 Volkswagen 1600TL Fastback. £35-£55/$55-$85.

164 Vauxhall Cresta Saloon. £90-£120/$140-$180.

164 Ford Zodiac MkIV Saloon. £90-£140/$125-$210.

165 Humber Hawk Saloon. £90-£120/$135-$180.

166 Sunbeam Rapier. £85-£120/$130-$180.

166 Renault 16 Saloon. £40-£60/$60-$90.

167 AC Aceca Coupé. £90-£120/$135-$180.

168 Singer Gazelle Saloon. £90-£110/$135-$170.

169 Ford Corsair 2000E Saloon. £60-£80/$90-$120.

171 Hudson Commodore Sedan, 'Highline' duotone. £110-£140/$170-$210.

172 Studebaker Land Cruiser. £100-£120/$150-$180.

173 Nash Rambler Station Wagon. £60-£80/$90-$120.

174 Hudson Hornet. £90-£110/$140-$170.

175 Hillman Minx Saloon. £90-£110/$135-$170.

175 Cadillac Eldorado. £45-£55/$70-$85.

176 Austin A105 saloon. £120-£150/$180-$220.

178 Plymouth Plaza. £110-£140/$165-$210.

179 Studebaker President. £90-£120/$140-$180.

179 Opel Commodore Coupé. £30-£50/$45-$75.

181 Volkswagen Saloon. £60-£80/$90-$120.

182 Porsche 356 Coupé. £90-£120/$140-$180.

183 Fiat 600 Saloon. £60-£80/$90-$120.

185 Alfa Romeo 1900 Sprint Coupé. £70-£90/$100-$140.

186 Mercedes Benz 220SE Saloon. £35-£55/$50-$80.

187 Volkswagen Karmann Ghia Coupé. £70-£90/$100-$140.

189 Triumph Herald Saloon. £70-£90/$100-$140.

189 Lamborghini Marzal. £30-£50/$45-$75.

190 Monteverdi 375L Coupé. £35-£45/$50-$75.

191 Dodge Royal Sedan. £90-£120/$140-$180.

192 De Soto Fireflite Sedan. £100-£140/$150-$210.

193 Rambler Cross Country Station Wagon. £80-£100/$120-$150.

194 Bentley S-Series Coupé. £80-£120/$120-$180.

195 Jaguar 3.4 litre Mark II. £80-£100/$120-$150.

196 Holden Special Sedan. £50-£70/$75-$100.

197 Morris Mini-Traveller. £60-£90/$90-$135.

197 Morris Mini-Traveller.

197 Morris Mini-Traveller.

197 Morris Mini-Traveller.

199 Austin 7 Countryman. £60-£90/$90-$135.

210 Alfa Romeo Tipo 33 Le Mans. £25-£35/$35-$50.

212 Ford Cortina Rally Car. £30-£40/$45-$60.

214 Hillman Imp Rally Car. £60-£75/$90-$110.

215 Ford GT Racing Car. £30-£40/$45-$60.

216 Ferrari Dino Coupé. £40-£60/$60-$90.

220 Ferrari P5 Coupé. £25-£30/$35-$45.

221 Chevrolet Corvette Stingray. £25-£35/$35-$50.

224 Mercedes-Benz C111 Coupé. £20-£25/$30-$45.

228 Super Sprinter Dragster. £20-£25/$30-$45.

370 Dragster Set. £40-£50/$60-$75.

405 Universal Jeep (was 25y). £60-£80/$90-$120.

448 Chevrolet El Camino Pick-Up with Trailers. £220-£280/$330-$420.

DUBLO

L to R: 067 Austin Taxi £65-£80/$90-$115; 065 Morris Pick-Up £45-£55/$65-$80; 064 Austin Lorry £45-£55/$65-$80; 063 Commer Van £45-£55/$65-$80; and 066 Bedford Flat Truck £50-£60/$70-$85.

L to R: 068 Royal Mail Van £75-£85/$100-$130; 069 Tractor £50-£60/$70-$85; 072 Bedford Articulated Flat Truck £60-£65/$85-$95; 076 Lansing Bagnall Tractor and Trailer £60-£65/$85-$95; 070 AEC Mercury Tanker "Shell-BP" £75-£85/$100-$120; 071 Volkswagen Delivery Van £60-£70/$85-$100.

FARM MACHINERY

22e The pre-war Fordson type Tractor. £250-£275/$375-$420.

27a Massey-Harris Tractor. £60-£80/$90-$120.

27b Halesowen Harvest Trailer. £25-£35/$40-$60.

27g Motocart - the rare dark green version. £50-£80/$75-$120.

27h Disc Harrow - the later 322 version in white. £15-£20/$20-$30.

27j Triple Gang Mower. £25-£30/$40-$50.

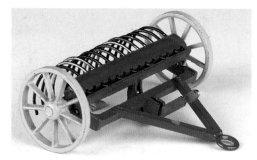

27k Hay Rake. £25-£30/$40-$50.

27n Field Marshall Tractor. £80-£100/$120-$150.

305 David Brown Tractor. £50-£80/$75-$120.

308 Leyland 308 Tractor - the rare blue version. £50-£80/$75-$120.

319 Week's Tipping Trailer. £25-£30/$35-$45.

105a, 105b, 105c, 105e and 107a. £15-£20/$20-$30 each.

FIGURES

3 Passengers Set. £80-£100/ $120-$150.

5 Train & Hotel Staff. £80-£100/ $120-$150.

6 Shepherd Set. £150-£175/$225-$250.

2 Farmyard Animals Set. £250-£275/$375-$420.

HONG KONG DINKY

57/001 Buick Riviera Coupé. £75-£95/$120-$150.

57/003 Chevrolet Impala. £75-£95/$120-$150.

PLANES

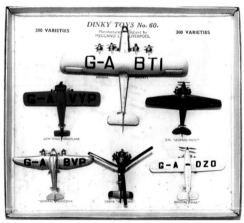

60 Aeroplanes - the 1st type without registration letters. £1500-£2000/$2300-$3000.

60 Aeroplanes - the 2nd type with registration letters. £900-£1200/$1400-$1800.

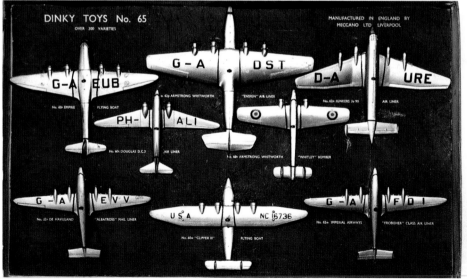

65 Presentation Aeroplane Set. £2000-£2250/$3000-$3500.

61 R.A.F. Aeroplanes. £5000-£750/$750-$1100.

63 Mayo Composite Aircraft (63b on top of 63a). £290-£390/$450-$575.

Examples of the camouflage livery (top: 68a, 60s, lower: 62d, 62h).

62g Long Range Bomber (post-war version of Flying Fortress). £100-£140/$150-$210.

67a Junkers Ju89 Heavy Bomber. £350-£450/$500-$650.

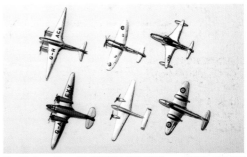

Top: 60g Comet Racer £70-£100/$100-$150; 70b Tempest II fighter £35-£50/$50-$75; 70f Shooting Star £25-£35/$40-$50; Lower: 62k King's Aeroplane £180-£250/$290-$380; 70d Twin Engined Fighter (Me110) £25-£35/$40-$50; 70e Gloster Meteor £25-£35/$40-$50.

70a Avro York £90-£140/$135-$220 and 70c Vickers Viking Airliners. £60-£80/$90-$120.

997 Caravelle 'Air France' £225-£275/$335-$400; and 998 Bristol Britannia 'Canadian Pacific' airliners. £200-£250/$300-$375.

62p *Armstrong Whitworth Airliner (G-ADSV) £130-£200/$200-$300; 62r Four Engined Liner £110-£150/$160-$225; 60w Flying Boat £180-£240/$270-$360.*

702 *D.H. Comet Airliner BOAC £100-£140/$150-$200; 706 Air France £110-£150/$160-$225; and 708 BEA Viscount £110-£150/$160-$225 Airliners.*

700 *Shetland Flying Boat £350-£480/$500-$720; with 737 P1B Lightning £50-£70/$75-$100; and 70b Tempest II £35-£50/$50-$75.*

Top: 738 D.H. 110 Sea Vixen £35-£45/$50-$75; 734 Supermarine Swift £35-£40/$50-$60; Lower: 736 Hawker Hunter £30-£45/$45-$70; 735 Gloster Javelin Delta Wing Fighter £35-£45/$50-$70.

715 *Bristol 173 (G-AUXR) £40-£55/$60-$80; and 716 Westland Sikorsky S.51 £35-£45/$50-$70 Helicopters.*

710 *Beechcraft S.35 Bonanza £45-£60/$70-$90.*

715 *Beechcraft C.55 Baron £35-£45/$50-$70; and 712 US Army T-42A £60-£80/$90-$120*

Top: 731 Jaguar £80-£100/$120-$150; 729 M.R.C.A. £40-£60/$60-$90; Lower: 725 Phantom (Royal Navy) £80-£100/$120-$150; 722 Hawker Harrier £70-£90/$100-$140.

PLANES

718 Hawker Hurricane £60-£80/$90-$120; 719 Spitfire Mk II £60-£80/$90-$120.

721 Junkers Ju.87B Stuka £60-£80/$90-$120; 734 P-47 Thunderbolt £130-£170/$200-$250; and 739 A6M5 Zero Sen £60-£80/$90-$120.

726 Messerschmitt Bf.109E £70-£90/$100-$140 – the later, rarer, livery is on the right £120-£150/$180-$225 (the size of the yellow paint areas on the wingtips varies).

724 Sea King Helicopter (US Navy) £50-£70/$75-$100; with the British Army version from Military Set 618 £55-£80/$90-$120.

PLANT AND CONSTRUCTION

25p Aveling-Barford Diesel Roller. £40-£60/$60-$90.

436 Atlas Copco Compressor Lorry (Ford). £55-£80/$80-$120.

437 Muir Hill 2WL Loader. £20-£30/$30-$45.

PLANT AND CONSTRUCTION

564 Elevator Loader £70-£90/$110-$140 - the more unusual version with colours reversed

959 Foden Dump Truck with Bulldozer Blade. £80-£100/$120-$150.

960 Albion Concrete Mixer Truck. £70-£80/$100-$120.

965 Euclid Rear Dump Truck. £45-£70/$70-$100.

965 Terex Rear Dump Truck. £160-£190/$240-$290.

975 Ruston Bucyrus Excavator. £200-£260/$300-$390.

SHIPS

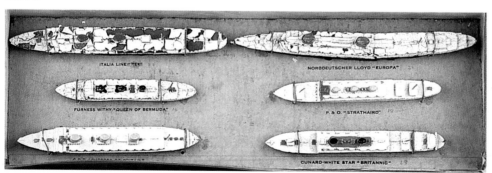

51 Famous Liners Set. £225-£270/$330-$400.

30f Ambulance. £90-£120/$135-$180.

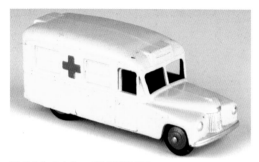

30h Daimler Ambulance. £50-£80/$75-$120.

30v Electric Dairy Van, NCB. £80-£100/$120-$150.

30v Electric Dairy Van, Express Dairies. £80-£90/$120-$135.

490 Express Dairy Van, Job's Dairies. £100-£120/$150-$180.

34b Royal Mail Van, late example with red roof. £80-£120/$120-$180.

36g Taxi. £60-£90/$90-$1350.

40h Austin Taxi, 1st version in blue. £80-£100/$120-$150.

255 Mersey Tunnel Police Van. £55-£70/$80-$100.

256 Police Patrol Car. £90-£110/$135-$165.

258 USA Police Car (Cadillac). £80-£110/$130-$165.

260 Royal Mail Van. £90-£120/$135-$180.

261 Telephone Service Van. £90-£120/$135-$180.

263 Super Criterion Ambulance. £45-£70/$65-$100.

268 Renault Dauphine Minicab. £100-£120/$150-$180.

269 Jaguar Motorway Police Car. £90-£110/$135-$165.

275 Brinks Armoured Car, 1st version. £110-£140/$1650-$210.

276 Airport Fire Tender. £45-£70/$65-$100.

277 Superior Criterion Ambulance. £55-£80/$80-$120.

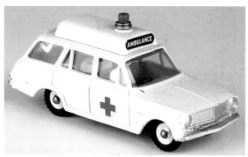

278 Vauxhall Victor Ambulance. £60-£80/$90-$120.

280 Midland Mobile Bank. £80-£100/$120-$150.

282 Austin 1800 Taxi. £45-£70/$65-$100.

581 Horse Box, British Railways. £100-£140/$150-$210.

582 Pullmore Car Transporter (note 3 rivets holding the trailer sides - the commoner version has only 1 at each end). £110-£130/$165-$200.

555 Fire Engine with Extending Ladder. £70-£90/$100-$135.

956 Turntable Fire Escape (Bedford). £100-£110/$150-$170.

956 Turntable Fire Escape (Berliet). £140-£160/$200-$240.

958 Snow Plough (Guy). £150-£200/$220-$300.

966 Marrell Multi-bucket Unit (Albion). £100-£120/$150-$180.

967 BBC TV Mobile Control Room. £110-£150/$165-$230.

968 BBC TV Roving Eye Vehicle. £110-£160/$165-$240.

969 BBC TV Extending Mast Vehicle. £125-£160/$185-$240.

977 Servicing Platform Vehicle. £140-£175/$200-$260.

978 Refuse Wagon (Bedford). £45-£70/$60-$100.

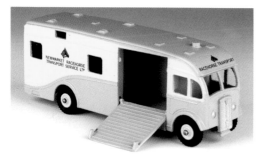

979 Racehorse Transport. £270-£320/$400-$480.

987 ABC TV Control Room. £170-£200/$250-$300.

TANKERS

988 ABC TV Transmitter Van. £190-£220/$280-$330.

25d Petrol Tank Wagon (type 4). £80-£180/$120-$160.

30p Petrol Tanker. £60-£80/$90-$120.

30p Petrol Tanker 'Mobilgas' (1st type decals). £110-£140/$165-$210.

30pa Petrol Tanker 'Castrol'. £140-£160/$210-$240.

30pb Petrol Tanker 'Esso'. £110-£140/$165-$210.

440 Petrol Tanker 'Mobilgas' (2nd type decals). £120-£140/$180-$210.

443 Petrol Tanker 'National Benzole'. £140-£160/$210-$240.

591 AEC Tanker 'Shell Chemicals Limited'. £130-£170/$200-$250.

504 Foden 14-ton Tanker (2nd type grille). £300-£400/$450-$600.

504 Foden 14-ton Tanker 'Mobilgas'. £275-£350/$400-$520.

942 Foden Tanker 'Regent'. £350-£400/$500-$600.

TANKERS

943 Leyland Octopus Tanker 'Esso'. £250-£300/$275-$450.

944 Shell-BP Fuel Tanker (Leyland). £180-£220/$270-$320.

TRAINS

798 Express Passenger train. £80-£120/$120-$180.

TRUCKS

14c Coventry Climax Fork Lift Truck. £30-£35/$45-$55.

14a BEV Electric Truck. £30-£40/$45-$60.

25a/3 Wagon (type 3). £50-£80/$75-$120.

25b Covered Wagon (type 4) – an unusual late all green example. £100-£120/$150-$180.

25e Tipping Wagon (type 4). £50-£80/$75-$120.

25f Marker Gardener's Wagon (type 4). £50-£80/$75-$120.

25t Flat Truck (type 3) and Trailer (25c + 25g). £100-£140/$150-$210.

25m Bedford End Tipper (a late 410 version). £130-£150/$200-$230.

25r Leyland Forward Control Lorry. £60-£80/$90-$120.

25v Refuse Wagon (a late 252 version with windows). £100-£150/$150-$220.

25w Bedford Truck. £90-£120/$135-$180.

25x Commer Breakdown Lorry. £70-£90/$100-$135.

30e Breakdown Car (post-war). £40-£60/$60-$90.

30m Dodge Rear Tipping Wagon. £80-£90/$120-$140.

30n Farm Produce Wagon. £80-£90/$120-$140.

30r Fordson Thames Flat Truck. £80-£100/$120-$150.

30s Austin Covered Wagon. £120-£140/$180-$210.

0w Hindle Smart Electric Articulated Lorry. £70-£90/$100-$135.

33e Dust Wagon (pre-war). £95-£110/$145-$165.

402 Bedford Coca Cola Lorry. £150-£180/$220-$270.

425 Bedford TK Coal Wagon. £100-£140/$150-$210.

431 Guy Warrior 4-ton Lorry. £350-£500/$500-$750.

432 Guy Warrior Flat Truck. £300-£400/$450-$600.

434 Bedford TK Crash Truck. £80-£100/$120-$150.

435 Bedford TK Tipper. £90-£120/$140-$180.

439 Ford D800 Snow Plough & Tipping Truck. £45-£70/$70-$100.

L to R: Foden 1st type cab £450-£600/$675-$900, Foden 2nd type, £250-£320/$375-$480; Leyland, £180-£230/$270-$350.

501 Foden Diesel 8-wheel Wagon (1st type). £450-£600/$675-$900.

502 Foden Flat Truck (1st type). £400-£500/$600-$750.

502 Foden Flat Truck (2nd type). £250-£320/$375-$480.

503 Foden Flat Truck with Tailboard (1st type). £650-£750/$950-$1150.

503 Foden Flat Truck with Tailboard (2nd type). £280-£340/$420-$500.

505 Foden Flat Truck with Chains (1st type). £750-£1000/$1100-$1500.

511 Guy 4-ton Lorry. £250-£400/$330-$400.

The early (left) Guy casting with the vertical sides to the number plate area, and; (right) the later triangulated type.

521 Bedford Articulated Lorry. £200-£260/$300-$400.

531 Leyland Comet Lorry (with tinplate back). £150-£200/$225-$300.

532 Leyland Comet Lorry with Hinged Tailboard. £110-£160/$165-$240.

533 Leyland Cement Wagon. £130-£160/$200-$290.

914 AEC Articulated Lorry. £90-£130/$135-$200.

925 Leyland Dump Truck. £120-£150/$180-$225.

934 Leyland Octopus Wagon. £180-£230/$270-$350.

935 Leyland Octopus Flat Truck with Chains. £750-£1000/$1100-$1500.

936 Leyland Test Chassis. £90-£100/$135-$150.

TRUCKS

908 Mighty Antar with Transformer. £550-£700/$800-$1000.

986 Mighty Antar with Propeller. £200-£280/$300-$420.

TV RELATED MODELS

513 Guy Flat Truck with Tailboard – a late model in an unusual colour, note the later "Supertoy" wheel hubs, £200-£260/$300-$400.

100 Lady Penelope's FAB 1. £170-£240/$250-$360.

101 Thunderbird 2 (Thunderbird 4 inside). £200-£250/$300-$375.

102 Joe's Car. £100-£130/$150-$200.

103 Spectrum Patrol Car. £90-£120/$140-$180.

104 Spectrum Pursuit Vehicle. £90-£120/$140-$180.

TV RELATED MODELS

105 Maximum Security Vehicle. £90-£120/$140-$180.

106 'Prisoner' Mini-Moke. £160-£200/$240-$300.

108 Sam's Car. £90-£120/$130-$180.

109 Gabriel's Model T Ford. £60-£90/$90-$140.

350 Tiny's Mini-Moke. £90-£110/$135-$165.

352 Ed Straker's Car. £80-£90/$120-$140.

354 Pink Panther's Jet Car. £35-£55/$50-$90.

280 Delivery Van. £50-£75/$75-$110.

31a Trojan 15cwt Van 'Esso'. £110-£150/$165-$225.

31b Trojan 15cwt Van 'Dunlop'. £110-£150/$165-$225.

31c Trojan 15cwt van 'Chivers'. £110-£150/$165-$225.

31d Trojan 15cwt Van 'Oxo'. £180-£220/$270-$330.

454 Trojan 15cwt Van 'Cydrax'. £110-£150/$165-$225.

455 Trojan 15cwt Van 'Brooke Bond'. £110-£150/$165-$225.

450 Bedford TK Box Van 'Castrol'. £120-£160/$180-$240.

465 Morris Van 'Capstan'. £170-£200/$260-$300.

470 Austin Van 'Shell - BP'. £100-£130/$150-$200.

471 Austin Van 'Nestlé's'. £100-£130/$150-$200.

472 Austin Van 'Raleigh'. £100-£150/$150-$225.

480 Bedford Van 'Kodak'. £100-£130/$150-$200.

481 Bedford Van 'Ovaltine'. £100-£130/$150-$200.

482 Bedford Van 'Dinky Toys'. £100-£120/$150-$180.

34c Loudspeaker Van. £50-£80/$75-$1200.

514 Guy Van 'Slumberland'. £250-£350/$375-$525.

514 Guy Van 'Lyons'. £750-£1000/$1100-$1500.

514 Guy Van 'Weetabix'. £1200-£1600/$1800-$2400.

514 Guy Van 'Spratts'. £300-£450/$450-$675.

918 Guy Van 'Ever Ready'. £190-£250/$290-$375.

919 Guy Van 'Golden Shred'. £500-£750/$800-$1100.

920 Guy Warrior Van 'Heinz'. £1200-£1500/$1800-$2200.

923 Bedford Van 'Heinz' with bean tin. £250-£350/$375-$525.

923 Bedford Van 'Heinz' with ketchup bottle. £900-£1200/$1350-$1800.

930 Bedford Pallet-Jekta Van. £140-£180/$210-$270.

273 RAC Patrol Minivan. £130-£170/$200-$250.

VANS

274 A.A. Patrol Minivan. £130-£170/$200-$250.

274 Minivan 'Joseph Mason Paints'. £500-£600/$750-$900.

492 Election Mini Van. £200-£250/$300-$375.

MISCELLANEOUS AND SUNDRY ITEMS

L to R: 12a Pillar Box £10-£15/$15-$20; 42a Police Hut £25-£35/$35-$50; 12c Telephone Box £25-£30/$35-$45; 12d Telegraph Messenger £20-£25/$30-$40; 13 Cook's Man £25-£30/$40-$45; 12e Postman £20-£25/$30-$40; 47d Belisha Beacon £7-£10/$10-$15.

47 Road Signs. £80-£90/ $120-$140.

772 British Road Signs (24). £150-£200/$220-$300.

771 International Road Signs. £90-£120/$130-$180.

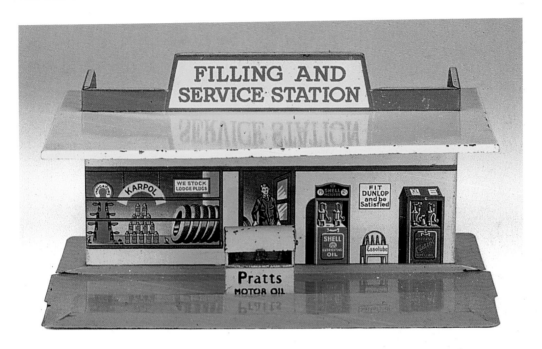

48 Filling & Service Station £300-£400/$450-$600.

49 Petrol Pumps Set. £100-£130/$150-$200.

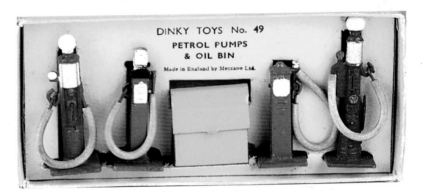

37a Civilian Motorcyclist £25-£35/$35-$50; 42b Police Motor Cycle Patrol £40-£50/$60-$75; 37b Police Motorcyclist £25-£35/$35-$50; 44b AA Motor Cycle Patrol £40-£60/$60-$90.

Examples of the boxes used by Dinky in the main collectable era. The early 'box of 6' is at the bottom on the right with the typical 'Supertoy' blue and white striped box on the left. The 157 Jaguar box is an example of what is universally known as the 'yellow box'.

34a Air Mail Service Car, 31 Holland Coahccraft Van and 60y Thompson Aircraft Refuelling Tender. Examples of some of the rarer pre-war toys which now turn up almost exclusively in auctions. (The 34a has been restored but the others are original).

290 SRN-6 Hovercraft. £25-£30/$35-$45.

Figures

The early figure sets were inherited from the range of Modelled Miniatures, an adjunct to the Hornby 'O' gauge railway system. These were beautifully painted little figures about 39mm tall. Later they were replaced by a series about 35mm tall. Both versions confusingly had the same catalogue number. The smaller figures were re-introduced after the war but with less detailed painting.

Postmen, Policemen, 'AA' and 'RAC' guides came along later in 1935 to 1938 as parts of gift sets. These figures are covered in the section MISCELLANEOUS in this book as part of the sets.

The wide range of military figures were designed for the early army vehicles. They are of course compatible with the 600 series of military vehicles also.

Some of the figures were re-numbered and kept in the American catalogue long after sales ceased in the UK.

AA GUIDE DIRECTING TRAFFIC
See under 'Miscellaneous' *Ref no:* 44c *Production Period:* 1935-1941

AA GUIDE SALUTING
See under 'Miscellaneous' *Ref no:* 44d *Production Period:* 1935-1941

ARMOURED CORPS PERSONNEL
Reissue for US only *Ref no:* 150 *Reno:* to 600 *Production Period:* 1952-1955 *Colour:* Khaki *Market Value:* £140-£160/$200-$240

ARMOURED CORPS PERSONNEL
Ref no: 600 *Reno:* of 150

BUSINESS MAN (LEFT HAND UP)
Ref no: 3b *Production Period:* 1932-1937/9 *Colour:* Dark blue *Market Value:* £30-£35/$45-$50

BUSINESS MAN (LEFT HAND+CASE)
Ref no: 3b *Production Period:* 1937/9-1941 *Colour:* Brown, later grey *Market Value:* £20-£25/$30-$40

COOK'S MAN
Ref no: 013 *Reno:* of 13a

COOK'S MAN
Ref no: 13a *Reno:* to 013 *Production Period:* 1952-1956 *Colour:* Blue *Market Value:* £25-£30/$40-$45

DOG
Ref no: 6b *Production Period:* 1934-1940 *Colour:* Black & white *Market Value:* £20-£25/$30-$40

DRIVER (OIL CAN IN RIGHT HAND)
Ref no: 1d *Production Period:* 1931-1939 *Colour:* Light blue *Market Value:* £30-£35/$45-$50

DRIVER (OIL CAN IN RIGHT HAND)
Postwar: Engine Driver *Ref no:* 1d *Production Period:* 1939-1941 *Colour:* Light blue *Market Value:* £15-£20/$25-$30

ELECTRICIAN
Ref no: 4a *Production Period:* 1932-1939 *Colour:* White & blue *Market Value:* £30-£35/$45-$50

ELECTRICIAN
Ref no: 4a *Production Period:* 1939-1941 *Colour:* Blue *Market Value:* £20-£25/$30-$40

ENGINE ROOM ATTENDANT
Ref no: 4e *Production Period:* 1932-1939 *Colour:* Light blue *Market Value:* £30-£35/$45-$50

ENGINE ROOM ATTENDANT
Ref no: 4e *Production Period:* 1939-1941 *Colour:* Light blue *Market Value:* £20-£25/$30-$40

ENGINEERING STAFF
35mm *Ref no:* 004 *Reno:* of 4

ENGINEERING STAFF
4a, 2 x 4b (1 of each colour), 4c, 4d, 4e, large about 39mm tall *Ref no:* 4 *Production Period:* 1932-1939 *Colour:* Cream base *Market Value:* £250-£275/$375-$425

ENGINEERING STAFF
4a, 2 x 4b (1 of each colour), 4c, 4d, 4e, small about 35mm tall *Ref no:* 4 *Production Period:* 1939-1941 *Colour:* Buff base *Market Value:* £100-£130/$150-$200

ENGINEERING STAFF
Reissue 4a, 4b, 4c, 4d, 4e, small about 35mm tall *Ref no:* 4 *Reno:* to 004 *Production Period:* 1952-1956 *Colour:* Main colours as prewar but less detailed *Market Value:* £100-£130/$150-$200

FARMYARD ANIMALS
Ref no: 002 *Reno:* of 2

FARMYARD ANIMALS (SET)
Contents: 2 x 2a, 2 x 2b, 2c, 2d. marked Hornby to 1934 then Dinky Toys *Ref no:* 2 *Reno:* to 002 *Production Period:* 1932-1952 *Market Value:* £250-£275/$375-$420

FEMALE HIKER
Ref no: 3d *Production Period:* 1932-1937/9 *Colour:* White & blue *Market Value:* £30-£35/$45-$50

FEMALE HIKER
Ref no: 3d *Production Period:* 1937/9-1941 *Colour:* White & blue, 1940 all blue *Market Value:* £20-£25/$30-$40

FIRE STATION PERSONNEL
Ref no: 008 *Production Period:* 1960-1967 *Colour:* Blue *Market Value:* £60-£80/$75-$120

FITTER

Ref no: 4b *Production Period:* 1932-1939 *Colour:* Dark blue until 1935 then light blue, or brown, all with white sleeves *Market Value:* £30-£35/$45-$50

FITTER

Ref no: 4b *Production Period:* 1939-1941 *Colour:* White & light blue *Market Value:* £20-£25/$30-$40

GREASER

Ref no: 4d *Production Period:* 1932-1939 *Colour:* Brown *Market Value:* £30-£35/$45-$50

GREASER

Ref no: 4d *Production Period:* 1939-1941 *Colour:* Brown *Market Value:* £20-£25/$30-$40

GUARD (FLAG IN LEFT HAND)

Ref no: 1b *Production Period:* 1931-1939 *Colour:* Dark blue *Market Value:* £30-£35/$45-$50

GUARD (FLAG IN RIGHT HAND)

Ref no: 1b *Production Period:* 1939-1941 *Colour:* Dark blue *Market Value:* £15-£20/$25-$30

HALL'S DISTEMPER ADVERTISEMENT

Ref no: 13 *Production Period:* 1931-1941 *Colour:* White: 1 with blue brush, 1 with green *Market Value:* £300-£400/$450-$600

HOTEL PORTER·

Ref no: 5c *Production Period:* 1932-1937/9 *Colour:* Red jacket, blue & red cases + 1 green with orange & red *Market Value:* £30-£35/$45-$55

HOTEL PORTER

Ref no: 5c *Production Period:* 1937/9-1941 *Market Value:* £20-£25/$30-$40

MALE HIKER (NO WALKING STICK)

Ref no: 3c *Production Period:* 1937/9-1941 *Colour:* Brown *Market Value:* £20-£25/$30-$40

MALE HIKER (WALKING STICK)

Ref no: 3c *Production Period:* 1932-1937/9 *Colour:* Brown *Market Value:* £30-£35/$45-$50

NEWSBOY (RUNNING)

Ref no: 3e *Production Period:* 1932-1937/9 *Colour:* Brown *Market Value:* £30-£35/$45-$50

NEWSBOY (STANDING)

Ref no: 3e *Production Period:* 1937/9-1941 *Colour:* Blue *Market Value:* £20-£25/$30-$40

PASSENGERS

35mm *Ref no:* 003 *Reno:* of 3

PASSENGERS

OO gauge 6 figures *Ref no:* 053 *Reno:* of 1003

PASSENGERS

3a, 3b, 3c, 3d, 3e, 3f , large about 39mm tall *Ref no:* 3 *Production Period:* 1932-1937/9 *Colour:* Cream base *Market Value:* £250-£275/$375-$425

PASSENGERS

3a, 3b, 3c, 3d, 3e, 3f , small about 35mm tall *Ref no:* 3 *Production Period:* 1937/9-1941 *Colour:* Buff base *Market Value:* £150-£180/$225-$270

PASSENGERS

Reissue 3a, 3b, 3c, 3d, 3e, 3f , small about 35mm tall, less detailed painting *Ref no:* 3 *Reno:* to 003 *Production Period:* 1952-1956 *Market Value:* £80-£100/$140-$160

PASSENGERS (SET OF 6) OO GAUGE

Ref no: 1003 *Reno:* to 053 *Production Period:* 1952-1959 *Colour:* Various colours *Market Value:* £70-£90/$100-$130

PETROL PUMP ATTENDANTS SET

Ref no: 007 *Production Period:* 1960-1967 *Colour:* White *Market Value:* £30-£40/$45-$60

POINT DUTY POLICEMAN

See under 'Miscellaneous' *Ref no:* 42d *Production Period:* 1936-1941

POINT DUTY POLICEMAN (IN WHITE COAT)

See under 'Miscellaneous' *Ref no:* 42c *Production Period:* 1936-1941

PORTER (STANDING)

Ref no: 1f *Production Period:* 1939-1941 *Colour:* Dark blue *Market Value:* £15-£20/$25-$30

PORTER (WALKING)

Ref no: 1f *Production Period:* 1931-1939 *Colour:* Dark blue *Market Value:* £30-£35/$45-$50

PORTER WITH BAGS (ONE ROUND)

Ref no: 1e *Production Period:* 1931-1939 *Colour:* Dark blue *Market Value:* £30-£35/$45-$50

PORTER WITH BAGS (TWO OBLONG)

Ref no: 1e *Production Period:* 1939-1941 *Colour:* Dark blue *Market Value:* £15-£20/$25-$30

POSTMAN

Ref no: 012 *Reno:* of 12e

POSTMAN

See under 'Miscellaneous' *Ref no:* 12e *Production Period:* 1938-1941

POSTMAN

Ref no: 12e *Reno:* to 012 *Production Period:* 1952-1957 *Colour:* Blue, brown bag *Market Value:* £20-£25/$30-$40

PRIVATE SEATED/ARMOURED CORPS PRIVATE

12x150b in khaki, 604 US market only *Ref no:* 150b *Reno:* to 604 *Production Period:* 1952-1955 *Market Value:* £50-£60/$75-$90

PULLMAN CAR CONDUCTOR

Ref no: 5a *Production Period:* 1932-1937/9 *Colour:* White & blue *Market Value:* £30-£35/$45-$50

PULLMAN CAR CONDUCTOR

Postwar: Dining Car Conductor *Ref no:* 5a *Production Period:* 1937/9-1941 *Market Value:* £20-£25/$30-$40

PULLMAN CAR WAITER

Ref no: 5b *Production Period:* 1932-1937/9 *Colour:* White & blue *Market Value:* £30-£35/$45-$50

PULLMAN CAR WAITER

Postwar: Dining Car Waiter *Ref no:* 5b *Production Period:* 1937/9-1941 *Market Value:* £20-£25/$30-$40

RAC GUIDE DIRECTING TRAFFIC
See under 'Miscellaneous' *Ref no:* 43c *Production Period:* 1935-1941

RAC GUIDE SALUTING
See under 'Miscellaneous' *Ref no:* 43d *Production Period:* 1935-1941

RAILWAY PASSENGERS
OO gauge 11 plastic figures + 1 seat, various colours *Ref no:* 052 *Production Period:* 1961-1969 *Market Value:* £25-£35/$40-$50

RAILWAY STAFF
OO gauge 12 plastic figures *Ref no:* 050 *Production Period:* 1961-1969 *Market Value:* £25-£35/$40-$50

RAILWAY STATION PERSONNEL
OO gauge 4 plastic figures + 8 station furniture, various colours *Ref no:* 054 *Production Period:* 1962-1971 *Market Value:* £35-£45/$40-$50

ROAD MAINTENANCE PERSONNEL
Ref no: 010 *Production Period:* 1962-1966 *Market Value:* £60-£80/$75-$120

ROYAL ARTILLERY GUNLAYER (SEATED HANDS OUT)
Ref no: 160c *Production Period:* 1939-1941 *Colour:* Khaki *Market Value:* £15-£20/$20-$30

ROYAL ARTILLERY GUNLAYER (SEATED HANDS OUT)
Ref no: 160c *Production Period:* 1952-1952 *Colour:* Khaki *Market Value:* £15-£20/$20-$30

ROYAL ARTILLERY GUNLAYER (STANDING HANDS AT SIDES)
Ref no: 160d *Production Period:* 1939-1941 *Colour:* Khaki *Market Value:* £15-£20/$20-$30

ROYAL ARTILLERY GUNNER (SEATED HANDS ON THIGHS)
Ref no: 160b *Production Period:* 1939-1941 *Colour:* Khaki *Market Value:* £15-£20/$20-$30

ROYAL ARTILLERY GUNNER (SEATED HANDS ON THIGHS)
Ref no: 160b *Reno:* to 608 *Production Period:* 1952-1955 *Colour:* Khaki *Market Value:* £15-£20/$20-$30

ROYAL ARTILLERY NCO (HANDS ON CHEST)
Ref no: 160a *Production Period:* 1939-1941 *Colour:* Khaki *Market Value:* £15-£20/$20-$30

ROYAL ARTILLERY PERSONNEL
160a, 2x160b, 160c, 2x160d *Ref no:* 160 *Reno:* to 606 *Production Period:* 1939-1941 *Market Value:* £140-£170/$200-$250

ROYAL ARTILLERY PERSONNEL
Reissue for US market only *Ref no:* 160 *Reno:* to 606 *Production Period:* 1952-1955

ROYAL ARTILLERY PERSONNEL
Ref no: 606 *Reno:* of 160

ROYAL ARTILLERY SEATED GUNNER
Ref no: 608 *Reno:* of 160b

ROYAL TANK CORPS DRIVER
Ref no: 150d *Production Period:* 1937-1941 *Colour:* Dark blue *Market Value:* £20-£25/$30-$40

ROYAL TANK CORPS NCO (WALKING)
Ref no: 150e *Production Period:* 1937-1941 *Colour:* Dark blue *Market Value:* £20-£25/$30-$40

ROYAL TANK CORPS OFFICER
Ref no: 150a *Production Period:* 1937-1941 *Colour:* Khaki, dark blue beret *Market Value:* £20-£25/$30-$40

ROYAL TANK CORPS PERSONNEL
150a, 2x150b, 2x150c, 150e *Ref no:* 150 *Production Period:* 1937-1941 *Market Value:* £140-£160/$200-$240

ROYAL TANK CORPS PRIVATE
Ref no: 604 *Reno:* of 150b

ROYAL TANK CORPS PRIVATE (SEATED)
Ref no: 150b *Production Period:* 1937-1941 *Colour:* Dark blue *Market Value:* £20-£25/$30-$40

ROYAL TANK CORPS PRIVATE (STANDING)
Ref no: 150c *Production Period:* 1937-1941 *Colour:* Dark blue *Market Value:* £20-£25/$30-$40

SERVICE STATION PERSONNEL
Ref no: 009 *Production Period:* 1962-1966 *Colour:* Mainly white *Market Value:* £60-£80/$75-$120

SHEPHERD
Ref no: 6a *Production Period:* 1934-1940 *Colour:* Dark brown hat, cream base *Market Value:* £30-£35/$45-$50

SHEPHERD SET
Ref no: 006 *Reno:* of 6

SHEPHERD SET
6a, 6b, 4 x 2d *Ref no:* 6 *Production Period:* 1934-1940 *Colour:* 3 x 2d cream, 1 x 2d black *Market Value:* £225-£275/$330-$420

SHEPHERD SET
Ref no: 6 *Reno:* to 006 *Production Period:* 1952-1956 *Colour:* 6a Shepherd green hat & base 6b Dog black, 4 x 2d sheep cream *Market Value:* £150-£175/$225-$250

STATION MASTER (LONG COAT)
Ref no: 1a *Production Period:* 1931-1939 *Colour:* Dark blue *Market Value:* £30-£35/$45-$50

STATION MASTER (LONG COAT)
Ref no: 1a *Production Period:* 1939-1941 *Colour:* Dark blue *Market Value:* £15-£20/$25-$30

STATION STAFF
35mm *Ref no:* 001 *Reno:* of 1

STATION STAFF
OO gauge 6 figures *Ref no:* 051 *Reno:* of 1001

STATION STAFF
1a, 1b, 1c, 1d, 1e, 1f, large about 39mm tall, orange base *Ref no:* 1 *Production Period:* 1931-1939 *Market Value:* £250-£275/$375-$425

STATION STAFF
1a, 1b, 1c, 1d, 1e, 1f, small about 35mm tall, buff base *Ref no:* 1 *Reno:* 1 *Production Period:* 1939-1941 *Market Value:* £175-£200/$275-$320

STATION STAFF
Reissue 1a, 1b, 1c, 1d, 1e, small about 35mm tall, dark blue with fawn base *Ref no:* 1 *Reno:* to 001 *Production Period:* 1952-1956 *Market Value:* £100-£130/$150-$200

STATION STAFF (SET OF 6) OO GAUGE
Ref no: 1001 *Reno:* to 051 *Production Period:* 1952-1959 *Colour:* Blue *Market Value:* £70-£90/$100-$130

STOREKEEPER
Ref no: 4c *Production Period:* 1932-1939 *Colour:* Brown *Market Value:* £30-£35/$45-$50

STOREKEEPER
Ref no: 4c *Production Period:* 1939-1941 *Colour:* Brown *Market Value:* £20-£25/$30-$40

TELEGRAPH MESSENGER
Ref no: 011 *Reno:* of 12d

TELEGRAPH MESSENGER
See under 'Miscellaneous' *Ref no:* 12d *Production Period:* 1938-1941

TELEGRAPH MESSENGER
Ref no: 12d *Reno:* to 011 *Production Period:* 1952-1957 *Colour:* Blue *Market Value:* £20-£25/$30-$40

TICKET COLLECTOR (OPEN ARMS)
Ref no: 1c *Production Period:* 1931-1939 *Colour:* Dark blue *Market Value:* £30-£35/$45-$50

TICKET COLLECTOR (RIGHT ARM OUT)
Ref no: 1c *Production Period:* 1939-1941 *Colour:* Dark blue *Market Value:* £15-£20/$25-$30

TRAIN & HOTEL STAFF
35mm *Ref no:* 005 *Reno:* of 5

TRAIN & HOTEL STAFF
5a, 2 x 5b, 2 x 5c large about 39mm tall *Ref no:* 5 *Production Period:* 1932-1937/39 *Colour:* Cream base *Market Value:* £250-£275/$375-$425

TRAIN & HOTEL STAFF
5a, 2 x 5b, 2 x 5c small about 35mm tall *Ref no:* 5 *Production Period:* 1937/39-1941 *Colour:* Buff base *Market Value:* £100-£130/$150-$200

TRAIN & HOTEL STAFF
5a, 2 x 5b, 2 x 5c small about 35mm tall *Ref no:* 5 *Reno:* to 005 *Production Period:* 1952-1956 *Colour:* Main colours as prewar but less detailed painting *Market Value:* £80-£100/$120-$150

WOMAN & CHILD (CHILD ON LEFT)
Postwar: Mother & Child *Ref no:* 3a *Production Period:* 1937/9-1941 *Colour:* Green *Market Value:* £25-£30/$30-$45

WOMAN & CHILD (CHILD ON RIGHT)
Ref no: 3a *Production Period:* 1932-1937/9 *Colour:* Green, red & yellow *Market Value:* £30-£35/$45-$50

WOMAN (OBLONG CASE)
Ref no: 3f *Production Period:* 1932-1937/9 *Colour:* Red & white *Market Value:* £30-£35/$45-$50

WOMAN (ROUND CASE)
Ref no: 3f *Production Period:* 1937/9-1941 *Colour:* Red, later brown *Market Value:* £20-£25/$30-$40

Hong Kong Dinky

This collection of 6 models was produced in Hong Kong in 1965 when Meccano, owned by Lines Bros since 1963 who had their own range of 1/42 scale models as Spot-On, were looking for a cheaper way of production. The venture was not successful and only a relatively small number were made. The construction method and detailing followed Spot-On tradition rather than Dinky. The models themselves remain highly collectable.

There was also a series of small scale cars, the Mini-Dinkies, produced in Hong Kong in 1968 but only probably one or two batches were made. They suffer very badly from metal fatigue and do not really feature as part of the main Dinky production.

BUICK RIVIERA COUPÉ
Ref no: 57/ 001 *Production Period:* 1965-1966 *Colour:* Blue, white roof *Market Value:* £75-£95/$120-$150

CHEVROLET CORVAIR MONZA COUPÉ
Ref no: 57/ 002 *Production Period:* 1965-1965 *Colour:* Red, black roof *Market Value:* £90-£110/$130-$160

CHEVROLET IMPALA
Ref no: 57/003 *Production Period:* 1965-1966 *Colour:* Yellow, white roof *Market Value:* £75-£95/$120-$150

CHEVROLET IMPALA
Ref no: 57/003 *Production Period:* 1965-1966 *Colour:* All yellow *Market Value:* £110-£130/$160-$200

FORD THUNDERBIRD
Ref no: 57/005 *Production Period:* 1965-1965 *Colour:* Blue, white roof *Market Value:* £90-£110/$130-$160

OLDSMOBILE 88
Ref no: 57/004 *Production Period:* 1965-1965 *Colour:* White, blue roof *Market Value:* £100-£130/$140-$160

RAMBLER CLASSIC STATION WAGON
Ref no: 57/ 006 *Production Period:* 1965-1965 *Colour:* Green, silver trim *Market Value:* £75-£95/$120-$150

Kits of Dinky Toys

In an attempt to widen the appeal of their product, Dinky launched a selection of their models in kit form. These used standard castings and parts but were supplied unpainted and unassembled, but with the necessary paint and sometimes decals to complete the model. The paints and decals were usually different from the standard factory finished model. The kits were never popular, the packaging seemed to attract dust and damage, so they are not very collectable today, except possibly they may have some novelty value for some.

It is unfortunate that these have been used by some unscrupulous collectors and dealers to create rare, pre-production samples in odd colours. Some of these fakes are so good they even appear in auctions and fool a lot of people. Beware.

ARMY LAND ROVER
Casting of 344 *Ref no:* 1032 *Production Period:* 1975-1976 *Market Value:* £10-£15/$15-$20

ATLANTEAN BUS
Casting of 295 *Ref no:* 1018 *Production Period:* 1974-1976 *Market Value:* £20-£25/$30-$40

BEACH BUGGY
Casting of 227 *Ref no:* 1014 *Production Period:* 1975-1976 *Market Value:* £10-£15/$15-$20

CHIEFTAIN TANK
Casting of 683 *Ref no:* 1037 *Production Period:* 1974-1978 *Market Value:* £10-£15/$15-$20

FERRARI 312-B2
Casting of 226 *Ref no:* 1012 *Production Period:* 1973-1976 *Market Value:* £10-£15/$15-$20

FORD D800 TIPPER TRUCK
Casting of 438 *Ref no:* 1029 *Production Period:* 1971-1978 *Market Value:* £20-£25/$30-$40

FORD ESCORT POLICE CAR
Casting of 270 *Ref no:* 1004 *Production Period:* 1971-1976 *Market Value:* £25-£30/$30-$40

FORD MEXICO
Casting of 168 *Ref no:* 1006 *Production Period:* 1973-1976 *Market Value:* £25-£30/$30-$40

FORD TRANSIT VAN
Casting of 407 *Ref no:* 1025 *Production Period:* 1971-1975 *Market Value:* £20-£25/$30-$40

HAWKER HURRICANE MK11C
Casting of 718 *Ref no:* 1041 *Production Period:* 1973-1975 *Market Value:* £25-£35/$30-$40

JENSEN FF
Casting of 188 *Ref no:* 1007 *Production Period:* 1971-1975 *Market Value:* £25-£30/$30-$40

LAND ROVER BREAKDOWN CRANE
Casting of 442 *Ref no:* 1030 *Production Period:* 1974-1976 *Market Value:* £15-£20/$20-$30

LEOPARD TANK
Casting of 692 *Ref no:* 1036 *Production Period:* 1975-1978 *Market Value:* £10-£15/$15-$20

LOTUS F.1 RACING CAR
Casting of 225 *Ref no:* 1009 *Production Period:* 1971-1975 *Market Value:* £10-£15/$15-$20

LUNAR ROVING VEHICLE
Casting of 355 *Ref no:* 1027 *Production Period:* 1972-1975 *Market Value:* £10-£15/$15-$20

MERCEDES-BENZ 600
Casting of 128 *Ref no:* 1008 *Production Period:* 1973-1978 *Market Value:* £15-£20/$20-$30

MESSERSCHMITT B.F.109E
Casting of 726 *Ref no:* 1044 *Production Period:* 1972-1975 *Market Value:* £20-£30/$30-$40

MOBILE GUN
Casting of 654 *Ref no:* 1034 *Production Period:* 1975-1978 *Market Value:* £10-£15/$15-$20

MOTOR PATROL BOAT
Casting of 675 *Ref no:* 1050 *Production Period:* 1975-1978 *Market Value:* £10-£15/$15-$20

MULTI-ROLE COMBAT AIRCRAFT
Casting of 729 *Ref no:* 1045 *Production Period:* 1975-1975 *Market Value:* £10-£15/$15-$20

ROLLS ROYCE PHANTOM V LIMOUSINE
Casting of 152 *Ref no:* 1001 *Production Period:* 1971-1976 *Market Value:* £15-£20/$20-$30

ROUTEMASTER BUS
Casting of 289 *Ref no:* 1017 *Production Period:* 1971-1976 *Market Value:* £20-£25/$30-$40

S.E.P.E.C.A.T. JAGUAR
Casting of 731 *Ref no:* 1043 *Production Period:* 1974-1975 *Market Value:* £10-£15/$15-$20

SCORPION TANK
Casting of 690 *Ref no:* 1038 *Production Period:* 1975-1978 *Market Value:* £10-£15/$15-$20

SEA KING HELICOPTER
Casting of 724, no capsule *Ref no:* 1040 *Production Period:* 1971-1978 *Market Value:* £25-£35/$30-$40

SINGLE DECKER BUS
Casting of 283 *Ref no:* 1023 *Production Period:* 1972-1978 *Market Value:* £20-£25/$30-$40

SPITFIRE MK II
Asting of 719 *Ref no:* 1042 *Production Period:* 1971-1978
Market Value: £25-£35/$30-$40

STRIKER ANTI-TANK VEHICLE
Casting of 691 *Ref no:* 1035 *Production Period:* 1975-1976 *Market Value:* £10-£15/$15-$20

U.S. JEEP
Casting of 615 Jeep only *Ref no:* 1033 *Production Period:* 1971-1976 *Market Value:* £10-£15/$15-$20

VOLKWAGEN 1300 SEDAN
Casting of 129 *Ref no:* 1003 *Production Period:* 1971-1974 *Market Value:* £15-£20/$20-$30

VOLVO 1800S
Casting of 116 *Ref no:* 1002 *Production Period:* 1971-1974 *Market Value:* £15-£20/$20-$30

Miscellaneous

This section contains all the models which do not fit into any of the main categories, or are types of models of which insufficient different items were made to warrant a section of their own.

Street furniture, doll's house furniture, various super gift sets, caravans, motorcycles, some space models, accessories and similar are to be found here. The Police, Royal Mail and 'AA' and 'RAC' road service sets are particularly desirable. The boxes hold the contents in a display with a scenic background. With the advent of colour photocopying onto cardboard in recent years many of these sets have been refurbished with new inner display panels so keep a watch for new parts.

'30 MILE LIMIT' SIGN
Ref no: 47e Production Period: 1935-1941 Colour: White underside of base Market Value: £10-£15/$15-$20

'BEND' SIGN
Early Z-bend, later left curve Ref no: 47k Production Period: 1935-1941 Colour: White underside of base Market Value: £10-£15/$15-$20

'CROSSING NO GATES' SIGN
Ref no: 47s Production Period: 1935-1941 Colour: White underside of base Market Value: £10-£15/$15-$20

'DERESTRICTION' SIGN
Ref no: 47f Production Period: 1935-1941 Colour: White underside of base Market Value: £10-£15/$15-$20

'DOLLY VARDEN' DOLL'S HOUSE
Leatherboard, no catalogue number allocated Ref no: 101/4* Production Period: 1936-1940 Market Value: £600-£900/$900-$1

'MAJOR ROAD AHEAD' SIGN
Ref no: 47r Production Period: 1935-1941 Colour: White underside of base Market Value: £10-£15/$15-$20

'NO ENTRY' SIGN
Ref no: 47q Production Period: 1935-1941 Colour: White underside of base Market Value: £10-£15/$15-$20

'ROAD JUNCTION' SIGN
Ref no: 47p Production Period: 1935-1941 Colour: White underside of base Market Value: £10-£15/$15-$20

'ROUNDABOUT' SIGN
Ref no: 47t Production Period: 1935-1941 Colour: White underside of base Market Value: £10-£15/$15-$20

'SCHOOL' SIGN
Ref no: 47g Production Period: 1935-1941 Colour: White underside of base Market Value: £10-£15/$15-$20

'STEEP HILL' SIGN
Ref no: 47h Production Period: 1935-1941 Colour: White underside of base Market Value: £10-£15/$15-$20

4-BERTH CARAVAN
Windows enlarged in 1963 Ref no: 188 Production Period: 1961-1963 Colour: Green & cream or blue & cream Market Value: £35-£45/$50-$65

4-BERTH CARAVAN WITH TRANSPARENT ROOF
Casting of 188 with green transparent roof Ref no: 117 Production Period: 1963-1969 Colour: Blue & cream or yellow & cream Market Value: £30-£50/$45-$75

AA BOX
Printed tinplate with signs on top: London, Liverpool, Glasgow Ref no: 44a Production Period: 1935-1941 Colour: Black with yellow printing, white roof Market Value: £90-£110/$135-$165

AA BOX, MOTOR CYCLE PATROL AND GUIDES
Contents: 44a, 44b, 44c, 44d Ref no: 44 Production Period: 1935-1941 Market Value: £280-£320/$420-$480

AA GUIDE DIRECTING TRAFFIC
Ref no: 44c Production Period: 1935-1941 Colour: Tan with blue sash Market Value: £25-£30/$40-$45

AA GUIDE SALUTING
Ref no: 44d Production Period: 1935-1941 Colour: Tan with blue sash Market Value: £25-£30/$40-$45

AA MOTOR CYCLE PATROL
Sidecar with pointed nose Ref no: 44a Production Period: 1935-1941 Colour: Black motorcycle, yellow sidecar with 'AA', blue sash over rider's right shoulder Market Value: £70-£90/$100-$130

AA MOTOR CYCLE PATROL
From 1950-1954/5 US market only, 1959 reissued as 270 Ref no: 44b Reno: to 045 & 270 Production Period: 1948-1963 Colour: Black motorcycle, yellow sidecar 'AA' Market Value: £40-£60/$60-$90

AA MOTOR CYCLE PATROL
US Market only Ref no: 045 Reno: of 44b

AA MOTORCYCLE PATROL
Ref no: 270 Reno: of 44b

ANWB MOTOR CYCLE PATROL
Casting of 44b/270, Dutch market as 270 but with 'ANWB' badge transfer Ref no: 272 Production Period: c1955 Market Value: £100-£120/$150-$190

BATH
Gold taps Ref no: 104a Production Period: 1936-1940 Colour: Pink & white or light green & white Market Value: £30-£35/$45-$60

BATH MAT
Rubber *Ref no:* 104b *Production Period:* 1936-1940 *Colour:* Pink & white or light green & white *Market Value:* £10-£15/$15-$20

BATHROOM FURNITURE
Contents : 104a, 104b, 104c, 104d, 104e, 104f. *Ref no:* 104 *Production Period:* 1936-1940 *Market Value:* £200-£250/$300-$375

BED
Ref no: 102a *Production Period:* 1936-1940 *Colour:* Green or pink *Market Value:* £25-£30/$35-$45

BEDROOM FURNITURE
Contents : 102a, 102b, 102c, 102d, 102e, 102f. *Ref no:* 102 *Production Period:* 1936-1940 *Market Value:* £200-£250/$300-$375

BELISHA BEACON
1948 SA market, 1950-1954/5 US market *Ref no:* 47d *Reno:* to 777 *Production Period:* 1948-1963 *Colour:* Black underside of base *Market Value:* £7-£10/$10-$15

BELISHA BEACON
Ref no: 777 *Reno:* of 47d

BELISHA SAFETY BEACON
Ref no: 47d *Production Period:* 1935-1941 *Colour:* White underside of base *Market Value:* £7-£10/$10-$15

BLAZING INFERNO
Dinky Builda, card *Ref no:* 002 *Production Period:* 1979 *Colour:* Grey & flame *Market Value:* £5-£10/$10-$15

BOWSER PETROL PUMP
Ref no: 49a *Production Period:* 1935-1941 *Colour:* Green *Market Value:* £25-£30/$35-$45

BRITISH ROAD SIGNS (24)
Contains: contents of 766, 767, 768, 769 *Ref no:* 772 *Production Period:* 1959-1964 *Market Value:* £150-£200/$220-$300

BRITISH ROAD SIGNS (COUNTRY SET A)
6 signs, different castings from 47 *Ref no:* 766 *Production Period:* 1959-1963 *Colour:* White base, black & white with red *Market Value:* £40-£60/$60-$90

BRITISH ROAD SIGNS (COUNTRY SET B)
7 signs, different castings from 47 *Ref no:* 767 *Production Period:* 1959-1964 *Colour:* White base, black & white with red *Market Value:* £40-£60/$60-$90

BRITISH ROAD SIGNS (TOWN SET A)
8 signs, different castings from 47 *Ref no:* 768 *Production Period:* 1959-1963 *Colour:* White base, black & white with red *Market Value:* £40-£60/$60-$90

BRITISH ROAD SIGNS (TOWN SET B)
9 signs, different castings from 47 *Ref no:* 769 *Production Period:* 1959-1963 *Colour:* White base, black & white with red *Market Value:* £40-£60/$60-$90

CARAVAN
Ref no: 190 *Production Period:* 1956-1964 *Colour:* Orange with cream, blue with cream *Market Value:* £35-£45/$50-$75

CARAVAN TRAILER
See under 'CARS' *Ref no:* 30g *Production Period:* 1936-1941

CARVER CHAIR
Ref no: 101c *Production Period:* 1936-1940 *Colour:* Walnut finish *Market Value:* £15-£20/$23-$30

CHAIR
Raised 'leather' cushion *Ref no:* 101d *Production Period:* 1936-1940 *Colour:* Walnut finish *Market Value:* £10-£15/$15-$20

CHAIR
Flat seat, casting as 103e *Ref no:* 102f *Production Period:* 1936-1940 *Colour:* Green or pink *Market Value:* £10-£15/$15-$20

CHAIR
Casting as 102f *Ref no:* 103e *Production Period:* 1936-1940 *Colour:* Light blue & white or green & cream *Market Value:* £10-£15/$15-$20

COSMIC INTERCEPTOR
Made for Marks & Spencer Xmas 1979 *Ref no:* 363 *Production Period:* 1979 *Colour:* Red & white *Market Value:* £35-£40/$50-$60

DINING-ROOM FURNITURE
Contents : 101a, 101b, 2x101c, 4x101d. *Ref no:* 101 *Production Period:* 1936-1940 *Market Value:* £200-£250/$300-$375

DRESSING CHEST
Tinplate back *Ref no:* 102d *Production Period:* 1936-1940 *Colour:* Green or pink *Market Value:* £20-£25/$30-$40

DRESSING TABLE
Tinplate mirror *Ref no:* 102c *Production Period:* 1936-1940 *Colour:* Green or pink *Market Value:* £25-£30/$35-$45

DRESSING TABLE STOOL
Ref no: 102e *Production Period:* 1936-1940 *Colour:* Green or pink *Market Value:* £15-£20/$20-$30

ELECTRIC COOKER
Tinplate back *Ref no:* 103c *Production Period:* 1936-1940 *Colour:* Light blue & white or green & cream *Market Value:* £35-£40/$50-$60

FILLING AND SERVICE STATION
Tinplate *Ref no:* 48 *Production Period:* 1935-1941 *Colour:* Yellow printed walls *Market Value:* £300-£400/$450-$600

FIRE STATION
Plastic, lighting kit 787 *Ref no:* 954 *Production Period:* 1961-1964 *Colour:* Red, yellow & brick *Market Value:* £240-£280/$350-$420

GARAGE
Printed tinplate *Ref no:* 45 *Production Period:* 1935-1941 *Colour:* Cream, green doors & base, orange tiled roof *Market Value:* £300-£400/$450-$600

HEALEY SPORTS BOAT
As 796, boat only *Ref no:* 797 *Production Period:* 1961-1963 *Market Value:* £10-£15/$15-$20

HEALEY SPORTS BOAT ON TRAILER
Plastic boat with cream hull & green deck *Ref no:* 796 *Production Period:* 1960-1968 *Colour:* Orange trailer *Market Value:* £25-£30/$35-$45

INTERNATIONAL ROAD SIGNS
12 signs *Ref no:* 771 *Production Period:* 1953-1964 *Colour:* Silver with white, cream, red, blue & black painted face on signs *Market Value:* £90-£120/$130-$180

KITCHEN CABINET
Tinplate back *Ref no:* 103b *Production Period:* 1936-1940 *Colour:* Light blue & white or green & cream *Market Value:* £35-£40/$50-$60

KITCHEN FURNITURE
Contents : 103a, 103b, 103c, 103d, 103e. *Ref no:* 103 *Production Period:* 1936-1940 *Market Value:* £200-£250/$300-$375

LAMP STANDARD DOUBLE ARM
Plastic lamp, metal base *Ref no:* 756 *Production Period:* 1960-1964 *Colour:* Grey & fawn *Market Value:* £25-£40/$45-$60

LAMP STANDARD SINGLE ARM
Plastic lamp, metal base *Ref no:* 755 *Production Period:* 1960-1964 *Colour:* Grey & fawn *Market Value:* £20-£30/$30-$45

LAND ROVER TRAILER
Ref no: 27m *Reno:* to 341 *Production Period:* 1952-1973 *Colour:* Orange, green or later red *Market Value:* £20-£25/$30-$35

LAND ROVER TRAILER
Ref no: 341 *Reno:* of 27m

LARGE TRAILER
Ref no: 428 *Reno:* of 551, to 9

LARGE TRAILER
Reissue *Ref no:* 551 *Reno:* to 428 *Production Period:* 1967-1971 *Colour:* Red *Market Value:* £35-£40/$50-$60

LEFT-HAND 'CORNER' SIGN
Ref no: 47m *Production Period:* 1935-1941 *Colour:* White underside of base *Market Value:* £10-£15/$15-$20

LINEN BASKET
Hinged lid *Ref no:* 104e *Production Period:* 1936-1940 *Colour:* Pink & white or light green & white *Market Value:* £25-£30/$40-$45

LOADING RAMP FOR PULLMORE CAR TRANSPORTER
Tinplate, for 582/982 Bedford Car Transporter *Ref no:* 994 *Reno:* to 794 *Production Period:* 1954-1964 *Colour:* Light blue *Market Value:* £15-£20/$20-$30

LUNAR ROVING VEHICLE
2 white plastic astronauts *Ref no:* 355 *Production Period:* 1972-1975 *Colour:* Metallic blue *Market Value:* £30-£40/$45-$60

MOTOR CYCLE PATROL
US Market only *Ref no:* 043 *Reno:* of 42b

MOTOR CYCLE PATROL
Sidecar with passenger *Ref no:* 42b *Production Period:* 1936-1941 *Colour:* Dark blue motorcycle, dark green sidecar *Market Value:* £70-£90/$100-$135

MOTOR CYCLE PATROL
1950-1954/5 US market only *Ref no:* 42b *Reno:* to 043 *Production Period:* 1948-1954/5 *Colour:* Dark blue motorcycle, dark green sidecar *Market Value:* £40-£50/$60-$75

MOTOR CYCLIST (CIVILIAN)
Ref no: 37a *Production Period:* 1937-1941 *Colour:* Blue, green or maroon rider on black cycle *Market Value:* £30-£40/$45-$60

MOTOR CYCLIST (CIVILIAN)
1950-54/5 in US catalogue only renumbered 041 *Ref no:* 37a *Reno:* to 041 *Production Period:* 1948-1954 *Colour:* Green, gloss green or grey rider, black cycle *Market Value:* £25-£35/$35-$50

MOTOR CYCLIST (POLICE)
White rubber wheels *Ref no:* 37b *Production Period:* 1937-1941 *Colour:* Blue rider, black cycle *Market Value:* £30-£40/$45-$60

MOTOR CYCLIST (POLICE)
1950-54/5 in US catalogue only renumbered 042 *Ref no:* 37b *Reno:* to 042 *Production Period:* 1948-1954 *Colour:* Blue rider, black cycle *Market Value:* £25-£35/$35-$50

MOTORCYCLIST (CIVILIAN)
US Market only *Ref no:* 041 *Reno:* of 37a

MOTORCYCLIST (POLICE)
US Market only *Ref no:* 042 *Reno:* of 37b

NASA SPACE SHUTTLE
With plastic booster rocket *Ref no:* 364 *Production Period:* 1979 *Colour:* White, stickers: 'United States' *Market Value:* £60-£80/$90-$120

NASA SPACE SHUTTLE
Without plastic booster rocket *Ref no:* 364 *Production Period:* 1979 *Colour:* White, stickers: 'United States' *Market Value:* £25-£30/$40-$45

NASA SPACE SHUTTLE
With plastic kit or card load *Ref no:* 366 *Production Period:* 1979 *Colour:* White *Market Value:* £25-£30/$40-$45

OIL BIN
Mazac with opening tinplate cover *Ref no:* 49e *Production Period:* 1935-1941 *Colour:* Yellow. Black 'Pratts Motor Oil' *Market Value:* £45-£50/$65-$75

OIL BIN
(Postwar) no lettering *Ref no:* 49e *Market Value:* £25-£30/$35-$45

PAVEMENT SET
Card, 18 pieces *Ref no:* 46 *Production Period:* 1937-1941 *Colour:* Dark grey *Market Value:* £120-£180/$180-$270

PAVEMENT SET
Card, 18 pieces *Ref no:* 46 *Production Period:* 1948-1950 *Colour:* Stone *Market Value:* £100-£150/$150-$220

PAVEMENT SET

Card, 24 pieces *Ref no:* 754 *Production Period:* 1958-1962 *Colour:* Grey & fawn *Market Value:* £40-£60/$60-$90

PEDESTAL HAND BASIN

Tinplate mirror, gold taps *Ref no:* 104c *Production Period:* 1936-1940 *Colour:* Pink & white or light green & white *Market Value:* £35-£40/$45-$50

PETROL PUMP STATION (BP)

Plastic with 4 metal pump bodies, BP sign *Ref no:* 783 *Production Period:* 1960-1965 *Colour:* Grey base, cream & green kiosk *Market Value:* £50-£70/$75-$100

PETROL PUMP STATION (ESSO)

Esso & Esso Extra Pumps, Esso sign *Ref no:* 781 *Production Period:* 1955-1964 *Colour:* Tan base, red & white *Market Value:* £50-£70/$75-$100

PETROL PUMP STATION (SHELL)

Plastic with 4 metal pump bodies, Shell sign *Ref no:* 782 *Production Period:* 1960-1970 *Colour:* Grey base, cream & green kiosk *Market Value:* £50-£70/$75-$100

PETROL PUMPS SET

Contents : 49a, 49b, 49c, 49d, 49e. White rubber hoses *Ref no:* 49 *Production Period:* 1935-1941 *Market Value:* £150-£200/$220-$300

PETROL PUMPS SET

Yellow plastic hoses, in UK catalogue until 1953 then US market only *Ref no:* 49 *Reno:* to 780 *Production Period:* 1948-1955 *Market Value:* £100-£130/$150-$200

PILLAR BOX (AIRMAIL)

Casting of 12a *Ref no:* 12b *Production Period:* 1935-1941 *Colour:* Blue, blue oval 'Air Mail' *Market Value:* £35-£45/$50-$65

PILLAR BOX (EIIR)

EIIR cast in *Ref no:* 760 *Production Period:* 1954-1960 *Colour:* Red & black *Market Value:* £25-£30/$45-$50

PILLAR BOX (GPO)

Cast oval on top of box *Ref no:* 12a *Production Period:* 1935-1941 *Colour:* Red, yellow oval 'Post Office' *Market Value:* £25-£30/$35-$45

POINT DUTY POLICEMAN

Ref no: 42d *Production Period:* 1936-1941 *Colour:* Dark blue, white gauntlets *Market Value:* £25-£30/$40-$45

POINT DUTY POLICEMAN (IN WHITE COAT)

Ref no: 42c *Production Period:* 1936-1941 *Colour:* White long coat *Market Value:* £25-£30/$40-$45

POLICE BOX

1954 US market only *Ref no:* 42a *Reno:* to 751 *Production Period:* 1948-1960 *Colour:* Dark blue *Market Value:* £25-£35/$35-$50

POLICE BOX

Ref no: 751 *Reno:* of 42a

POLICE CONTROLLED CROSSING

Plastic, policeman revolves *Ref no:* 753 *Production Period:* 1962-1966 *Colour:* Grey base, black & white *Market Value:* £80-£100/$120-$150

POLICE HUT, MOTOR CYCLE PATROL AND POLICEMAN

Contents : 42a, 42b, 42c, 42d *Ref no:* 42 *Production Period:* 1936-1941 *Market Value:* £200-£250/$300-$375

POLICE HUT/BOX

Ref no: 42a *Production Period:* 1936-1941 *Colour:* Dark blue *Market Value:* £35-£45/$50-$65

POSTAL SET

Contents : 12a, 12b, 12c, 12d, 12e, 34b (see Section 12) *Ref no:* 12 *Production Period:* 1938-1941 *Market Value:* £500-£600/$750-$900

POSTERS FOR ROAD HOARDINGS

Paper, 6 different *Ref no:* 763 *Production Period:* 1959-1964 *Colour:* Various *Market Value:* £25-£30/$45-$50

POSTERS FOR ROAD HOARDINGS

Paper, 6 different *Ref no:* 764 *Production Period:* 1959-1964 *Colour:* Various *Market Value:* £25-£30/$45-$50

POSTMAN

Ref no: 012 *Reno:* of 12e

POSTMAN

Ref no: 12e *Production Period:* 1938-1941 *Colour:* Dark blue *Market Value:* £20-£25/$30-$40

POSTMAN

Ref no: 12e *Reno:* to 012 *Production Period:* 1952-1957 *Colour:* Blue, brown bag *Market Value:* £20-£25/$30-$40

RAC BOX

Printed tinplate *Ref no:* 43a *Production Period:* 1935-1941 *Colour:* Blue with white & black *Market Value:* £70-£90/$100-$140

RAC BOX, MOTOR CYCLE PATROL AND GUIDES

Contents : 43a, 43b, 43c, 43d *Ref no:* 43 *Production Period:* 1935-1941 *Market Value:* £250-£300/$375-$450

RAC GUIDE DIRECTING TRAFFIC

Ref no: 43c *Production Period:* 1935-1941 *Colour:* Blue with red sash *Market Value:* £25-£30/$40-$45

RAC GUIDE SALUTING

Ref no: 43d *Production Period:* 1935-1941 *Colour:* Blue with red sash *Market Value:* £25-£30/$40-$45

RAC MOTOR CYCLE PATROL

Sidecar with rounded nose *Ref no:* 43b *Production Period:* 1935-1941 *Colour:* Black motor cycle with red sash over rider's left shoulder *Market Value:* £70-£90/$100-$130

RAMP FOR PULLMORE CAR TRANSPORTER

Ref no: 794 *Reno:* of 994

REFRIGERATOR

Tinplate insert with food *Ref no:* 103a *Production Period:* 1936-1940 *Colour:* Light blue & white or green & cream *Market Value:* £35-£40/$50-$60

RIGHT-HAND 'CORNER' SIGN

Ref no: 47n *Production Period:* 1935-1941 *Colour:* White underside of base *Market Value:* £10-£15/$15-$20

ROAD HOARDINGS
Plastic, with 6 posters *Ref no: 765 Production Period:* 1959-1963 *Colour:* Green *Market Value:* £60-£80/$90-$120

ROAD REPAIR WARNING BOARDS
Plastic: Road Up, Keep Left, Stop, Go, Danger..., No Entry *Ref no: 778 Production Period:* 1962-1967 *Market Value:* £15-£20/$25-$30

ROAD SIGNS
Contents: 47e, 47f, 47g, 47h, 47k, 47m, 47n, 47p, 47q, 47r, 47s, 47t. Triangle at top filled in *Ref no: 47 Production Period:* 1935-1941 *Market Value:* £180-£220/$270-$330

ROAD SIGNS
Triangles open, 1950-1954/5 US market only *Ref no: 47 Reno:* to 770 *Production Period:* 1948-1954 *Colour:* Black underside of base *Market Value:* £80-£90/$120-$140

ROAD SIGNS (12)
US market *Ref no: 770 Reno:* of 47

ROBOT FOUR-FACE
SA market *Ref no: 47b Production Period:* 1948-1948 *Colour:* Black underside of base *Market Value:* £10-£15/$15-$20

ROBOT FOUR-FACE (RIGHT ANGLE)
SA market *Ref no: 47c Production Period:* 1948-1948 *Colour:* Black underside of base *Market Value:* £10-£15/$15-$20

ROBOT TWO-FACE (BACK TO BACK)
2nd version of 47c for SA market *Ref no: 47y Production Period:* 1948-1948 *Market Value:* £10-£15/$15-$20

SRN-6 HOVERCRAFT
Casting used for 281 Military Hovercraft *Ref no: 290 Production Period:* 1970-1976 *Colour:* Metallic red then red *Market Value:* £25-£30/$35-$45

SERVICE STATION
Plastic, lighting kit 787 *Ref no: 785 Production Period:* 1960-1963 *Colour:* Tan & red *Market Value:* £150-£200/$220-$300

SHELL PETROL PUMP
Ref no: 49d Production Period: 1935-1941 *Colour:* Red *Market Value:* £25-£30/$35-$45

SIDEBOARD
Tinplate back *Ref no: 101b Production Period:* 1936-1940 *Colour:* Walnut finish *Market Value:* £35-£40/$50-$65

SPACE BATTLE CRUISER
Marked 'Made in England' only *Ref no: 367 Production Period:* 1979 *Colour:* White *Market Value:* £35-£40/$50-$60

SPACE BATTLE CRUISER
Made for Marks & Spencer for Xmas 1979 *Ref no: 367 Production Period:* 1979 *Colour:* Dark blue *Market Value:* £35-£40/$50-$60

SPACE WAR STATION
Dinky Builda, card *Ref no: 001 Production Period:* 1979 *Colour:* Silver grey *Market Value:* £5-£10/$10-$15

STOOL
Ref no: 104d Production Period: 1936-1940 *Colour:* Pink & white or light green & white *Market Value:* £15-£20/$20-$30

TS MOTOR CYCLE PATROL
Casting of 44b/270, Belgian market as 270 but with 'TS' badge transfer *Ref no: 271 Production Period:* c1955 *Market Value:* £100-£120/$150-$190

TABLE
Ref no: 101a Production Period: 1936-1940 *Colour:* Walnut finish *Market Value:* £25-£30/$35-$45

TABLE
Ref no: 103d Production Period: 1936-1940 *Colour:* Light blue & white or green & cream *Market Value:* £25-£30/$40-$45

TELEGRAPH MESSENGER
Ref no: 011 Reno: of 12d

TELEGRAPH MESSENGER
Ref no: 12d Production Period: 1938-1941 *Colour:* Dark blue *Market Value:* £20-£25/$30-$40

TELEGRAPH MESSENGER
Ref no: 12d Reno: to 011 *Production Period:* 1952-1957 *Colour:* Blue *Market Value:* £20-£25/$30-$40

TELEPHONE BOX
Ref no: 12c Production Period: 1936-1941 *Colour:* Cream, later red *Market Value:* £35-£40/$50-$60

TELEPHONE BOX
1954 US market only *Ref no: 12c Reno:* to 750 *Production Period:* 1946-1962 *Colour:* Red with silver windows *Market Value:* £25-£30/$35-$45

TELEPHONE BOX
Ref no: 750 Reno: of 12c

THEO PETROL PUMP
Ref no: 49c Production Period: 1935-1941 *Colour:* (Prewar) royal blue. (Postwar) brown *Market Value:* £25-£30/$35-$45

TOILET
Hinged lid *Ref no: 104f Production Period:* 1936-1940 *Colour:* Pink & white or light green & white *Market Value:* £35-£40/$50-$60

TRAFFIC SIGNAL 4-FACE
Ref no: 773 Reno: of 47a

TRAFFIC SIGNAL FOUR-FACE
With yellow beacon on top *Ref no: 47a Production Period:* 1935-1941 *Colour:* White underside of base *Market Value:* £10-£15/$15-$20

TRAFFIC SIGNAL FOUR-FACE/ROBOT FOUR-FACE
With yellow beacon, late 1956 replaced with finial, 1950-1954/5 US market *Ref no: 47a Reno:* to 773 *Production Period:* 1948-1963 *Colour:* Black underside of base, from mid-1959 all white base *Market Value:* £10-£15/$15-$20

TRAFFIC SIGNAL THREE-FACE
Ref no: 47b Production Period: 1935-1941 *Colour:* White underside of base *Market Value:* £10-£15/$15-$20

TRAFFIC SIGNAL TWO-FACE
Faces back to back *Ref no:* 47c *Production Period:* 1935-1941 *Colour:* White underside of base *Market Value:* £10-£15/$15-$20

TRAFFIC SIGNAL TWO-FACE
Faces at right angles *Ref no:* 47c *Production Period:* 1935-1941 *Colour:* White underside of base *Market Value:* £10-£15/$15-$20

TRAILER
Tinplate drawbar *Ref no:* 25g *Production Period:* 1935-1941 *Colour:* Dark blue or green *Market Value:* £35-£45/$50-$65

TRAILER
Wire drawbar *Ref no:* 25g *Reno:* to 429 *Production Period:* 1946-1963 *Colour:* Stone, light blue, orange, red or dark green *Market Value:* £20-£25/$30-$35

TRAILER
Ref no: 429 *Reno:* of 25g

TRAILER
Ref no: 951 *Reno:* of 551

TRAILER/LARGE TRAILER
Ref no: 551 *Reno:* to 951 & 428 *Production Period:* 1948-1964 *Colour:* Green or grey *Market Value:* £35-£40/$50-$60

TRIDENT STAR FIGHTER
Ref no: 362 *Production Period:* 1979 *Colour:* Black *Market Value:* £35-£40/$50-$60

TYRE RACK WITH TYRES
21 treaded tyres *Ref no:* 786 *Production Period:* 1960-1967 *Colour:* Green metal rack, Dunlop *Market Value:* £30-£40/$45-$60

WARDROBE
Tinplate back *Ref no:* 102b *Production Period:* 1936-1940 *Colour:* Green or pink *Market Value:* £25-£30/$35-$45

WAYNE PETROL PUMP
Ref no: 49b *Production Period:* 1935-1941 *Colour:* Light blue *Market Value:* £25-£30/$35-$45

ZYGON MARAUDER
Casting of 367 but marked 'Dinky Toys' *Ref no:* 368 *Reno:* of 367 *Production Period:* 1979 *Colour:* White *Market Value:* £35-£40/$50-$60

ZYGON PATROLLER
Casting of 363 Cosmic Interceptor *Ref no:* 363 *Production Period:* 1979 *Colour:* Red & white *Market Value:* £35-£40/$50-$60

ZYGON/GALACTIC WAR CHARIOT
2 white plastic astronauts *Ref no:* 361 *Production Period:* 1979 *Colour:* Metallic green & silver *Market Value:* £35-£40/$50-$60

Planes

The collecting of aeroplanes was restricted to the plane enthusiast for many years but there has been a great upsurge in the last 10 years of interest in planes generally. Now they have at least as great a following as a lot of the other categories of collecting.

The pre-war Dinky planes are intrinsically beautiful shapes with often very attractive colour schemes. The small scale of these models enables a lot of models to be displayed in a small area. Old drawing office plan chests are ideal for this purpose if you can find any.

The thin wings and tails of the planes make the models very prone to warping and cracking due to metal fatigue. This has caused most of the late pre-war planes to be rare because so many of them just crumble as you look at them. However, it is fair to say that if it has not fatigued by now, then it probably is not going to fall apart in the future unless you drop it!

There are many, many super colour variations on the early Dinkies, only the main ones can be listed here for space reasons. Often the castings were used for more than one catalogue number. This gives rise to similar models with different names under the wing and sometimes without a name at all, which can make identification difficult. The cross referencing in the table should alleviate this problem.

The new post-war production up to about 1950 almost seems to have been painted from the same can of aluminium paint, except for a few late examples which have a very shiny silver finish.

The mid 1950s saw the airliners and private owner light planes come along. There are not very many variations on these. Some military planes in camouflage were also made then. The top of the range was the 992 Avro Vulcan which was made in aluminium. A small quantity only was made because of casting problems and this batch was sold in Canada.

The 'Big Planes' of the 1970s are a group on their own. They have working features, missiles, rockets, etc and you either like them or you don't. They are now getting to be very collectable.

A6M5 ZERO-SEN
Motor driven propeller *Ref no:* 739 *Production Period:* 1975-1978 *Colour:* Metallic blue-green, grey lower *Market Value:* £60-£80/$90-$120

AEROPLANES/BRITISH AEROPLANES
Contents : 60a, 60b, 60c, 60d, 60e, 60f (1st versions) *Ref no:* 60 *Production Period:* 1934-1936 *Market Value:* £1500-£2000/$2300-$3000

AEROPLANES/BRITISH AEROPLANES
Contents : with black registration letters (except 60f), 60a gold, 60b green, 60c white, 60d red, 60e silver, 60f gold with blue *Ref no:* 60 *Production Period:* 1936-1941 *Market Value:* £900-£1200/$1400-$1800

AIRCRAFT IN SERVICE CAMOUFLAGE
Contains: 68a, 68b, 2x60n, 2x62a, 3x62h, 62t *Ref no:* 68 *Production Period:* 1940-1941 *Market Value:* £2600-£3500/$3900-$5200

AIRSPEED ENVOY
Ref no: 62m *Production Period:* 1938-1941 *Colour:* Various colours/registrations *Market Value:* £140-£170/$210-$250

AIRSPEED ENVOY KING'S AEROPLANE
Casting of 62m, with new name under wing *Ref no:* 62k *Production Period:* 1938-1941 *Colour:* Silver, red & blue, G-AEXX *Market Value:* £180-£250/$290-$380

ARMSTRONG WHITWORTH AIR LINER
Casting of 62p with new name under wing *Ref no:* 62p *Production Period:* 1945-1949 *Colour:* Silver with registrations, or blue, grey or green with contrasting trim *Market Value:* £130-£200/$200-$300

ARMSTRONG WHITWORTH ENSIGN LINER IN SERVICE CAMOUFLAGE
Casting of 62p *Ref no:* 68a *Production Period:* 1940-1941 *Colour:* Camouflage *Market Value:* £220-£270/$330-$400

ARMSTRONG WHITWORTH WHITLEY BOMBER
See 62t *Ref no:* 60v *Production Period:* 1937-1941 *Colour:* Silver *Market Value:* £180-£220/$270-$330

ARMSTRONG WHITWORTH WHITLEY BOMBER CAMOUFLAGED
Casting of 60v *Ref no:* 62t *Production Period:* 1939-1941 *Colour:* Camouflage *Market Value:* £210-£270/$320-$400

ARMY CO-OPERATION AUTOGIRO
Casting of 60f *Ref no:* 66f *Production Period:* 1940-1941 *Colour:* Silver grey with red, white & blue roundels *Market Value:* £200-£250/$300-$380

ATLANTIC FLYING BOAT
Casting of 60r *Ref no:* 60x *Production Period:* 1937-1941 *Colour:* 60r in bright colours with registration letters *Market Value:* £340-£450/$500-$675

AVRO VULCAN DELTA WING BOMBER
Numbered 749 on drawing but catalogued and boxed as 992 *Ref no: 749 Reno:* to 992

AVRO VULCAN DELTA WING BOMBER
Aluminium, poor castings resulted in a small quantity only being exported to Canada *Ref no: 992 Production Period:* 1955-1956 *Colour:* Silver, transfers: RAF roundels on wings & nose *Market Value:* £1750-£2250/$2600-$3300

AVRO YORK AIRLINER
Name under wing *Ref no: 70a Reno:* to 704 *Production Period:* 1946-1949 *Colour:* Silver, G-AGJC *Market Value:* £90-£140/$135-$220

AVRO YORK AIRLINER
Name under wing *Ref no: 70a Reno:* to 704 *Production Period:* 1952-1959 *Market Value:* £90-£140/$135-$220

AVRO YORK AIRLINER
Ref no: 704 *Reno:* of 70a

BEECHCRAFT C55 BARON
Casting used for 712 *Ref no: 715 Production Period:* 1968-1976 *Colour:* White with yellow wingtips, from 1971/2 red with yellow tips *Market Value:* £35-£45/$50-$70

BEECHCRAFT S.35 BONANZA
2 suitcases till 1971 *Ref no: 710 Production Period:* 1965-1976 *Colour:* White/red, yellow/bronze, white/blue, N8695M, from 1975 N4480W *Market Value:* £45-£60/$70-$90

BELL POLICE HELICOPTER
Police Accident board *Ref no: 732 Production Period:* 1974-1979 *Colour:* Blue, white tinplate, orange plastic *Market Value:* £40-£50/$60-$75

BOEING 737 LUFTHANSA
Ref no: 717 Production Period: 1970-1975 *Colour:* White with blue tail, white engines, from 1971 blue engines *Market Value:* £50-£70/$75-$100

BOEING FLYING FORTRESS
Ref no: 62g Production Period: 1939-1941 *Colour:* Silver, some grey *Market Value:* £170-£210/$250-$320

BRISTOL 173 HELICOPTER
Red rotors *Ref no: 715 Production Period:* 1956-1962 *Colour:* Light blue/green, later turquoise, G-AUXR *Market Value:* £40-£55/$60-$80

BRISTOL BLENHEIM BOMBER
Blenheim Bomber under wing. See 62d *Ref no: 62b Production Period:* 1940-1941 *Colour:* Silver *Market Value:* £100-£150/$150-$220

BRISTOL BLENHEIM BOMBER CAMOUFLAGED
Casting of 62b *Ref no: 62d Production Period:* 1940-1941 *Colour:* Camouflage *Market Value:* £125-£175/$190-$265

BRISTOL BRITANNIA AIRLINER
Canadian pacific, cf-cza *Ref no: 998 Production Period:* 1959-1965 *Colour:* Silver & white with blue lines *Market Value:* £225-£275/$335-$400

BRISTOL BRITANNIA AIRLINER
Canadian pacific, cf-cza *Ref no: 998 Production Period:* 1959-1965 *Colour:* Silver or metallic grey with white and red lines *Market Value:* £200-£250/$300-$375

BRITISH 40-SEATER AIR LINER
Ref no: 62x Production Period: 1939-1941 *Colour:* 62p in bright colours with regisration G-AZCA *Market Value:* £250-£320/$375-$480

BUNDESMARINE SEA KING HELICOPTER
Casting of 724 *Ref no: 736 Production Period:* 1973-1978 *Colour:* Grey with red engine casting & tailfin *Market Value:* £60-£90/$80-$130

CAMOUFLAGED AEROPLANE SET
Contents : 66a, 66b, 66c, 66d, 66e, 66f - all as 60 set but camouflaged *Ref no: 66 Production Period:* 1940-1941 *Market Value:* £2100-£2700/$3200-$4000

CARAVELLE SE210 AIRLINER
French Dinky 60F but made in England *Ref no: 997 Production Period:* 1962-1965 *Colour:* Silver with white upper, Air France, F-BGNY *Market Value:* £225-£275/$335-$400

CIERVA AUTOGIRO
Open cockpit, pilot added 1936. See 66f *Ref no: 60f Production Period:* 1934-1941 *Colour:* Gold with blue rotor & tailplane tips *Market Value:* £150-£200/$220-$300

DH 110 SEA VIXEN FIGHTER
Ref no: 738 Production Period: 1960-1965 *Colour:* Medium sea grey with white lower surfaces *Market Value:* £35-£45/$50-$75

DH COMET AEROPLANE
Ref no: 60g Production Period: 1935-1941 *Colour:* Red with gold trim, gold with red, silver with blue, from 1936 red, silver or gold with G-ACSR *Market Value:* £110-£170/$160-$250

DH COMET JET AIRLINER
Early: white fin G-ALYV Later: blue fin G-ALYX *Ref no: 702 Reno:* to 999 *Production Period:* 1954-1955 *Colour:* White & blue, BOAC livery *Market Value:* £100-£140/$150-$200

DH COMET JET AIRLINER
Ref no: 999 Reno: of 702

DH LEOPARD MOTH
Ref no: 60b Production Period: 1934-1936 *Colour:* Green, yellow tips & tail *Market Value:* £180-£230/$270-$350

DH LEOPARD MOTH
1939 name added, from 1939/40 windows filled in. See 66b *Ref no: 60b Production Period:* 1936-1941 *Colour:* Green, G-ACPT in black *Market Value:* £150-£200/$220-$300

DE HAVILLAND ALBATROSS MAIL LINER
DH Albatross under wing. See 62w, 68b *Ref no: 62r Production Period:* 1939-1941 *Colour:* Silver G-AEVV *Market Value:* £200-£225/$300-$350

DIVE BOMBER FIGHTER
Casting of 60b with new name under wing *Ref no: 66b Production Period:* 1940-1941 *Colour:* Dark camouflage, dark green underside *Market Value:* £225-£275/$340-$400

DOUGLAS DC3 AIR LINER
Ref no: 60t *Production Period:* 1938-1941 *Colour:* Silver PH-ALI *Market Value:* £230-£290/$350-$430

EMPIRE FLYING BOAT
Plastic rollers, see 60x, 63a *Ref no:* 60r *Production Period:* 1937-1941 *Colour:* Silver, 13 different name/registration combinations *Market Value:* £275-£400/$400-$600

EMPIRE FLYING BOAT
Name under wing, brass roller *Ref no:* 60r *Production Period:* 1945-1949 *Colour:* Silver, G-ADHM, G-ADUV, or G-ADVB *Market Value:* £210-£260/$300-$400

ENSIGN CLASS AIRLINER
See 62x, 68a *Ref no:* 62p *Production Period:* 1938-1941 *Colour:* Silver, with 6 different names/registrations *Market Value:* £180-£225/$270-$340

F-4K PHANTOM DER BUNDESLUFTWAFFE
Casting of 725, German & Austrian market only *Ref no:* 733 *Production Period:* 1973-1973 *Colour:* Dark grey with matt grey/green camouflage *Market Value:* £120-£150/$180-$225

F-4K PHANTOM II
White plastic missiles, black nosecone *Ref no:* 725 *Production Period:* 1972-1977 *Colour:* Ultramarine blue with light blue under *Market Value:* £80-£100/$120-$150

FAIREY BATTLE BOMBER
1940 undercarriage deleted. See 60s *Ref no:* 60n *Production Period:* 1937-1941 *Colour:* Silver, some grey *Market Value:* £160-£200/$240-$300

FAIREY BATTLE BOMBER (CAMOUFLAGED)
Casting of 60n without undercarriage *Ref no:* 60s *Production Period:* 1939-1941 *Colour:* Light camouflage with roundels on both wings, later dark camouflage *Market Value:* £170-£225/$250-$300

FLYING BOAT
Ref no: 60w *Production Period:* 1945-1949 *Colour:* Silver *Market Value:* £130-£150/$200-$230

FLYING BOAT
Ref no: 60w *Production Period:* 1945-1949 *Colour:* Some blue, light or dark green *Market Value:* £180-£240/$270-$360

FLYING BOAT CLIPPER III
Ref no: 60w *Production Period:* 1938-1941 *Colour:* Silver, USA NC 16736 *Market Value:* £180-£220/$270-$330

FOUR-ENGINED FLYING BOAT
Casting of 60h *Ref no:* 60m *Production Period:* 1936-1941 *Colour:* 60h in various bright colours and registrations *Market Value:* £220-£300/$330-$450

FOUR-ENGINED LINER
Casting of 62r with new name under wing *Ref no:* 62r *Production Period:* 1945-1949 *Colour:* Grey, light blue, silver, fawn, some G-ATPV *Market Value:* £110-£150/$160-$225

FROBISHER CLASS LINER IN SERVICE CAMOUFLAGE
Casting of 62r/62w *Ref no:* 68b *Production Period:* 1940-1941 *Colour:* Camouflage *Market Value:* £220-£270/$330-$400

GENERAL MONOSPAR
Ref no: 60e *Production Period:* 1934-1936 *Colour:* Silver with blue tips & tail *Market Value:* £180-£230/$270-$350

GENERAL MONOSPAR
See 66e *Ref no:* 60e *Production Period:* 1936-1941 *Colour:* Silver, G-ABVP in black *Market Value:* £150-£200/$220-$300

GIANT HIGH SPEED MONOPLANE
Ref no: 62y *Production Period:* 1939-1941 *Colour:* 62n in bright colours with registration D-AZBK *Market Value:* £190-£250/$285-$375

GIANT HIGH SPEED MONOPLANE
Ref no: 62y *Production Period:* 1946-1949 *Colour:* Light green, mid-green, grey, or silver, G-ATBK, no window transfers *Market Value:* £140-£180/$210-$270

GLOSTER GLADIATOR BIPLANE
1939 name added *Ref no:* 60p *Production Period:* 1937-1941 *Colour:* Silver, some grey *Market Value:* £160-£200/$240-$300

GLOSTER JAVELIN DELTA WING FIGHTER
Ref no: 735 *Production Period:* 1955-1966 *Colour:* Medium grey & dark green camouflage *Market Value:* £35-£45/$50-$70

GLOSTER METEOR TWIN-JET FIGHTER
Name under wing *Ref no:* 70e *Reno:* to732 *Production Period:* 1946-1949 *Colour:* Silver *Market Value:* £25-£35/$40-$50

GLOSTER METEOR TWIN-JET FIGHTER
Name under wing *Ref no:* 70e *Reno:* to732 *Production Period:* 1952-1962 *Market Value:* £25-£35/$40-$50

GLOSTER METEOR TWIN-JET FIGHTER
Ref no: 732 *Reno:* of 70e

HAWKER HARRIER
Undercarriage linked to swivelling jet exhausts *Ref no:* 722 *Production Period:* 1970-1979 *Colour:* Metallic blue with variable green shading *Market Value:* £70-£90/$100-$140

HAWKER HUNTER
Ref no: 736 *Production Period:* 1955-1963 *Colour:* Medium grey & dark green camouflage *Market Value:* £30-£45/$45-$70

HAWKER HURRICANE MKIIC
Cannon noise *Ref no:* 718 *Production Period:* 1972-1975 *Colour:* Grey with dark green shading *Market Value:* £60-£80/$90-$120

HAWKER HURRICANE SINGLE SEAT FIGHTER
See 62h *Ref no:* 62s *Production Period:* 1939-1941 *Colour:* Silver *Market Value:* £110-£160/$160-$240

HAWKER SIDDELEY HS125 EXECUTIVE JET
Casting used for 728 RAF Dominie *Ref no:* 723 *Production Period:* 1970-1975 *Colour:* White, yellow lower & wings, later white upper the rest metallic blue *Market Value:* £35-£50/$50-$75

HEAVY BOMBER

Casting of 60a with new name under wing *Ref no: 66a Production Period:* 1940-1941 *Colour:* Dark camouflage, dark green underside *Market Value:* £400-£450/$600-$680

HURRICANE

Ref no: 62s *Production Period:* 1945-1949 *Colour:* Silver *Market Value:* £80-£110/$120-$170

HURRICANE SINGLE SEATER FIGHTER CAMOUFLAGED

See 62s *Ref no:* 62h *Production Period:* 1939-1941 *Colour:* Camouflage *Market Value:* £150-£190/$225-$285

IMPERIAL AIRWAYS FROBISHER CLASS LINER

Casting of 62r with new name under wing, see 68b *Ref no:* 62w *Production Period:* 1939-1941 *Colour:* Silver, G-AFDI, G-AFDJ, & G-AFDK *Market Value:* £200-£225/$300-$350

IMPERIAL AIRWAYS LINER

Ref no: 60a *Production Period:* 1934-1936 *Colour:* Gold with blue sunray pattern on wing *Market Value:* £275-£350/$400-$525

IMPERIAL AIRWAYS LINER

From 1939 name under wing, see 66a *Ref no:* 60a *Production Period:* 1936-1941 *Colour:* Gold, G-ABTI in black *Market Value:* £275-£340/$400-$500

JUNKERS JU90 AIRLINER

See 62y, 67a *Ref no:* 62n *Production Period:* 1938-1941 *Colour:* Silver, D-AURE, D-AIVI, window transfers *Market Value:* £225-£300/$340-$450

JUNKERS JU.87B STUKA

Dropping cap-firing bomb *Ref no:* 721 *Production Period:* 1969-1979 *Colour:* Service green upper surfaces, duck egg blue under, yellow nose band & tailfin *Market Value:* £60-£80/$90-$120

JUNKERS JU89 HEAVY BOMBER

Casting of 62n with new name under wing *Ref no:* 67a *Production Period:* 1940-1941 *Colour:* Black, light blue under, white crosses on wings *Market Value:* £350-£450/$500-$650

LIGHT RACER

Light Racer under wing *Ref no:* 60g *Production Period:* 1945-1949 *Colour:* Yellow, red or silver, G-RACE *Market Value:* £70-£100/$100-$150

LIGHT TOURER

Briefly Percival Tourer under wing then Light Tourer *Ref no:* 60k *Production Period:* 1945-1949 *Colour:* Dark or light green, red or silver *Market Value:* £90-£150/$130-$220

LIGHT TRANSPORT

Casting of 62m, Light Transport under wing *Ref no:* 62m *Production Period:* 1945-1949 *Colour:* Silver, red or blue G-ATMH *Market Value:* £80-£110/$120-$160

LONG RANGER BOMBER

Long Range Bomber under wing *Ref no:* 62g *Production Period:* 1945-1949 *Colour:* Silver *Market Value:* £100-£140/$150-$210

LOW WING MONOPLANE

Open cockpit *Ref no:* 60d *Production Period:* 1934-1936 *Colour:* Red with cream tips & tail *Market Value:* £180-£230/$270-$350

LOW WING MONOPLANE

Pilot's head added. See 66d *Ref no:* 60d *Production Period:* 1936-1941 *Colour:* Red, G-AVYP in black *Market Value:* £150-£200/$220-$300

MAIA

Casting as 60r with tinplate frame on upper wing, Mayo Composite under wing *Ref no:* 63a *Production Period:* 1939-1941 *Colour:* Silver G-ADHK Maia *Market Value:* £200-£275/$300-$400

MAYO COMPOSITE

63a fitted with cradle to hold 63b *Ref no:* 63 *Production Period:* 1939-1941 *Colour:* 63a and 63b in box *Market Value:* £290-£390/$450-$575

MEDIUM BOMBER

Medium Bomber under wing *Ref no:* 62b *Production Period:* 1945-1949 *Colour:* Silver *Market Value:* £80-£125/$120-$190

MEDIUM BOMBER

Casting of 60e *Ref no:* 66e *Production Period:* 1940-1941 *Colour:* Dark camouflage, dark green under wing *Market Value:* £225-£275/$340-$400

MEDIUM BOMBER (MIRROR PAIR)

Casting of 60n *Ref no:* 60s *Production Period:* 1937-1940 *Colour:* Light camouflage, black undersurface, roundel on one wing *Market Value:* £340-£400/$500-$600

MESSERSCHMITT BF109E

Battery driven propeller *Ref no:* 726 *Production Period:* 1972-1975 *Colour:* Desert sand with spots of green on upper casting, *Market Value:* £70-£90/$100-$140

MESSERSCHMITT BF109E

Battery driven propeller *Ref no:* 726 *Production Period:* 1975 *Colour:* Dark grey-green with yellow nose, rudder & wingtips *Market Value:* £120-£150/$180-$225

P-47 THUNDERBOLT

Motor driven prop *Ref no:* 734 *Production Period:* 1975-1978 *Colour:* Gloss silver with gloss black engine cowling & stripe *Market Value:* £130-£170/$200-$250

P.1B LIGHTNING FIGHTER

Black plastic nose *Ref no:* 737 *Production Period:* 1959-1968 *Colour:* Silver *Market Value:* £50-£70/$75-$100

PANAVIA MULTI-ROLE COMBAT AIRCRAFT

Swing-wing linked to undercarriage *Ref no:* 729 *Production Period:* 1974-1975 *Colour:* Grey with dull green camouflage *Market Value:* £40-£60/$60-$90

PERCIVAL GULL

Ref no: 60c *Production Period:* 1934-1936 *Colour:* White with blue tips & tail *Market Value:* £180-£230/$270-$350

PERCIVAL GULL

1939/40 side windows filled in, see 60k, 66c *Ref no:* 60c *Reno:* to 60k *Production Period:* 1936-1941 *Colour:* White, G-ADZO in black *Market Value:* £150-£200/$220-$300

PERCIVAL GULL MONOPLANE
Casting of 60c *Ref no: 60k Production Period:* 1936-1941 *Colour:* Blue, silver wings & tailplane, G-ADZO in blue (Mollison) or black (Brooks) *Market Value:* £220-£270/$330-$400

PRESENTATION AEROPLANE SET
Contents : 60g, 62h (or 62a), 62k, 62m, 62s, 63b *Ref no:* 64 *Production Period:* 1939-1941 *Market Value:* £800-£1100/$1200-$1650

PRESENTATION AEROPLANE SET
Contents : 60r, 60t, 60v, 60w, 62n, 62p, 62r, 62w *Ref no:* 65 *Production Period:* 1939-1941 *Market Value:* £2000-£2250/$3000-$3500

RAF AEROPLANES
Contents : 60h, 2x60n, 2x60p *Ref no:* 61 *Production Period:* 1937-1941 *Market Value:* £500-£750/$750-$1100

RAF DOMINIE
Casting of 723 HS125 *Ref no:* 728 *Production Period:* 1972-1975 *Colour:* Mid-metallic blue, mid green camouflage *Market Value:* £40-£60/$60-$90

SEPECAT JAGUAR
Ref no: 731 *Production Period:* 1973-1975 *Colour:* Light metallic blue with dull green camouflage *Market Value:* £40-£60/$60-$90

SEA KING HELICOPTER
Apollo space capsule *Ref no:* 724 *Production Period:* 1971-1979 *Colour:* White upper, metallic blue lower *Market Value:* £50-£70/$75-$100

SEAPLANE
No tinplate clip, new name under wing *Ref no:* 63b *Production Period:* 1945-1949 *Colour:* Silver G-AVKW *Market Value:* £40-£70/$60-$100

SEAPLANE
No tinplate clip, new name under wing *Ref no:* 63b *Production Period:* 1952-1957 *Market Value:* £40-£70/$60-$100

SEAPLANE
Ref no: 700 *Reno:* of 63b

SEAPLANE MERCURY
Tinplate clip under fuselage *Ref no:* 63b *Production Period:* 1939-1941 *Colour:* Silver G-ADHJ Mercury *Market Value:* £90-£130/$130-$200

SHETLAND FLYING BOAT
Marked 'Supertoy' under casting but no number *Ref no:* 701 *Production Period:* 1947-1949 *Colour:* Silver, G-AGVD *Market Value:* £350-£480/$520-$720

SHOOTING STAR JET FIGHTER
Name under wing *Ref no:* 70f *Reno:* to 733 *Production Period:* 1947-1949 *Colour:* Silver *Market Value:* £25-£35/$40-$50

SHOOTING STAR JET FIGHTER
Name under wing *Ref no:* 70f *Reno:* to 733 *Production Period:* 1952-1962 *Market Value:* £25-£35/$40-$50

SHOOTING STAR JET FIGHTER
Ref no: 733 *Reno:* of 70f

SINGAPORE FLYING BOAT
Early: lead hull then mazac. Early: no roller, later roller. See 60m *Ref no:* 60h *Production Period:* 1936-1941 *Colour:* Silver, some grey *Market Value:* £200-£300/$300-$400

SPIFIRE MKII
No motor driven propeller *Ref no:* 741 *Production Period:* 1978-1979 *Colour:* As 719 *Market Value:* £60-£80/$90-$120

SPITFIRE
Casting with long nose & bubble cockpit *Ref no:* 62a *Production Period:* 1945-1949 *Colour:* Silver *Market Value:* £80-£110/$120-$160

SPITFIRE FUND SPITFIRE
Casting of 62a above with ring cast in tail *Ref no:* 62a* *Production Period:* 1941-1941 *Colour:* Various colours *Market Value:* A

SPITFIRE MK II DIAMOND JUBILEE OF THE RAF
For Diamond Jubilee of the Royal Air Force, not in catalogue. Casting of 741 *Ref no:* 700 *Production Period:* 1979-1979 *Colour:* Chromed, mounted on green plastic plinth *Market Value:* £120-£150/$180-$225

SPITFIRE MKII
Motor driven prop *Ref no:* 719 *Production Period:* 1969-1978 *Colour:* Green with brown shading on upper surfaces *Market Value:* £60-£80/$90-$120

SUPERMARINE SWIFT
Ref no: 734 *Production Period:* 1955-1962 *Colour:* Medium grey & dark green camouflage *Market Value:* £35-£40/$50-$60

TEMPEST II FIGHTER
Name under wing *Ref no:* 70b *Reno:* to 730 *Production Period:* 1946-1949 *Colour:* Silver *Market Value:* £35-£50/$50-$75

TEMPEST II FIGHTER
Name under wing *Ref no:* 70b *Reno:* to 730 *Production Period:* 1952-1955 *Market Value:* £35-£50/$50-$75

TEMPEST II FIGHTER
Ref no: 730 *Reno:* of 70b

TORPEDO DIVE BOMBER
Casting of 60d with new name under wing *Ref no:* 66d *Production Period:* 1940-1941 *Colour:* Light or dark camouflage, dark green underside *Market Value:* £225-£275/$340-$400

TWIN-ENGINED FIGHTER
Name under wing *Ref no:* 70d *Reno:* to 731 *Production Period:* 1946-1949 *Colour:* Silver *Market Value:* £25-£35/$40-$50

TWIN-ENGINED FIGHTER
Name under wing *Ref no:* 70d *Reno:* to 731 *Production Period:* 1952-1955 *Market Value:* £25-£35/$40-$50

TWIN-ENGINED FIGHTER
Ref no: 731 *Reno:* of 70d

TWO-SEATER FIGHTER
Casting of 60c with new name under wing *Ref no:* 66c
Production Period: 1940-1941 *Colour:* Light or dark
camouflage, dark green underside *Market Value:* £225-
£275/$340-$400

US AIR FORCE F-4 PHANTOM II
Casting of 725, yellow missiles *Ref no:* 727 *Production
Period:* 1976-1977 *Colour:* Greyish brown with olive green
camouflage *Market Value:* £230-£280/$350-$420

US ARMY T-42A
715 C55 Baron with plastic wingtip tanks *Ref no:* 712
Production Period: 1972-1977 *Colour:* Green drab *Market
Value:* £60-£80/$90-$120

US NAVY PHANTOM II
Casting of 725 *Ref no:* 730 *Production Period:* 1972-1975
Colour: Mid-grey, white undersurfaces, AC on fin *Market
Value:* £80-£100/$120-$150

VICKERS SUPERMARINE SPITFIRE
CAMOUFLAGED
Casting of 62a *Ref no:* 62e *Production Period:* 1940-1941
Colour: Camouflage *Market Value:* £150-£190/$225-
$285

VICKERS VISCOUNT AIRLINER (AIR
FRANCE)
706 cast under wing *Ref no:* 706 *Production Period:* 1956-
1957 *Colour:* Silver & white, F-BGNL *Market Value:* £110-
£150/$160-$225

VICKERS VISCOUNT AIRLINER (BEA)
Without number under wing, replaced 706 *Ref no:* 708
Production Period: 1957-1965 *Colour:* Silver & white, later
metallic grey & white, G-AOJA *Market Value:* £110-
£150/$160-$225

VICKERS-SUPERMARINE SPITFIRE
Casting with short nose, see 62*a, 62e *Ref no:* 62a
Production Period: 1940-1941 *Colour:* Silver *Market
Value:* £110-£160/$160-$240

VIKING AIRLINER
Name under wing *Ref no:* 70c *Reno:* to 705 *Production
Period:* 1947-1949 *Colour:* Silver or grey, G-AGOL *Market
Value:* £60-£80/$90-$120

VIKING AIRLINER
Name under wing *Ref no:* 70c *Reno:* to 705 *Production
Period:* 1952-1962 *Market Value:* £60-£80/$90-$120

VIKING AIRLINER
Ref no: 705 *Reno:* of 70c

WESTLAND SIKORSKY S51 HELICOPTER
Ref no: 716 *Production Period:* 1957-1962 *Colour:* Dark
red, G-ATWX *Market Value:* £35-£45/$50-$70

Plant (Construction)

This is the section for road making equipment, cranes, excavators and such heavy machinery. In general these models are fairly uninspiring and are not thought to be very desirable by collectors at large. There are two items however which are very sought after, the 975 Ruston Bucyrus Excavator, which has a plastic body, and the 900 Site Building Gift Set. These models were only in production for a maximum of four years but are very hard to find.

ALBION LORRY-MOUNTED CONCRETE MIXER
Ref no: 960 Production Period: 1960-1967 *Colour:* Orange truck, yellow & blue mixer *Market Value:* £70-£80/$100-$120

ATLAS COPCO COMPRESSOR LORRY
Ref no: 436 *Production Period:* 1963-1969 *Colour:* Yellow *Market Value:* £55-£80/$80-$120

ATLAS DIGGER
Ref no: 984 *Production Period:* 1974-1979 *Colour:* Yellow, red & black *Market Value:* £35-£45/$50-$65

AVELING BARFORD CENTAUR DUMP TRUCK
Ref no: 924 *Production Period:* 1972-1976 *Colour:* Red cab, yellow back *Market Value:* £45-£55/$70-$85

AVELING-BARFORD DIESEL ROLLER
Ref no: 25p Reno: to 251 *Production Period:* 1948-1963 *Colour:* Green with red roller *Market Value:* £40-£60/$60-$90

AVELING-BARFORD DIESEL ROLLER
Ref no: 251 *Reno:* of 25p

AVELING-BARFORD DIESEL ROLLER
Ref no: 279 *Production Period:* 1965-1979 *Colour:* Orange with green rollers, yellow with silver rollers *Market Value:* £40-£60/$60-$90

BLAW-KNOX BULLDOZER
Casting of 563 with dozer blade *Ref no:* 561 *Reno:* to 961 *Production Period:* 1949-1964 *Colour:* Red or yellow *Market Value:* £70-£90/$100-$140

BLAW-KNOX BULLDOZER
Ref no: 961 *Reno:* of 561

BLAW-KNOX HEAVY TRACTOR
Casting used for 561/961 *Ref no:* 563 *Reno:* to 963 *Production Period:* 1948-1959 *Colour:* Red or orange *Market Value:* £40-£60/$90-$120

COLES 20-TON LORRY MOUNTED CRANE
Ref no: 972 *Production Period:* 1955-1968 *Colour:* Orange lorry, yellow crane *Market Value:* £70-£100/$100-$150

COLES MOBILE CRANE
Ref no: 571 *Reno:* to 971 *Production Period:* 1949-1965 *Colour:* Yellow & black *Market Value:* £70-£90/$100-$140

COLES MOBILE CRANE
Ref no: 971 *Reno:* of 571

EATON YALE ARTICULATED TRACTOR SHOVEL
Ref no: 973 *Production Period:* 1971-1976 *Colour:* Yellow & orange *Market Value:* £25-£35/$35-$50

ELEVATOR LOADER
Black rubber belt *Ref no:* 564 *Reno:* to 964 *Production Period:* 1952-1969 *Colour:* Yellow with blue chute or blue with yellow *Market Value:* £60-£90/$90-$140

ELEVATOR LOADER
Ref no: 964 *Reno:* of 564

EUCLID REAR DUMP TRUCK
Ref no: 965 *Production Period:* 1955-1969 *Colour:* Yellow *Market Value:* £45-£70/$70-$100

FODEN DUMP TRUCK WITH BULLDOZER BLADE
Ref no: 959 *Production Period:* 1961-1968 *Colour:* Red, silver *Market Value:* £80-£100/$120-$150

GOODS YARD CRANE
Some with cast iron base *Ref no:* 752 *Reno:* to 973 *Production Period:* 1953-1959 *Colour:* Yellow with blue base *Market Value:* £40-£60/$60-$90

GOODS YARD CRANE
Ref no: 973 *Reno:* of 752

HEAVY TRACTOR
Ref no: 963 *Reno:* of 563

JOHNSON 2-TON DUMPER
Ref no: 430 *Production Period:* 1977-1979 *Colour:* Orange & red *Market Value:* £25-£30/$40-$50

JONES FLEETMASTER CANTILEVER CRANE
Ref no: 970 *Production Period:* 1967-1976 *Colour:* Red, yellow or metallic red *Market Value:* £60-£80/$90-$120

MICHIGAN 180 III TRACTOR DOZER
Ref no: 976 *Production Period:* 1968-1977 *Colour:* Yellow with red parts. *Market Value:* £25-£35/$35-$50

MUIR HILL 2WL LOADER
Ref no: 437 *Production Period:* 1962-1979 *Colour:* Red with grey, yellow with yellow *Market Value:* £20-£30/$30-$45

MUIR HILL LOADER AND TRENCHER
Ref no: 967 *Production Period:* 1973-1978 *Colour:* Yellow & orange *Market Value:* £25-£35/$35-$50

MUIR-HILL DUMP TRUCK
Ref no: 562 *Reno:* to 962 *Production Period:* 1948-1966
Colour: Yellow *Market Value:* £40-£60/$90-$120

MUIR-HILL DUMPER
Ref no: 962 *Reno:* of 562

ROAD GRADER
Ref no: 963 *Production Period:* 1973-1976 *Colour:*
Orange & yellow *Market Value:* £23-£35/$40-$60

RUSTON BUCYRUS EXCAVATOR
Plastic body *Ref no:* 975 *Production Period:* 1963-1967
Colour: Red, yellow & grey *Market Value:* £200-
£260/$300-$390

SHOVEL DOZER
Ref no: 977 *Production Period:* 1973-1978 *Colour:* Yellow
& red *Market Value:* £25-£35/$35-$50

SITE BUILDING GIFT SET
Contents : 437 Muir Hill 2wl Loader, 960 Albion Concrete
Mixer, 961 Blaw-Knox Bulldozer, 962 Muir Hill Dumper,
965 Euclid Dump Truck *Ref no:* 900 *Production Period:*
1964-1968 *Market Value:* £800-£1200/$1200-$1800

TEREX DUMP TRUCK
Casting as 965 Euclid *Ref no:* 965 *Production Period:*
1969-1970 *Colour:* Yellow *Market Value:* £160-
£190/$240-$290

Service Vehicles

This is a large and very important group of models. Fire engines, police cars, taxis, ambulances, refuse trucks and all similar types of public service vehicles. In fact virtually everything except buses, which have their own section.

The description of the individual models in the table below should be sufficient to identify each one. There is one area though where some clarification is probably needed - the Ford Transit vans. There are three basic casting types, each of which gets a separate catalogue number:

Type 1: 1967-74, 2 opening rear doors, opening passenger door
Type 2: 1975-78, as 1 but lifting rear door, no opening passenger door
Type 3: 1978-79, as 2 but headlights in line with protruding grille.

This gives the type order, but NOT in numerical order, as:

Ambulance: 276 as type 2, 274 as type 3
Fire Appliance: 286 as type 1, 271 as type 2
Police Van: 287 as type 1, 272 as type 2, 269 as type 3.

This seems to be more complicated than necessary, perhaps it explains why Dinky ceased production in 1979 in rather a state of disarray. There are also some 'Falck' versions made for the Danish market only.

The large majority of the models in this section owe their origin to castings seen elsewhere in Truck or Cars sections, but there are some unique items. The BBC and ATV TV vans are a case in point, these are super models with attractive liveries and accessories and are justly respected by collectors. There are also two special vans in this group, 274 Minivan 'Mason Paints' and the 275 Armoured Van 'Manriques'. These are both genuine factory produced promotional vehicles and are very rare. Some of the castings are used on different catalogue numbers, the Superior ambulance body being an example.

'CONVOY' FIRE RESCUE TRUCK
Ref no: 384 Production Period: 1977-1979 Colour: Red, white escape Market Value: £15-£20/$20-$30

AA PATROL MINI VAN
Plug in plastic roof sign Ref no: 274 Production Period: 1964-1972 Colour: Yellow, from 1971 with white roof Market Value: £130-£175/$200-$250

ABC TV CONTROL ROOM
Casting of 967 BBC with camera & operator Ref no: 987 Production Period: 1962-1969 Colour: Light blue & light grey, ABC Television on sides Market Value: £170-£200/$250-$300

ABC TV TRANSMITTER VAN
Casting as 968 BBC Roving Eye Vehicle + plastic dish from 969 Ref no: 988 Production Period: 1962-1968 Colour: Light blue & light grey, ABC-TV Market Value: £190-£220/$280-$330

AEC HOYNOR CAR TRANSPORTER
10 chocks in sealed bag Ref no: 974 Production Period: 1968-1975 Colour: Blue cab, yellow & red trailer, 'Silcock & Colling' Market Value: £55-£80/$80-$120

AIRPORT FIRE RESCUE TENDER
Casting of 266 Ref no: 263 Production Period: 1978-1979 Colour: Yellow Market Value: £35-£50/$50-$75

AIRPORT FIRE TENDER
Casting of 259 Ref no: 276 Production Period: 1962-1969 Colour: Red Market Value: £45-£70/$65-$100

AMBULANCE
Ref no: 24a Production Period: 1934-1941 Colour: See under 'CARS'

AMBULANCE
Ref no: 30f Production Period: 1935-1941 Colour: See under 'CARS'

AMBULANCE
Closed windows Ref no: 30f Production Period: 1946-1948 Colour: Grey or cream with black chassis Market Value: £90-£120/$135-$180

ARMOURED CAR 'LUIS R PICASO MANRIQUES'
As 275, Mexican promotional Ref no: 275 Production Period: 1976-1976 Colour: Dark grey with black base Market Value: £550-£750/$800-$1100

AUSTIN 1800 TAXI
Casting of 171 Ref no: 282 Production Period: 1967-1968 Colour: Blue & white Market Value: £45-£70/$65-$100

AUSTIN TAXI
Ref no: 40h Reno: to 254 Production Period: 1951-1962 Colour: Blue, yellow, green & yellow, black Market Value: £80-£100/$120-$150

AUSTIN TAXI
Ref no: 254 Reno: of 40h

BBC TV EXTENDING MAST VEHICLE
Plastic dish on tinplate mast Ref no: 969 Production Period: 1959-1964 Colour: Dark green, with BBC crest on sides Market Value: £125-£160/$185-$240

BBC TV MOBILE CONTROL ROOM
Ref no: 967 *Production Period:* 1959-1964 *Colour:* Dark green, with BBC crest on sides *Market Value:* £110-£150/$165-$230

BBC TV ROVING EYE VEHICLE
With camera man on roof, aerial *Ref no:* 968 *Production Period:* 1959-1964 *Colour:* Dark green, with BBC crest on sides *Market Value:* £110-£160/$165-$240

BEDFORD REFUSE WAGON
Ref no: 252 *Reno:* of 25v

BEDFORD VAN (AA)
410 with headboard *Ref no:* 412 *Production Period:* 1974-1979 *Colour:* Light yellow, later dark *Market Value:* £25-£30/$40-$50

BEDFORD VAN (ROYAL MAIL)
Ref no: 410 *Production Period:* 1972-1979 *Colour:* Red *Market Value:* £20-£25/$30-$40

BRINKS ARMOURED CAR (WITH GOLD BULLION)
2 plastic crates with gold bars *Ref no:* 275 *Production Period:* 1964-1969 *Colour:* Grey with dark blue base *Market Value:* £110-£140/$165-$210

BRINKS TRUCK
As 275 above but no drivers or gold *Ref no:* 275 *Production Period:* 1979-1979 *Colour:* Dark grey with white roof & blue base *Market Value:* £45-£70/$65-$100

BRITISH RAILWAYS HORSEBOX
Ref no: 981 *Reno:* of 581

CANADIAN FIRE CHIEF'S CAR
Casting of 173 *Ref no:* 257 *Production Period:* 1960-1969 *Colour:* Red *Market Value:* £60-£80/$90-$120

CAR CARRIER
Aluminium back *Ref no:* 984 *Production Period:* 1958-1965 *Colour:* Red with grey runways, 'Dinky Autoservice' *Market Value:* £130-£160/$200-$240

CAR CARRIER (AUTO TRANSPORTERS)
Casting of 984 Car Carrier *Ref no:* 989 *Production Period:* 1963-1965 *Colour:* Yellow cab, light grey back & blue runways *Market Value:* £1100-£1400/$1600-$2000

CAR CARRIER AND TRAILER
984 car carrier, 985 trailer *Ref no:* 983 *Production Period:* 1958-1963 *Market Value:* £220-£270/$330-$400

CAR TRANSPORTER GIFT SET
In 1969 catalogue but not issued *Ref no:* 950

CRASH SQUAD GIFT SET
Contents: 244 Plymouth Police Car, 732 Bell Police Helicopter *Ref no:* 299 *Production Period:* 1979-1979 *Market Value:* £45-£55/$70-$80

DAIMLER AMBULANCE
Ref no: 30h *Reno:* to 253 *Production Period:* 1950-1964 *Colour:* Cream, or white *Market Value:* £50-£80/$75-$120

DAIMLER AMBULANCE
Ref no: 253 *Reno:* of 30h

ERF FIRE TENDER
White wheeled escape *Ref no:* 266 *Production Period:* 1976-1979 *Colour:* Red, later metallic red *Market Value:* £45-£70/$65-$95

ELECTRIC DAIRY VAN
'Express Dairy' renumbered 490 *Ref no:* 30v *Reno:* to 490 *Production Period:* 1949-1960 *Colour:* Cream with red bed or grey with blue *Market Value:* £80-£90/$120-$135

ELECTRIC DAIRY VAN
'Express Dairy' *Ref no:* 490 *Reno:* of 30v

ELECTRIC VAN (NCB)
'NCB' *Ref no:* 30v *Reno:* 491 *Production Period:* 1950-1960 *Colour:* Grey with blue bed *Market Value:* £80-£100/$120-$150

ELECTRIC VAN (NCB)
'NCB' *Ref no:* 491 *Reno:* of 30v

EMERGENCY SERVICES GIFT SET
Contents: 258 USA Police Car (Fairlane), 263 Criterion Ambulance, 277 ditto with flashing light, 276 Airport Fire Tender, 008 Fire Station Personnel, 2 Ambulancemen from 007, 1 Policeman *Ref no:* 298 *Production Period:* 1963-1964 *Market Value:* £800-£1000/$1200-$1500

EMERGENCY SQUAD GIFT SET
In 1979 catalogue but not issued *Ref no:* 302 *Production Period:* 1979

FIAT 2300 PATHÉ NEWS CAMERA CAR
Casting of 172 Fiat 2300, camera, tripod & man *Ref no:* 281 *Production Period:* 1967-1969 *Colour:* Black *Market Value:* £90-£110/$135-$165

FIRE ENGINE
Tinplate ladder *Ref no:* 259 *Production Period:* 1961-1969 *Colour:* Red, silver ladder *Market Value:* £70-£90/$100-$135

FIRE ENGINE WITH EXTENDING LADDER
Ref no: 555 *Reno:* to 955 *Production Period:* 1952-1969 *Colour:* Red *Market Value:* £70-£90/$100-$135

FIRE ENGINE WITH EXTENDING LADDER
Ref no: 955 *Reno:* of 555

FIRE RESCUE GIFT SET
Contents: 195 Range Rover Fire Chief, 282 Land Rover Fire Appliance, 384 'Convoy' Fire Rescue Truck *Ref no:* 304 *Production Period:* 1978-1979 *Market Value:* £70-£100/$100-$150

FIRE SERVICES GIFT SET
Contents: 257 canadian fire chief's car, 555/955 fire engine, 956 turntable fire escape (bedford) *Ref no:* 957 *Production Period:* 1959-1964 *Market Value:* £370-£450/$550-$670

FORD PANDA POLICE CAR
Casting of 168 Ford *Ref no:* 270 *Production Period:* 1969-1976 *Colour:* Blue with white doors *Market Value:* £50-£60/$75-$90

FORD TRANSIT AMBULANCE
Replacing 276 Transit *Ref no:* 274 *Production Period:* 1978-1979 *Colour:* White *Market Value:* £30-£35/$45-$60

FORD TRANSIT AMBULANCE
As 271, replaced by 274 *Ref no: 276 Production Period:* 1976-1978 *Colour:* White *Market Value:* £30-£35/$45-$55

FORD TRANSIT FIRE APPLIANCE
Replacing 286 *Ref no: 271 Production Period:* 1975-1976 *Colour:* Red *Market Value:* £50-£70/$75-$100

FORD TRANSIT FIRE APPLIANCE
Replaced by 271 *Ref no: 286 Production Period:* 1969-1974 *Colour:* Metallic red, then red *Market Value:* £55-£80/$80-$120

FORD ZODIAC POLICE CAR
Casting of 164 *Ref no: 255 Production Period:* 1967-1971 *Colour:* White *Market Value:* £55-£70/$80-$100

HAPPY CAB
Casting as 115 *Ref no: 120 Production Period:* 1979-1979 *Colour:* White, yellow & blue *Market Value:* £30-£50/$45-$75

HORSE BOX
Aluminium, British Railways renumbered to 981 *Ref no: 581 Reno:* to 980, 981 *Production Period:* 1953-1960 *Colour:* Maroon *Market Value:* £100-£140/$150-$210

HORSE BOX
Express Horse Van. US issue *Ref no: 980 Reno:* of 581 *Production Period:* 1953-1960 *Colour:* Maroon *Market Value:* £380-£430/$550-$650

JAGUAR MOTORWAY POLICE CAR
Casting of 195 Jaguar 3.4 with rooflight, aerial & 2 figures *Ref no: 269 Production Period:* 1962-1965 *Colour:* White or matt white *Market Value:* £90-£110/$135-$165

JOB'S DAIRY VAN
Special made at the request of Job's Dairy *Ref no: 30v Production Period:* 1960-1960 *Colour:* Cream with red, 'Job's Dairy' in red *Market Value:* £100-£120/$150-$180

JOHNSON ROAD SWEEPER
Casting of 451 without opening doors *Ref no: 449 Production Period:* 1977-1979 *Colour:* Orange with metallic green, lime green with black *Market Value:* £45-£55/$70-$85

JOHNSON ROAD SWEEPER
Opening doors. Replaced by 449 *Ref no: 451 Production Period:* 1971-1977 *Colour:* Orange & metallic green *Market Value:* £45-£55/$70-$85

LAND ROVER FIRE APPLIANCE
Ref no: 282 Production Period: 1973-1979 *Colour:* Red *Market Value:* £30-£35/$45-$60

LONDON AUSTIN TAXI
Cast boot detail until 1977 *Ref no: 284 Production Period:* 1972-1979 *Colour:* Black or dark blue *Market Value:* £30-£40/$45-$60

MARREL MULTI-BUCKET UNIT
Uses chassis of 960 *Ref no: 966 Production Period:* 1960-1964 *Colour:* Yellow with grey bucket *Market Value:* £100-£120/$150-$180

MERRYWEATHER MARQUIS FIRE ENGINE
Ref no: 285 Production Period: 1969-1979 *Colour:* Metallic red then red *Market Value:* £45-£70/$65-$100

MERSEY TUNNEL POLICE VAN
Ref no: 255 Production Period: 1955-1961 *Colour:* Red *Market Value:* £55-£70/$80-$100

MIDLAND MOBILE BANK
Ref no: 280 Production Period: 1966-1968 *Colour:* White & silver *Market Value:* £80-£100/$120-$150

MIGHTY ANTAR LOW LOADER AND PROPELLER
Brown plastic propeller, casting of 660 Tank Transporter *Ref no: 986 Production Period:* 1959-1964 *Colour:* Red tractor, grey trailer *Market Value:* £200-£280/$300-$420

MINI VAN 'JOSEPH MASON PAINTS'
Made for Joseph Mason, 1969 *Ref no: 274 Production Period:* 1969-1969 *Colour:* Maroon *Market Value:* £500-£600/$750-$900

MINI-COOPER 'S' POLICE CAR
Ref no: 250 Production Period: 1967-1975 *Colour:* White, Police on doors in black *Market Value:* £45-£55/$65-$80

MOTORWAY SERVICES GIFT SET
Contents: 257 Canadian Fire Chief's Car, 263, later 277 Criterion Ambulance, 269 Jaguar Motorway Police, 276 Airport Fire Tender, 434 Bedford TK Crash Truck *Ref no: 299 Production Period:* 1963-1967 *Market Value:* £900-£1100/$1350-$1650

PLYMOUTH POLICE CAR
Casting as 201 & 278 *Ref no: 244 Production Period:* 1977-1979 *Colour:* Dark blue & white, Police on side in white *Market Value:* £20-£25/$30-$40

PLYMOUTH TAXI
Casting of 178 Pymouth *Ref no: 265 Production Period:* 1960-1966 *Colour:* Yellow with red roof, fare details on doors *Market Value:* £90-£110/$135-$165

PLYMOUTH TAXI
Casting of 178 Pymouth *Ref no: 266 Production Period:* 1960-1966 *Colour:* Yellow with red roof, '450 Metro Cab' *Market Value:* £100-£130/$150-$200

PLYMOUTH YELLOW CAB
Casting of 244 Plymouth *Ref no: 278 Production Period:* 1978-1979 *Colour:* Yellow *Market Value:* £20-£25/$30-$40

POLICE ACCIDENT UNIT
Replacing 287 Transit *Ref no: 272 Production Period:* 1975-1978 *Colour:* White *Market Value:* £35-£40/$50-$60

POLICE ACCIDENT UNIT (FORD TRANSIT)
Replaced 272 Accident Unit *Ref no: 269 Production Period:* 1978-1979 *Colour:* White with red stripes, 'Police' *Market Value:* £35-£40/$50-$60

POLICE ACCIDENT UNIT (TRANSIT)
Replaced by 272 *Ref no: 287 Production Period:* 1967-1974 *Colour:* Orange lower, cream upper, later white with red panels *Market Value:* £55-£80/$80-$120

POLICE LAND ROVER
Casting of 344 *Ref no: 277 Production Period:* 1978-1979 *Colour:* Dark blue & white *Market Value:* £20-£30/$30-$45

POLICE MINI CLUBMAN
Casting of 178 *Ref no:* 255 *Production Period:* 1977-1979
Colour: Blue with white doors *Market Value:* £30-£35/$45-
$55

POLICE PATROL CAR
Casting of 165 *Ref no:* 256 *Production Period:* 1960-1964
Colour: Black *Market Value:* £90-£110/$135-$165

POLICE RANGE ROVER
Casting of 192 *Ref no:* 254 *Production Period:* 1971-1979
Colour: White with red stripes *Market Value:* £30-
£40/$45-$60

POLICE VEHICLES GIFT SET
Contents: 250 Mini-Cooper 'S', 254 Range Rover Police,
287 Accident Unit then 272 Police Accident Unit *Ref no:*
294 *Production Period:* 1973-1976 *Market Value:* £110-
£150/$165-$220

POLICE VEHICLES GIFT SET
Contents: 250 Mini-Cooper 'S', 255 Ford Zodiac police,
287 Accident Unit *Ref no:* 297 *Production Period:* 1967-
1972 *Market Value:* £150-£180/$220-$270

POST OFFICE SERVICES GIFT SET
Contents: 12c/750 Telephone Box, 12d/011 Telegraph
Messenger, 12e/012 Postman, 260 Royal Mail Van, 261
Telephone Services Van *Ref no:* 299 *Production Period:*
1957-1959 *Market Value:* £400-£500/$600-$750

PULLMORE CAR TRANSPORTER
Ref no: 982 *Reno:* of 582

PULLMORE CAR TRANSPORTER WITH FOUR CARS
Contents: 154 Hillman Minx, 156 Rover 75, 161 Austin
Somerset (all 2-tone versions), 162 Ford Zephyr, 582/982
Pullmore Car Transporter, 994/794 Ramp *Ref no:* 990
Production Period: 1957-1958 *Market Value:* £1250-
£1600/$1900-$2400

PULLMORE CAR TRANSPORTER, WITH RAMP
Ref no: 582 *Reno:* to 982 *Production Period:* 1953-1964
Colour: Blue with fawn tracks for cars or all blue *Market
Value:* £90-£110/$135-$165

RAC PATROL MINI VAN
Plug in plastic roof sign *Ref no:* 273 *Production Period:*
1965-1969 *Colour:* Blue with white roof *Market Value:*
£130-£170/$200-$250

RCMP CAR
Casting of 173 Pontiac *Ref no:* 252 *Production Period:*
1969-1974 *Colour:* Blue, white front doors *Market Value:*
£45-£55/$65-$80

RCMP PATROL CAR
Casting of 148 Ford *Ref no:* 264 *Production Period:* 1962-
1965 *Colour:* Dark blue, white front doors *Market Value:*
£70-£90/$100-$135

RCMP PATROL CAR
Casting of 147 Cadillac 62 *Ref no:* 264 *Production Period:*
1965-1968 *Colour:* Dark blue, white front doors *Market
Value:* £80-£100/$120-$150

RACEHORSE TRANSPORT
Casting of 581, 2 plastic horses *Ref no:* 979 *Production
Period:* 1961-1964 *Colour:* Light grey and yellow *Market
Value:* £270-£320/$400-$480

RANGE ROVER AMBULANCE
Casting of 192 *Ref no:* 268 *Production Period:* 1973-1976
Colour: White *Market Value:* £25-£40/$35-$60

RANGE ROVER FIRE CHIEF
Casting of 192 *Ref no:* 195 *Production Period:* 1971-1978
Colour: Red or metallic red *Market Value:* £35-£45/$50-
$70

REFUSE WAGON
2 grey plastic dustbins with lids *Ref no:* 978 *Production
Period:* 1964-1979 *Colour:* Metallic green or green, yellow
or lime green *Market Value:* £45-£70/$60-$100

RENAULT DAUPHINE MINICAB
Ref no: 268 *Production Period:* 1962-1967 *Colour:* Red
Market Value: £100-£120/$150-$180

ROVER 3500 POLICE CAR
Casting of 180 Rover *Ref no:* 264 *Production Period:* 1979-
1979 *Colour:* White, yellow stripe *Market Value:* £20-
£25/$30-$40

ROYAL AIR MAIL SERVICE CAR
Ref no: 34a *Production Period:* 1935-1941 *Colour:* Blue,
'Air Mail' on door *Market Value:* £250-£300/$375-$450

ROYAL MAIL VAN
Open rear window, see Miscellaenous no.12 *Ref no:* 34b
Production Period: 1938-1941 *Colour:* Red with black
roof, bonnet & wings *Market Value:* £120-£150/$180-
$225

ROYAL MAIL VAN
Open then closed rear windows *Ref no:* 34b *Production
Period:* 1945-1952 *Colour:* As prewar 34b then all red
except black bonnet & front wings *Market Value:* £80-
£120/$120-$180

ROYAL MAIL VAN
Ref no: 260 *Production Period:* 1955-1961 *Colour:* Red
with black roof *Market Value:* £90-£120/$135-$180

SERVICING PLATFORM VEHICLE (COMMERCIAL)
Casting of 667 Missile Servicing Platform *Ref no:* 977
Production Period: 1960-1964 *Colour:* Cream truck with
red beanstalk *Market Value:* £140-£175/$200-$260

SILVER JUBILEE TAXI
Casting of 284 with boot detail removed *Ref no:* 241
Production Period: 1977-1977 *Colour:* Silver, Union Jack
on boot, crest on doors *Market Value:* £20-£25/$30-$40

SNOW PLOUGH
Casting of 431 Guy Warrior *Ref no:* 958 *Production Period:*
1961-1965 *Colour:* Yellow & black *Market Value:* £150-
£200/$220-$300

STREAMLINED FIRE ENGINE
Red tinplate ladder, from 1937 with tinplate base *Ref no:*
25h *Production Period:* 1936-1941 *Colour:* Red *Market
Value:* £130-£190/$200-$300

STREAMLINED FIRE ENGINE
Silver tinplate ladder *Ref no:* 25h *Reno:* to 250 *Production Period:* 1945-1962 *Colour:* Red *Market Value:* £60-£80/$90-$120

STREAMLINED FIRE ENGINE
Ref no: 250 *Reno:* of 25h

STREAMLINED FIRE ENGINE WITH FIREMEN
As 25h with 6 tinplate firemen on the tinplate base *Ref no:* 25k *Production Period:* 1937-1939 *Colour:* Red *Market Value:* £250-£320/$375-$480

SUPERIOR CADILLAC AMBULANCE
Flashing light *Ref no:* 267 *Production Period:* 1967-1971 *Colour:* Cream & red *Market Value:* £45-£70/$65-$100

SUPERIOR CADILLAC AMBULANCE
Casting as 267 *Ref no:* 288 *Production Period:* 1971-1979 *Colour:* White, red lower panels *Market Value:* £40-£50/$60-$75

SUPERIOR CRITERION AMBULANCE
Casting of 277 *Ref no:* 263 *Production Period:* 1962-1968 *Colour:* White *Market Value:* £45-£70/$65-$100

SUPERIOR CRITERION AMBULANCE
Casting as 263 with flashing light *Ref no:* 277 *Production Period:* 1962-1968 *Colour:* Metallic blue & white *Market Value:* £55-£80/$80-$120

TAXI WITH DRIVER
Open rear window *Ref no:* 36g *Production Period:* 1937-1941 *Colour:* Green, blue, red *Market Value:* £100-£180/$150-$270

TAXI WITH DRIVER
Some open, then closed rear window *Ref no:* 36g *Production Period:* 1946-1949 *Colour:* Green, light green, dark blue, red or maroon *Market Value:* £60-£90/$90-$135

TELEPHONE SERVICE VAN
Tinplate ladder *Ref no:* 261 *Production Period:* 1956-1961 *Colour:* Green with black roof *Market Value:* £90-£120/$135-$180

THOMPSON AIRCRAFT REFUELLING TENDER
Tinplate base held on by axles, white then black rubber wheels *Ref no:* 60y *Production Period:* 1938-1940 *Colour:* Red with black wings, gold transfer 'Shell Aviation Service' *Market Value:* £275-£340/$400-$500

TRAILER FOR CAR CARRIER
Ref no: 985 *Production Period:* 1958-1963 *Colour:* Red with grey runways, 'Dinky Autoservice' *Market Value:* £40-£70/$60-$100

TURNTABLE FIRE ESCAPE (BEDFORD)
Replaced by Berliet cab *Ref no:* 956 *Production Period:* 1958-1969 *Colour:* Red *Market Value:* £100-£110/$150-$170

TURNTABLE FIRE ESCAPE (BERLIET)
Replaced Bedford Cab *Ref no:* 956 *Production Period:* 1969-1973 *Colour:* Metallic red *Market Value:* £140-£160/$200-$240

UB TAXI
Casting as 120, only from United Biscuits *Ref no:* 115 *Production Period:* 1979-1979 *Colour:* Yellow, blue & black *Market Value:* £30-£50/$45-$75

USA POLICE CAR
Casting of 173 Pontiac *Ref no:* 251 *Production Period:* 1970-1972 *Colour:* White with black roof *Market Value:* £45-£55/$65-$80

USA POLICE CAR
Casting of 192 De Soto *Ref no:* 258 *Production Period:* 1960-1961 *Colour:* Black, white front doors *Market Value:* £80-£110/$120-$165

USA POLICE CAR
Casting of 191 Dodge *Ref no:* 258 *Production Period:* 1961-1962 *Colour:* Black, white front doors *Market Value:* £80-£110/$120-$165

USA POLICE CAR
Casting of 148 Ford *Ref no:* 258 *Production Period:* 1962-1966 *Colour:* Black, white front doors *Market Value:* £80-£110/$120-$165

USA POLICE CAR
Casting of 147 Cadillac *Ref no:* 258 *Production Period:* 1966-1968 *Colour:* Black, white front doors *Market Value:* £80-£110/$120-$165

VAUXHALL VICTOR AMBULANCE
Casting of 141 *Ref no:* 278 *Production Period:* 1964-1968 *Colour:* White *Market Value:* £60-£80/$90-$120

VOLVO POLICE CAR
Casting of 122 Volvo, policeman, dog etc *Ref no:* 243 *Production Period:* 1979-1979 *Colour:* White, red stripe on sides, Police headboard *Market Value:* £20-£25/$30-$40

Ships

The ships fall into two groups; the small scale waterline models of liners and warships produced between 1934 and 1941 and the large scale wheeled toy boats of the mid 1970s. Only 1 of the pre-war liners was re-issued post-war, 52a 'Queen Mary', and then only for two years. The pre-war ships suffer very badly from metal fatigue and are extremely difficult to find in reasonable condition. The later offerings are almost uncollectable.

'BRITANNIC'
Ref no: 51g *Production Period:* 1934-1940 *Colour:* Black hull, tan deck, white superstructure, black & tan funnels *Market Value:* £40-£45/$60-$70

'EMPRESS OF BRITAIN'
Ref no: 51d *Production Period:* 1934-1941 *Colour:* White, light stone funnels *Market Value:* £40-£45/$60-$70

'EUROPA'
Ref no: 51b *Production Period:* 1934-1941 *Colour:* Black hull, white deck, tan funnels *Market Value:* £40-£45/$60-$70

'QUEEN MARY'
With brass or red or yellow plastic rollers, rollers deleted by 1941 *Ref no:* 52a *Production Period:* 1934-1941 *Colour:* Black hull, white upper, red & black funnels *Market Value:* £60-£70/$90-$100

'QUEEN MARY'
With red or yellow rollers *Ref no:* 52a *Production Period:* 1947-1949 *Colour:* Black hull, white upper, red & black funnels *Market Value:* £35-£55/$50-$80

'QUEEN MARY'
Without rollers *Ref no:* 52b *Reno:* of 52, to 52 *Production Period:* 1935-1936 *Colour:* Black hull, white upper, red & black funnels *Market Value:* £35-£50/$50-$80

'QUEEN MARY'
Without rollers *Ref no:* 52m *Production Period:* 1936-1940 *Colour:* Black hull, white upper, red & black funnels *Market Value:* £30-£35/$50-$80

'QUEEN OF BERMUDA'
Ref no: 51f *Production Period:* 1934-1941 *Colour:* Light grey hull, white deck, red & black funnels *Market Value:* £40-£45/$60-$70

'REX'
Ref no: 51c *Production Period:* 1934-1941 *Colour:* Black hull, white deck, red, green & white funnels *Market Value:* £40-£45/$60-$70

'STRATHAIRD'
Ref no: 51e *Production Period:* 1934-1941 *Colour:* White, light stone funnels *Market Value:* £40-£45/$60-$70

AIR SEA RESCUE LAUNCH
With pilot & dinghy *Ref no:* 678 *Production Period:* 1974-1977 *Colour:* Black with grey & yellow, wheels *Market Value:* £15-£20/$20-$30

BATTLE CRUISER 'HOOD'
Ref no: 50a *Production Period:* 1934-1941 *Colour:* Grey *Market Value:* £30-£40/$45-$60

BATTLESHIP 'NELSON' CLASS
Casting has HMS Nelson or HMS Rodney below, later removed *Ref no:* 50b *Production Period:* 1934-1941 *Colour:* Grey *Market Value:* £30-£40/$45-$60

COASTGUARD AMPHIBIOUS MISSILE LAUNCH
From Gerry Anderson TV pilot 'The Investigator' *Ref no:* 674 *Production Period:* 1976-1978 *Colour:* White with blue, red & yellow *Market Value:* £15-£20/$20-$30

CRUISER 'DELHI'
Ref no: 50e *Production Period:* 1934-1941 *Colour:* Grey *Market Value:* £25-£30/$30-$45

CRUISER 'EFFINGHAM'
Ref no: 50c *Production Period:* 1934-1941 *Colour:* Grey *Market Value:* £30-£40/$45-$60

CRUISER 'YORK'
Ref no: 50d *Production Period:* 1934-1941 *Colour:* Grey *Market Value:* £25-£30/$30-$45

CUNARD WHITE STAR
'No 534'. No rollers (mid 1934) *Ref no:* 52 *Reno:* to 52b *Production Period:* 1934-1935 *Colour:* Black hull, white upper, red & black funnels *Market Value:* £60-£110/$100-$160

DESTROYER 'AMAZON' CLASS
No markings, 52mm long *Ref no:* 50h *Production Period:* 1934-1941 *Colour:* Grey *Market Value:* £15-£20/$20-$30

DESTROYER 'BROKE' CLASS
No markings, 57mm long *Ref no:* 50f *Production Period:* 1934-1941 *Colour:* Grey *Market Value:* £15-£20/$20-$30

FAMOUS LINERS
Contents : 51b, 51c, 51d, 51e, 51f, 51g *Ref no:* 51 *Production Period:* 1934-1941 *Market Value:* £225-£270/$330-$400

MK1 CORVETTE
Brown plastic deck, grey superstructure, wheels *Ref no:* 671 *Production Period:* 1975-1977 *Colour:* White hull with black stripes *Market Value:* £15-£20/$20-$30

MOTOR PATROL BOAT
Ref no: 675 *Production Period:* 1973-1977 *Colour:* Grey hull with cream, black & red wheels *Market Value:* £15-£20/$20-$30

OSA MISSILE BOAT
Ref no: 672 *Production Period:* 1976-1977 *Colour:* Light grey hull with white & black wheels *Market Value:* £15-£20/$20-$30

SHIPS OF THE BRITISH NAVY
Contents: 50a, 50b 'Nelson', 50b 'Rodney', 50c, 50d, 50e, 3x50f, 50g, 3x50h, 50k *Ref no:* 50 *Production Period:* 1934-1941 *Market Value:* £300-£380/$450-$550

SUBMARINE 'K' CLASS
No markings 57mm long, some catalogues confuse 50g & 50k *Ref no:* 50g *Production Period:* 1934-1941 *Colour:* Grey *Market Value:* £15-£20/$20-$30

SUBMARINE 'X' CLASS
No markings, 62mm long some catalogues confuse 50g & 50k *Ref no:* 50k *Production Period:* 1934-1941 *Colour:* Grey *Market Value:* £15-£20/$20-$30

SUBMARINE CHASER
Ref no: 673 *Production Period:* 1977-1978 *Colour:* Grey hull with white & black wheels *Market Value:* £15-£20/$20-$30

Tankers

This small group of petrol tankers are some of the prettiest Dinkies made. The pre-war 25d tankers were issued with the liveries of some petrol companies now long amalgamated, names like Power, Redline, but also with names which are still around, Shell, Texaco. For details of the casting variations listed as types 1 to 4 see under TRUCKS.

The small 30/440 series tankers were based on a Studebaker and very good they are too. They are highly collected in mint condition.

The large Foden and Leyland 8-wheel tankers are the top of the range and are magnificent.

There are a few promotional liveries to be found on the Leyland and AEC tankers but they can not all be confirmed as factory made. The ones listed here are genuine.

'CORN PRODUCTS' TANKER
Casting etc as 944 Shell-BP Tanker, 500 only made for Corn Products (Sales) Ltd *Ref no:* 944* *Production Period:* 1963-1963 *Colour:* White cab, black chassis, cream tank 'Corn Products' 'Sweeteners for Industry' *Market Value:* A

AEC FUEL TANKER (ESSO)
Cab as 914 AEC *Ref no:* 945 *Production Period:* 1966-1976 *Colour:* White, 'Esso' each side, early Tiger sticker on tail, later deleted *Market Value:* £60-£90/$90-$130

AEC TANKER
Ref no: 991 *Reno:* of 591

AEC TANKER (SHELL CHEMICALS)
Ref no: 591 *Reno:* to 991 *Production Period:* 1952-1958 *Colour:* Red cab, yellow tank top 'Shell Chemicals Ltd', later 'Shell Chemicals', Shell logo on tail *Market Value:* £130-£170/$200-$250

FODEN 14-TON TANKER (1ST GRILLE)
Replaced by 504 2nd grille *Ref no:* 504 *Production Period:* 1948-1952 *Colour:* Red with fawn tank or dark blue with light blue *Market Value:* £400-£500/$600-$750

FODEN 14-TON TANKER (2ND GRILLE)
Cab with stylised grille with horizontal barring *Ref no:* 504 *Production Period:* 1952-1953 *Colour:* Red with fawn tank, also dark blue with light blue *Market Value:* £300-£400/$450-$600

FODEN 14-TON TANKER (MOBILGAS)
Ref no: 504 *Reno:* to 941 *Production Period:* 1953-1956 *Colour:* Red 'Mobilgas' in white, Mobiloil logo *Market Value:* £275-£350/$400-$520

FODEN S20 FUEL TANKER
Cab as 432 Foden *Ref no:* 950 *Production Period:* 1978-1979 *Colour:* Red & white 'Burmah' or 'Shell' *Market Value:* £60-£90/$90-$130

FODEN TANKER (MOBILGAS)
Ref no: 941 *Reno:* of 504

FODEN TANKER (REGENT)
Casting etc of 504/941 *Ref no:* 942 *Production Period:* 1955-1957 *Colour:* Dark blue with red, white & blue tank 'Regent' *Market Value:* £350-£400/$500-$600

LEYLAND OCTOPUS TANKER (ESSO)
Cab/chassis as 934 Leyland, tank as 941 *Ref no:* 943 *Production Period:* 1958-1964 *Colour:* Red, 'Esso Petroleum Company Ltd' in blue on white stripe *Market Value:* £250-£300/$375-$450

LUCAS OIL TANKER
Casting of 945, made for Lucas Services *Ref no:* 945* *Production Period:* 1977-1977 *Colour:* Green, Lucas Oil and chevron in white *Market Value:* £140-£180/$200-$270

PETROL TANK WAGON
Type 1. Tinplate radiator *Ref no:* 25d *Production Period:* 1934-1935 *Colour:* Red with no transfer, 'Shell-BP', green with 'Esso', 'Power' or 'Pratts', some red with 'Texaco' *Market Value:* £200-£400/$300-$600

PETROL TANK WAGON
Type 2. Cast radiator *Ref no:* 25d *Production Period:* 1935-1941 *Colour:* Red or green with black 'Petrol' *Market Value:* £100-£125/$150-$190

PETROL TANK WAGON
Type 2. Cast radiator *Ref no:* 25d *Production Period:* 1935-1941 *Colour:* Red 'Shell-BP', 'Mobiloil', 'Esso', 'Texaco', green 'Power', 'Castrol', dark blue 'Redline-Glico' *Market Value:* £250-£300/$375-$450

PETROL TANK WAGON
Type 2. Cast radiator *Ref no:* 25d *Production Period:* 1940-1941 *Colour:* Grey 'Pool' *Market Value:* £350-£400/$500-$600

PETROL TANK WAGON
Type 3 *Ref no:* 25d *Production Period:* 1945-1948 *Colour:* Red, green with black 'Petrol' *Market Value:* £80-£110/$120-$160

PETROL TANK WAGON
Type 3 *Ref no:* 25d *Production Period:* 1945-1948 *Colour:* Orange with black 'Petrol' *Market Value:* £100-£150/$150-$220

PETROL TANK WAGON
Type 4 *Ref no:* 25d *Production Period:* 1948-1950 *Colour:* Red, mid or light green with black 'Petrol' *Market Value:* £80-£110/$120-$160

PETROL TANK WAGON

Type 4 *Ref no:* 25d *Production Period:* 1948-1950 *Colour:* Orange with black 'Petrol' *Market Value:* £100-£150/$150-$220

PETROL TANKER

Ref no: 30p *Production Period:* 1950-1952 *Colour:* Red or green with black 'Petrol' *Market Value:* £60-£80/$90-$120

PETROL TANKER (CASTROL)

Ref no: 30pa *Reno:* to 441 *Production Period:* 1952-1960 *Colour:* Green 'Castrol ' *Market Value:* £140-£160/$210-$240

PETROL TANKER (CASTROL)

Ref no: 441 *Reno:* of 30pa

PETROL TANKER (ESSO)

Ref no: 30pb *Reno:* to 442 *Production Period:* 1952-1958 *Colour:* Red, 'Esso' *Market Value:* £110-£140/$165-$210

PETROL TANKER (ESSO)

Ref no: 442 *Reno:* of 30pb

PETROL TANKER (MOBILGAS)

Ref no: 30p *Reno:* to 440 *Production Period:* 1952-1961 *Colour:* Red, 'Mobilgas' white letters with blue borders then blue letters on white *Market Value:* £110-£140/$165-$210

PETROL TANKER (MOBILGAS)

Ref no: 440 *Reno:* of 30p

PETROL TANKER (NATIONAL BENZOLE)

Ref no: 443 *Production Period:* 1957-1959 *Colour:* Yellow 'National Benzole' *Market Value:* £140-£160/$210-$240

SHELL-BP FUEL TANKER

Cab/chassis as 934, plastic tank *Ref no:* 944 *Production Period:* 1963-1970 *Colour:* White with yellow cab Shell & BP logos *Market Value:* £180-£220/$270-$330

Trains

These are a series of diecast trains to a scale smaller scale than 'OO' gauge, produced originally as 'Modelled Miniatures' from 1932 and deleted as Dinky Toys at the start of the war. They were all issued in very attractive boxed sets and are rare in mint boxed condition, and therefore highly prized by collectors. Individual pieces in poor condition are not really wanted by anyone.

Post-war the Streamlined Train Set, 16, was re-issued as an Express Passenger Train in different, simpler, liveries. There was a set in 1972 but this was very child's toylike and rather ugly.

COACH
Mazac body, lead chassis, c1935 Mazac chassis. In sets or box of 6 Ref no: 20a Production Period: 1934-1940 Colour: Brown with cream roof, dark green with white roof Market Value: £30-£35/$45-$50

CRANE WAGON
Lead marked Hornby Series. In set or box of 6 Ref no: 21c Production Period: 1932-1934 Colour: Green with blue chassis Market Value: £80-£100/$120-$150

DINKY GOODS TRAIN SET
Individual printed card box, card tray with clear lid Ref no: 784 Production Period: 1972-1974 Colour: Blue loco, 1 x red truck, 1 x yellow Market Value: £30-£35/$45-$50

DOUBLE ARM SIGNAL
In set or box of 6 Ref no: 15b Production Period: 1937-1941 Colour: Red (Home), yellow (Distant) Market Value: £40-£50/$60-$70

EXPRESS PASSENGER TRAIN
Casting as prewar but closed windows. Brown box, 3 pieces in a stack Ref no: 16 Reno: to 798 Production Period: 1948-1959 Colour: Dark blue & black loco, pale brown coaches Market Value: £80-£120/$120-$180

EXPRESS PASSENGER TRAIN
No numbers, letters cast in, tinplate base. Yellow box, 3 pieces in a row, packing pieces Ref no: 798 Reno: of 16 Colour: Green & black loco, red & cream carriages, early with grey roof, B.R. transfer Market Value: £80-£120/$120-$180

GWR RAILCAR (EARLY RAIL AUTOCAR)
Lead, later Mazac, red or green plastic rollers. Box of 6 Ref no: 26 Production Period: 1934-1940 Colour: Green, blue yellow or brown with cream top, green with red, red with blue Market Value: £110-£150/$165-$220

GUARD'S VAN
Mazac body, lead chassis, c1935 Mazac chassis. In sets or box of 6 Ref no: 20b Production Period: 1934-1940 Colour: Brown with cream roof, dark green with white roof Market Value: £30-£35/$45-$50

HORNBY TRAIN SET
Contents: 21a, 21b, 21c, 21d, 21e, lead, marked Hornby Series. Box: red Hornby Series box, later Modelled Miniatures box with train on gradient on lid Ref no: 21 Production Period: 1932-1934 Market Value: £200-£225/$300-$350

JUNCTION SIGNAL
In set or box of 6 (3 of each) Ref no: 15c Production Period: 1937-1941 Colour: Red (Home), yellow (Distant) Market Value: £70-£80/$100-$120

LOCOMOTIVE
Mazac upper, lead chassis to c1935, then Mazac chassis from 21a Tank Locomotive. In sets or box of 6 Ref no: 17a Production Period: 1934-1940 Colour: Maroon or dark green with black chassis Market Value: £25-£35/$35-$50

LUMBER WAGON
Lead marked Hornby Series, c1934 marked Dinky Toys, c1935 Mazac. In sets or box of 6 Ref no: 21e Production Period: 1932-1941 Colour: Brown log with blue chassis, yellow log with red or black chassis Market Value: £30-£45/$45-$55

MIXED GOODS TRAIN SET
Contents: 21a, 21b, 21d, 21e, replaced set 21. Box: long blue box with scene (11/38) Ref no: 19 Production Period: 1934-1941 Market Value: £200-£225/$300-$350

PASSENGER TRAIN SET
Contents: 17a, 17b, 20a, 20b. Dinky Toys box with name and train on gradient on lid Ref no: 17 Production Period: 1934-1940 Market Value: £200-£225/$300-$340

RAILWAY SIGNALS
Contents: 2 x 15a, 15b Home, 15c Home, 15c Distant Ref no: 15 Production Period: 1937-1941 Colour: Poles white with black bases. Box yellow box, purple liner Market Value: £150-£200/$225-$300

SINGLE ARM SIGNAL
In set or box of 6 (3 of each) Ref no: 15a Production Period: 1937-1941 Market Value: £35-£40/$50-$60

STREAMLINED TRAIN SET
Open windows, LNER & 2509 cast on loco Box: box with drawing on lid, scenic packing piece Ref no: 16 Production Period: 1937-1941 Colour: Silver with red, orange, grey or blue, cream & red, light blue with dark blue Market Value: £225-£275/$330-$400

TANK GOODS TRAIN SET
Contents : 21a, 3 x 21b. Box: purple marble finished box, drawing on lid Ref no: 18 Production Period: 1934-1941 Market Value: £200-£225/$300-$350

TANK LOCOMOTIVE

Lead marked Hornby Series, c1934 marked Dinky Toys, c1935 Mazac. In sets or box of 6 *Ref no:* 21a *Production Period:* 1932-1941 *Colour:* Red & blue marked Hornby Series, then maroon or dark green with black chassis *Market Value:* £30-£35/$45-$50

TANK PASSENGER TRAIN SET

Contents : 21a, 2 x 20a, 20b. Box: Modelled Miniatures box with illustration, later blue & green Dinky Toys box with illustration on lid *Ref no:* 20 *Production Period:* 1934-1940 *Market Value:* £200-£225/$300-$350

TANK WAGON

Lead marked Hornby Series, c1934 marked Dinky Toys, c1935 Mazac. In sets or box of 6 *Ref no:* 21d *Production Period:* 1932-1941 *Colour:* Red or blue with black chassis *Market Value:* £30-£45/$45-$55

TENDER

Lead, c1935 Mazac. In sets or box of 6 *Ref no:* 17b *Production Period:* 1934-1940 *Colour:* Maroon or dark green to match engine *Market Value:* £20-£25/$30-$40

WAGON

Lead marked Hornby Series, c1934 marked Dinky Toys, c1935 Mazac. In sets or box of 6 *Ref no:* 21b *Production Period:* 1932-1941 *Colour:* Green with blue, red or black chassis then maroon with black chassis *Market Value:* £20-£25/$30-$40

Trucks

These are Dinky's basic commercial vehicles, the mainstay of the production of delivery and goods carrying vehicles. The first series, the 25, was in production from 1934 to 1950 with four main variations:

Type 1: tinplate radiator grille clipped to the front, types 2-4 have diecast radiator
Type 2: chassis has 3 triangular holes underneath
Type 3: chassis has 1 round hole underneath
Type 4: chassis has transmission details under, and a front bumper.

As with all 1941/45 models there is some overlap at this point; type 2 models have been issued post-war but this was not the norm.

There were many bright colours used from 1935 to 1941 in the same manner as on the 24, 30 and 36 series cars, and in the same way an attractive scheme rates more highly than a dull one. The ones listed here are the usual ones to be found.

The 33 series of Mechanical Horse & Trailer models was based on the little Scammell which was used extensively by the four railway operators in England. They were very manoeuvrable and well suited to working in narrow streets and yards. The top of the range undoubtedly were the 33R sets in the railway colours. These suffer from fatigue and are very rare now.

The 25 series was replaced by the 30 series in 1950 all of which were accurate models of contemporary trucks, and so named by Dinky. They are very well detailed and also have a variety of odd colour variations now coming to light. Some of these may not be genuine.

The first Supertoys were the Foden and Guy lorry ranges. These magnificent models were released in a wide combination of colours. Dinky at this time started to put little stickers on the ends of the now individual boxes to show the colour of the model inside. Later this information was printed integrally with the general box printing. This is now a very useful guide for the collector to check whether the model is in its original box or not. The early Guys and Fodens were held together by small screws and nuts at the rear so that it was easy to change liveries by swapping parts with other models. Later models were rivetted at this point but it is still easy enough to swap parts and produce 'rare' colours variations.

The Bedford, Leyland and Ford ranges were similarly produced in many colours, again the colour code on the box should match the model. Dinky renumbered some of these models twice, changing them from Supertoys to Dinky Toys as they did so. The purist will want to know which colour schemes relate to which catalogue number but for the general collector it is not realistic to differentiate between them.

'CONVOY' DUMPER TRUCK
Ref no: 382 *Production Period:* 1977-1979 *Colour:* Red & grey *Market Value:* £15-£20/$20-$30

'CONVOY' FARM TRUCK
Ref no: 381 *Production Period:* 1977-1979 *Colour:* Yellow & brown *Market Value:* £15-£20/$20-$30

'CONVOY' GIFT SET
380 'Convoy' Skip, 381 Farm, 382 Dumper Trucks *Ref no:* 399 *Production Period:* 1977-1979 *Market Value:* £35-£45/$50-$70

'CONVOY' NCL TRUCK
Ref no: 383 *Production Period:* 1978-1979 *Colour:* Yellow *Market Value:* £30-£35/$45-$60

'CONVOY' ROYAL MAIL TRUCK
Ref no: 385 *Production Period:* 1977-1979 *Colour:* Red *Market Value:* £25-£30/$35-$45

'CONVOY' SKIP TRUCK
Ref no: 380 *Production Period:* 1977-1979 *Colour:* Yellow & orange *Market Value:* £15-£20/$20-$30

'CONVOY' TRUCK 'AVIS'
In 1979 catalogue but not issued *Ref no:* 386

'CONVOY' TRUCK PICKFORDS
In 1979 catalogue but not issued *Ref no:* 387

AEC ARTICULATED LORRY
Cast grille, later silver foil grille *Ref no:* 914 *Production Period:* 1965-1970 *Colour:* Red cab, grey back, 'British Road Services' *Market Value:* £90-£130/$135-$200

AEC WITH FLAT TRAILER
As 914 *Ref no:* 915 *Production Period:* 1973-1975 *Colour:* Orange & white 'Truck Hire Co Liverpool' *Market Value:* £75-£90/$110-$135

AUSTIN COVERED WAGON
Casting of 30j with tinplate tilt as 25b *Ref no:* 30s *Reno:* to 413 *Production Period:* 1950-1960 *Colour:* Dark blue with blue or cream tilt, maroon with cream, maroon with red *Market Value:* £120-£140/$180-$210

AUSTIN COVERED WAGON
Ref no: 413 *Reno:* of 30s

AUSTIN WAGON
Ref no: 30j *Reno:* to 412 *Production Period:* 1950-1960 *Colour:* Blue, maroon *Market Value:* £80-£90/$120-$140

AUSTIN WAGON
Ref no: 412 *Reno:* of 30j

BEV ELECTRIC TRUCK
Standing driver *Ref no:* 14a *Reno:* to 400 *Production Period:* 1948-1960 *Colour:* Blue, grey, dark blue *Market Value:* £30-£40/$45-$60

BEV ELECTRIC TRUCK
Ref no: 400 *Reno:* of 14a

BEDFORD ARTICULATED LORRY
Ref no: 409 *Reno:* of 521/921

BEDFORD ARTICULATED LORRY
Ref no: 521 *Reno:* to 921 & 409 *Production Period:* 1948-1963 *Colour:* Red or yellow with black wings *Market Value:* £100-£150/$150-$210

BEDFORD ARTICULATED LORRY
Ref no: 921 *Reno:* of 521 to 409

BEDFORD COCA COLA LORRY
6 brown plastic crates *Ref no:* 402 *Production Period:* 1966-1968 *Colour:* Red with white roof *Market Value:* £150-£180/$220-$270

BEDFORD END TIPPER
Ref no: 25m *Reno:* to 410 *Production Period:* 1948-1963 *Colour:* Green, orange, red or cream *Market Value:* £70-£90/$100-$140

BEDFORD END TIPPER
Ref no: 25m *Reno:* to 410 *Production Period:* 1948-1963 *Colour:* Red with cream back, yellow with blue *Market Value:* £130-£150/$200-$255

BEDFORD END TIPPER
Ref no: 410 *Reno:* of 25m

BEDFORD REFUSE WAGON
Ref no: 25v *Reno:* to 252 *Production Period:* 1948-1964 *Colour:* Fawn with green shutters *Market Value:* £80-£100/$120-$150

BEDFORD REFUSE WAGON
Ref no: 25v *Reno:* to 252 *Production Period:* 1960-1964 *Colour:* Lime green with black, orange cab, light grey back, green shutters *Market Value:* £140-£180/$210-$270

BEDFORD TK COAL WAGON
Plastic scales & 6 sacks of coal *Ref no:* 425 *Production Period:* 1964-1968 *Colour:* Red *Market Value:* £100-£140/$150-$210

BEDFORD TK CRASH TRUCK
Black plastic hubs *Ref no:* 434 *Production Period:* 1964-1972 *Colour:* 1. White with green flash 'Top Rank' 2. Red with black roof & grey back 'Autoservices' *Market Value:* £80-£100/$120-$150

BEDFORD TK TIPPER
Plastic drop-down flaps & tailboard *Ref no:* 435 *Production Period:* 1964-1970 *Colour:* Various multi-colour combinations *Market Value:* £90-£120/$140-$180

BEDFORD TRUCK
Ref no: 25w *Reno:* to 411 *Production Period:* 1949-1960 *Colour:* Green *Market Value:* £90-£120/$135-$180

BEDFORD TRUCK
Ref no: 411 *Reno:* of 25w

BIG BEDFORD LORRY
Ref no: 408 *Reno:* of 522/922

BIG BEDFORD LORRY
Ref no: 522 *Reno:* to 922 & 408 *Production Period:* 1952-1963 *Colour:* Maroon with fawn back or blue with yellow *Market Value:* £125-£175/$190-$270

BIG BEDFORD LORRY
Ref no: 922 *Reno:* of 522 to 408

BOX VAN
Cast chassis with tinplate box *Ref no:* 33d *Production Period:* 1935-1941 *Colour:* Green, no transfer *Market Value:* £150-£170/$200-$250

BOX VAN
Cast chassis with tinplate box *Ref no:* 33d *Production Period:* 1935-1941 *Colour:* Green, 'Meccano' *Market Value:* £200-£250/$300-$375

BOX VAN
Cast chassis with tinplate box *Ref no:* 33d *Production Period:* 1935-1941 *Colour:* Green or blue, 'Hornby Trains'

BREAKDOWN CAR (TRUCK)
Ref no: 30e *Production Period:* 1935-1941 *Colour:* See under 'CARS'

BREAKDOWN CAR (TRUCK)
Closed rear window *Ref no:* 30e *Production Period:* 1945-1948 *Colour:* Grey, green or red *Market Value:* £40-£60/$60-$80

BREAKDOWN LORRY
Later Commer Breakdown Lorry *Ref no:* 25x *Reno:* to 430 *Production Period:* 1950-1963 *Colour:* Tan cab with green back, grey with blue, brown with green, 'Dinky Service' in black or white *Market Value:* £70-£90/$100-$135

COLES HYDRA TRUCK 150T
Ref no: 980 *Production Period:* 1972-1979 *Colour:* Yellow with black wings *Market Value:* £35-£45/$50-$70

COMMER ARTICULATED TRUCK
Ref no: 406 *Production Period:* 1963-1966 *Colour:* Yellow cab, grey rear *Market Value:* £125-£150/$185-$220

COMMER BREAKDOWN LORRY
Ref no: 430 *Colour:* Tan with blue, red with light grey, cream with light blue *Market Value:* £100-£120/$150-$180

COMMER BREAKDOWN LORRY
Ref no: 430 *Reno:* of 25x

COMMER CONVERTIBLE ARTICULATED TRUCK
Blue plastic tarpaulin, 406 Commer Artic with 2 interchangeable plastic inserts *Ref no:* 424 *Production Period:* 1963-1966 *Colour:* Yellow cab, grey rear, white stake sides, blue tilt *Market Value:* £140-£170/$210-$250

COMMERCIAL MOTOR VEHICLES
Contents: 25a Wagon, 25b Covered Wagon, 25c Flat Truck, 25d Petrol Tanker, 25e Tipping Wagon, 25f Market Gardener's Wagon *Ref no:* 25 *Production Period:* 1934-1937 *Market Value:* A

COMMERCIAL MOTOR VEHICLES
Contents: 25b Covered Wagon, 25d Petrol Tanker, 25e Tipping Wagon, 25f Market Gardener's Wagon, 25h Fire Engine *Ref no:* 25 *Production Period:* 1937-1941 *Market Value:* A

COMMERCIAL VEHICLES
Contents: 25a Wagon, 25b Covered Wagon, 25d Petrol Tank Wagon, 25f Market Gardener's Wagon, 29c Double Decker Bus (1st type), US, Canadian & SA markets *Ref no:* 1 *Production Period:* 1947-1949 *Market Value:* A

COMMERCIAL VEHICLES
Contents: 25m/410 Bedford End Tipper, 27d/340 Land Rover, 30n/343 Farm Produce Wagon, 30p/30pb Petrol Tanker, 30s/413 Austin Covered Wagon *Ref no:* 2 *Reno:* to 499 *Production Period:* 1952-1954 *Market Value:* £1700-£2000/$2500-$3000

COMMERCIAL VEHICLES
Contents: 25d Petrol Tank Wagon, 25f Market Gardener's Wagon, 29c Double Decker Bus (1st type), 25w Bedford Truck, 30e Breakdown Truck, US market *Ref no:* 4 *Production Period:* 1948-1948 *Market Value:* A

COMMERCIAL VEHICLES
Contents: 25h Streamlined Fire Engine, 29b Streamlined Bus, 29c Double Deck Bus, 30e Breakdown Truck, 36f Ambulance, US, SA market *Ref no:* 6 *Production Period:* 1947-1949 *Market Value:* A

COMMERCIAL VEHICLES
Ref no: 499 *Reno:* of 2

CONVEYANCER/CLIMAX FORK LIFT TRUCK
With pallets *Ref no:* 404 *Production Period:* 1967-1979 *Colour:* Red & yellow, orange & yellow *Market Value:* £25-£35/$35-$50

COVENTRY CLIMAX FORK LIFT TRUCK
Ref no: 14c *Reno:* to 401 *Production Period:* 1949-1964 *Colour:* Orange body, green forks *Market Value:* £30-£35/$45-$55

COVENTRY CLIMAX FORK LIFT TRUCK
Ref no: 401 *Reno:* of 14c

COVERED WAGON
Type 1. 25a with a tinplate tilt *Ref no:* 25b *Production Period:* 1934-1935 *Colour:* Blue with cream tilt *Market Value:* £120-£150/$180-$210

COVERED WAGON
Type 2 *Ref no:* 25b *Production Period:* 1935-1941 *Colour:* Green with green tilt, fawn with cream, red with red tilt *Market Value:* £100-£120/$150-$180

COVERED WAGON
Type 2 *Ref no:* 25b *Production Period:* 1935-1941 *Colour:* 1. Green with green tilt 'Carter Paterson... London' 2. Green with cream tilt 'Carter Paterson... Seaside' or 'Meccano' 3. Fawn with cream tilt 'Hornby Trains' *Market Value:* £400-£450/$600

COVERED WAGON
Type 3 *Ref no:* 25b *Production Period:* 1945-1948 *Colour:* Green with green or cream tilt, dark grey with light grey, blue with grey *Market Value:* £100-£120/$150-$180

COVERED WAGON
Type 4 *Ref no:* 25b *Production Period:* 1948-1950 *Colour:* Green with green or cream tilt, dark grey with light grey, cream with red tilt *Market Value:* £100-£120/$150-$180

COVERED WAGON
Type 4 *Ref no:* 25b *Production Period:* 1948-1950 *Colour:* Yellow with blue tilt *Market Value:* £120-£150/$180-$210

DODGE REAR TIPPING WAGON
Earlier Rear Tipping Wagon *Ref no:* 30m *Reno:* to 414 *Production Period:* 1950-1964 *Colour:* Orange cab & chassis with light green back, blue with grey *Market Value:* £80-£90/$120-$140

DODGE REAR TIPPING WAGON
Ref no: 414 *Reno:* of 30m

DUST WAGON
33c with tinplate insert *Ref no:* 33e *Production Period:* 1935-1941 *Colour:* Blue with yellow *Market Value:* £95-£110/$145-$165

FARM PRODUCE WAGON
Ref no: 30n *Reno:* to 343 *Production Period:* 1950-1964 *Colour:* Green cab & chassis with yellow back, yellow with green, red with blue *Market Value:* £80-£90/$120-$140

FARM PRODUCE WAGON
Ref no: 343 *Reno:* of 30n

FLAT TRUCK
Type 1 *Ref no:* 25c *Production Period:* 1934-1935 *Colour:* Dark blue *Market Value:* £110-£140/$165-$210

FLAT TRUCK
Type 2 *Ref no:* 25c *Production Period:* 1935-1941 *Colour:* Green, dark blue or stone *Market Value:* £100-£125/$150-$190

FLAT TRUCK
Type 3 *Ref no:* 25c *Production Period:* 1946-1948 *Colour:* Green, blue or grey *Market Value:* £50-£80/$75-$120

FLAT TRUCK
Type 4. 1948-50 as part of 25t only *Ref no:* 25c *Production Period:* 1948 *Colour:* Green, blue, orange or stone *Market Value:* £50-£80/$75-$120

FLAT TRUCK
Ref no: 33b *Production Period:* 1935-1941 *Colour:* Red, green, blue or yellow *Market Value:* £70-£90/$100-$135

FLAT TRUCK AND TRAILER
Type 3. 25c Truck & 25f Trailer *Ref no:* 25t *Production Period:* 1948-1948 *Colour:* Truck & trailer both stone or green *Market Value:* £100-£140/$150-$210

FLAT TRUCK AND TRAILER
Type 4. 25c Truck & 25f Trailer *Ref no:* 25t *Production Period:* 1948-1950 *Colour:* Truck & trailer both green, orange or blue *Market Value:* £100-£140/$150-$210

FODEN DIESEL 8-WHEEL WAGON
Ref no: 901 *Reno:* of 501

FODEN DIESEL 8-WHEEL WAGON (1ST GRILLE)

Type 1 *Ref no:* 501 *Production Period:* 1947-1952 *Colour:* Brown, dark blue, light grey, red with fawn back, light blue with dark blue *Market Value:* £450-£600/$675-$900

FODEN DIESEL 8-WHEEL WAGON (2ND GRILLE)

Type 2 *Ref no:* 501 *Reno:* to 901 *Production Period:* 1952-1957 *Colour:* Red with fawn back *Market Value:* £220-£280/$330-$420

FODEN DIESEL 8-WHEEL WAGON (2ND GRILLE)

Type 2 *Ref no:* 501 *Reno:* to 901 *Production Period:* 1952-1957 *Colour:* Dark blue with light *Market Value:* £450-£600/$675-$900

FODEN FLAT TRUCK

Ref no: 902 *Reno:* of 502

FODEN FLAT TRUCK (1ST GRILLE)

Type 1 *Ref no:* 502 *Production Period:* 1947-1952 *Colour:* Green, blue, orange cab/chassis with light green back *Market Value:* £400-£500/$600-$750

FODEN FLAT TRUCK (2ND GRILLE)

Type 2 *Ref no:* 502 *Reno:* to 902 *Production Period:* 1952-1960 *Colour:* Orange with green back, blue with red *Market Value:* £250-£320/$375-$480

FODEN FLAT TRUCK WITH CHAINS

Ref no: 905 *Reno:* of 505

FODEN FLAT TRUCK WITH CHAINS (1ST GRILLE)

Type 1 *Ref no:* 505 *Production Period:* 1952-1952 *Colour:* Green or maroon *Market Value:* £750-£1000/$1100-$1500

FODEN FLAT TRUCK WITH CHAINS (2ND GRILLE)

Type 2 *Ref no:* 505 *Reno:* to 905 *Production Period:* 1952-1964 *Colour:* Green, maroon or red with grey *Market Value:* £260-£320/$400-$500

FODEN FLAT TRUCK WITH TAILBOARD

Ref no: 903 *Reno:* of 503

FODEN FLAT TRUCK WITH TAILBOARD (1ST GRILLE)

Type 1 *Ref no:* 503 *Production Period:* 1947-1952 *Colour:* Grey body & cab on blue chassis, red with black chassis, dark blue with orange *Market Value:* £650-£750/$950-$1

FODEN FLAT TRUCK WITH TAILBOARD (2ND GRILLE)

Type 2 *Ref no:* 503 *Reno:* to 903 *Production Period:* 1952-1960 *Colour:* Blue with orange back, duotone green *Market Value:* £280-£340/$420-$500

FODEN FLAT TRUCK WITH TAILBOARD (2ND GRILLE)

Type 2 *Ref no:* 503 *Reno:* to 903 *Production Period:* 1952-1960 *Colour:* Blue with yellow *Market Value:* £550-£680/$800-$1000

FODEN TIPPING LORRY

Ref no: 432 *Production Period:* 1976-1979 *Colour:* White cab, yellow rear *Market Value:* £35-£45/$50-$70

FORD D800 SNOW PLOUGH & TIPPING TRUCK

Casting of 438 with snow plough from 958 *Ref no:* 439 *Production Period:* 1970-1978 *Colour:* Blue with red back, later blue with light blue *Market Value:* £45-£70/$70-$100

FORD D800 TIPPER TRUCK

Opening doors *Ref no:* 438 *Production Period:* 1970-1976 *Colour:* Red with yellow *Market Value:* £35-£45/$50-$70

FORD D800 TIPPER TRUCK

As 438 but no opening doors *Ref no:* 440 *Production Period:* 1977-1978 *Colour:* All-red or red with yellow back *Market Value:* £35-£45/$50-$70

FORDSON THAMES FLAT TRUCK

Later Thames Flat Truck *Ref no:* 30r *Reno:* to 422 *Production Period:* 1951-1960 *Colour:* Red or dark green, also reddish brown *Market Value:* £80-£100/$120-$150

GUY 4-TON LORRY

Ref no: 431 *Reno:* of 511/911

GUY 4-TON LORRY

Ref no: 511 *Reno:* to 911 & 431 *Production Period:* 1947-1958 *Colour:* Green or brown *Market Value:* £250-£450/$375-$675

GUY 4-TON LORRY

Ref no: 511 *Reno:* to 911 & 431 *Production Period:* 1947-1958 *Colour:* 2-tone blue or red & fawn *Market Value:* £220-£270/$330-$400

GUY 4-TON LORRY

Ref no: 911 *Reno:* of 511

GUY FLAT TRUCK

Ref no: 432 *Reno:* of 512/ 912

GUY FLAT TRUCK

Ref no: 512 *Reno:* to 912 & 432 *Production Period:* 1947-1958 *Colour:* Yellow, maroon, brown or grey *Market Value:* £250-£450/$375-$675

GUY FLAT TRUCK

Ref no: 512 *Reno:* to 912 & 432 *Production Period:* 1947-1958 *Colour:* Blue with red or red with blue *Market Value:* £220-£270/$330-$400

GUY FLAT TRUCK

Ref no: 912 *Reno:* of 512

GUY FLAT TRUCK WITH TAILBOARD

Ref no: 433 *Reno:* of 513/913

GUY FLAT TRUCK WITH TAILBOARD

Ref no: 513 *Reno:* to 913 & 433 *Production Period:* 1947-1958 *Colour:* Yellow, grey or green *Market Value:* £250-£350/$375-$500

GUY FLAT TRUCK WITH TAILBOARD

Ref no: 513 *Reno:* to 913 & 433 *Production Period:* 1947-1958 *Colour:* 2-tone green or blue with orange *Market Value:* £200-£260/$300-$400

GUY FLAT TRUCK WITH TAILBOARD

Ref no: 913 *Reno:* of 513

GUY WARRIOR 4-TON LORRY

Ref no: 431 *Production Period:* 1958-1964 *Colour:* Tan & green *Market Value:* £350-£500/$500-$750

GUY WARRIOR FLAT TRUCK
Ref no: 432 *Production Period:* 1958-1964 *Colour:* Green & red *Market Value:* £300-£400/$450-$600

GUY WARRIOR FLAT TRUCK WITH TAILBOARD
In 1958 catalogue but not issued *Ref no:* 433 *Production Period:* 1958-1958

HINDLE-SMART ELECTRIC ARTICULATED LORRY
Ref no: 30w *Reno:* to 421 *Production Period:* 1953-1959 *Colour:* Maroon, 'British Railways' *Market Value:* £70-£90/$100-$135

HINDLE-SMART ELECTRIC ARTICULATED LORRY
Ref no: 421 *Reno:* of 30w

LAND ROVER BREAKDOWN CRANE
Ref no: 442 *Production Period:* 1973-1979 *Colour:* White & red ' Motorway Rescue' *Market Value:* £25-£30/$40-$45

LEYLAND CEMENT WAGON
Ref no: 533 *Reno:* to 933 & 419 *Production Period:* 1953-1959 *Colour:* Yellow 'Portland Cement' 'Ferrocrete' *Market Value:* £130-£160/$200-$290

LEYLAND CEMENT WAGON
Ref no: 933 *Reno:* of 533 to 419

LEYLAND COMET LORRY
Ref no: 417 *Reno:* of 531/931

LEYLAND COMET LORRY
Ref no: 531 *Reno:* to 931 & 417 *Production Period:* 1949-1959 *Colour:* Red with yellow back, blue with brown, blue with yellow *Market Value:* £150-£200/$225-$300

LEYLAND COMET LORRY
Ref no: 931 *Reno:* of 531 to 417

LEYLAND COMET LORRY WITH HINGED TAILBOARD
Ref no: 418 *Reno:* of 532/ 932

LEYLAND COMET LORRY WITH HINGED TAILBOARD/WAGON
Ref no: 532 *Reno:* to 932 & 418 *Production Period:* 1952-1959 *Colour:* Green cab with orange back, blue with blue *Market Value:* £110-£160/$165-$240

LEYLAND COMET WAGON
Portland Cement *Ref no:* 419 *Reno:* of 533/ 933

LEYLAND COMET WAGON WITH HINGED TAILBOARD
Ref no: 932 *Reno:* of 532 to 418

LEYLAND DUMP TRUCK
Ref no: 925 *Production Period:* 1966-1969 *Colour:* White cab/chassis, red back *Market Value:* £120-£150/$180-$225

LEYLAND EIGHT-WHEELED TEST CHASSIS
3 metal weights marked 5 Tons *Ref no:* 936 *Production Period:* 1964-1969 *Colour:* Red cab, silver chassis *Market Value:* £90-£100/$135-$150

LEYLAND FORWARD CONTROL LORRY
Ref no: 25r *Reno:* to 420 *Production Period:* 1948-1961 *Colour:* Cream, orange, red or green *Market Value:* £60-£80/$90-$120

LEYLAND FORWARD CONTROL LORRY
Ref no: 420 *Reno:* of 25r

LEYLAND OCTOPUS FLAT TRUCK WITH CHAINS
Back as 505/905 Foden Flat Truck with Chains *Ref no:* 935 *Production Period:* 1964-1966 *Colour:* Green cab with grey back *Market Value:* £750-£1000/$1100-$1500

LEYLAND OCTOPUS FLAT TRUCK WITH CHAINS
Back as 505/905 Foden Flat Truck with Chains *Ref no:* 935 *Production Period:* 1964-1966 *Colour:* Blue cab with grey back *Market Value:* £1000-£1300/$1500-$2000

LEYLAND OCTOPUS WAGON
Back as 501/901 Foden Diesel 8-Wheel Wagon *Ref no:* 934 *Production Period:* 1956-1964 *Colour:* Yellow chassis/cab with green bands with green back *Market Value:* £180-£230/$270-$350

LEYLAND OCTOPUS WAGON
Back as 501/901 Foden Diesel 8-Wheel Wagon *Ref no:* 934 *Production Period:* 1956-1964 *Colour:* Blue chassis/cab with with cream back *Market Value:* £900-£1200/$1350-$1800

MARKET GARDENER'S VAN (WAGON)
Type 1 *Ref no:* 25f *Production Period:* 1934-1935 *Colour:* Green, yellow with green chassis *Market Value:* £110-£150/$165-$225

MARKET GARDENER'S VAN (WAGON)
Type 2 *Ref no:* 25f *Production Period:* 1935-1941 *Colour:* Yellow with green chassis or green with black *Market Value:* £100-£125/$150-$190

MARKET GARDENER'S VAN (WAGON)
Type 3 *Ref no:* 25f *Production Period:* 1945-1948 *Colour:* Green, yellow or orange *Market Value:* £50-£80/$75-$120

MARKET GARDENER'S VAN (WAGON)
Type 4 *Ref no:* 25f *Production Period:* 1948-1950 *Colour:* Green, yellow or orange *Market Value:* £50-£80/$75-$120

MECHANICAL HORSE
Postwar part of 33w *Ref no:* 33a *Production Period:* 1935-1941 *Colour:* Red, green, blue or yellow *Market Value:* £25-£45/$40-$70

MECHANICAL HORSE & OPEN WAGON
Ref no: 415 *Reno:* of 33w

MECHANICAL HORSE AND FIVE ASSORTED TRAILERS
Contents: 33a Mechanical Horse, 33b Flat Truck, 33c Open Wagon, 33d Box Van, 33e Dust Wagon, 33f Petrol Tank *Ref no:* 33 *Production Period:* 1935-1937 *Market Value:* £700-£900/$1000-$1400

MECHANICAL HORSE AND FOUR ASSORTED TRAILERS

Contents: 33a Mechanical Horse, 33b Flat Truck, 33c Open Wagon, 33e Dust Wagon, 33f Petrol Tank *Ref no:* 33 *Production Period:* 1937-1941 *Market Value:* £500-£700/$750-$1000

MECHANICAL HORSE AND OPEN WAGON

Ref no: 33w *Reno:* to 415 *Production Period:* 1945-1957 *Colour:* Various single & two-colour combinations *Market Value:* £70-£90/$100-$140

MERCEDES-BENZ TRUCK

917 without opening doors *Ref no:* 940 *Production Period:* 1977-1979 *Colour:* White cab, red chassis *Market Value:* £35-£40/$50-$60

MERCEDES-BENZ TRUCK & TRAILER

Replaced by 940 without opening doors *Ref no:* 917 *Production Period:* 1967-1976 *Colour:* Blue, yellow & white *Market Value:* £70-£90/$100-$135

MERCEDES-BENZ TRUCK & TRAILER 'MUNSTERLAND'

German margarine promo *Ref no:* 917 *Production Period:* 1976-1976 *Colour:* Dark green, white tilts 'Münsterland Qualitätsprodukte...' *Market Value:* £200-£250/$300-$375

MIGHTY ANTAR WITH PROPELLER

Low Loader as 660 Tank Transporter plus propellor load *Ref no:* 986 *Production Period:* 1959-1964 *Colour:* Red tractor, grey trailer *Market Value:* £200-£280/$300-$420

MIGHTY ANTAR WITH TRANSFORMER

Low Loader as 660 Tank Transporter + French Dinky 833 Transformer *Ref no:* 908 *Production Period:* 1962-1964 *Colour:* Yellow cab, grey trailer *Market Value:* £550-£700/$800-$1000

MOTOR TRUCK

Ref no: 22c *Production Period:* 1933-1935 *Colour:* See under 'CARS'

MOTOR TRUCK

Open rear window *Ref no:* 22c *Production Period:* 1935-1941 *Colour:* Red, green, blue *Market Value:* £40-£70/$60-$100

MOTOR TRUCK

Open, later closed rear window *Ref no:* 22c *Production Period:* 1945-1950 *Colour:* Red, green, brown *Market Value:* £25-£35/$40-$55

OPEN WAGON

Postwar part of 33w *Ref no:* 33c *Production Period:* 1935-1941 *Colour:* Red, green, blue or yellow *Market Value:* £25-£45/$40-$70

PETROL TANK

33b with tinplate tank *Ref no:* 33f *Production Period:* 1935-1941 *Colour:* Green with red tank or red with green *Market Value:* £100-£125/$150-$190

PETROL TANK

33b with tinplate tank *Ref no:* 33f *Production Period:* 1935-1941 *Colour:* Green with red tank 'Esso' or red with green 'Castrol' *Market Value:* £120-£160/$180-$240

RAILWAY MECHANICAL HORSE

Casting of 33a *Ref no:* 33Ra *Production Period:* 1935-1941 *Colour:* As 33r *Market Value:* £60-£70/$90-$100

RAILWAY MECHANICAL HORSE AND TRAILER VAN GWR

Ref no: 33a + 33d *Reno:* 33R *Production Period:* 1935-1941 *Colour:* Brown with cream, 'GWR Express Cartage Services' *Market Value:* £300-£360/$450-$550

RAILWAY MECHANICAL HORSE AND TRAILER VAN LMS

Ref no: 33a + 33d *Reno:* 33R *Production Period:* 1935-1941 *Colour:* Maroon lower with black cab roof & upper box, 'LMS' 'Express Parcels Traffic' *Market Value:* £300-£360/$450-$550

RAILWAY MECHANICAL HORSE AND TRAILER VAN LNER

Ref no: 33a + 33d *Reno:* 33R *Production Period:* 1935-1941 *Colour:* Blue with black, 'LNER', 'Express Parcels Service' *Market Value:* £300-£360/$450-$550

RAILWAY MECHANICAL HORSE AND TRAILER VAN SR

Ref no: 33a + 33d *Reno:* 33R *Production Period:* 1935-1941 *Colour:* Green with black, 'Southern Railway' 'Express Parcels Service' *Market Value:* £300-£360/$450-$550

RAILWAY TRAILER VAN

Casting of 33d *Ref no:* 33Rd *Production Period:* 1935-1941 *Colour:* As 33r *Market Value:* £180-£200/$270-$300

SIX-WHEELED WAGON

Casting of 151b, no tilt *Ref no:* 25s *Production Period:* 1938-1941 *Colour:* Brick red, dark blue, maroon *Market Value:* £80-£125/$120-$190

SIX-WHEELED WAGON

Ref no: 25s *Production Period:* 1945-1948 *Colour:* Brick red, green or dark blue, all with grey tilt *Market Value:* £70-£90/$100-$135

THAMES FLAT TRUCK

Ref no: 422 *Reno:* of 30r

TIPPING WAGON

Type 1 *Ref no:* 25e *Production Period:* 1934-1935 *Colour:* Maroon cab with yellow back *Market Value:* £110-£150/$165-$220

TIPPING WAGON

Type 2 *Ref no:* 25e *Production Period:* 1935-1941 *Colour:* Maroon cab with yellow back, brown with turquoise *Market Value:* £100-£125/$150-$190

TIPPING WAGON

Type 2 *Ref no:* 25e *Production Period:* 1945-1948 *Colour:* Grey, stone, green or yellow *Market Value:* £50-£80/$75-$120

TIPPING WAGON

Type 2 *Ref no:* 25e *Production Period:* 1948-1950 *Colour:* Grey, stone, green, brown, yellow *Market Value:* £50-£80/$75-$120

TRACTOR-TRAILER 'MCLEAN'

Plastic box van on a metal base *Ref no:* 948 *Production Period:* 1961-1967 *Colour:* Red cab, grey trailer, 'Trucking mclean Company' *Market Value:* £140-£175/$210-$260

WAGON

Type 1 *Ref no:* 25a *Production Period:* 1934-1935 *Colour:* Maroon, green or blue *Market Value:* £110-£140/$165-$210

WAGON

Type 2 *Ref no:* 25a *Production Period:* 1935-1941 *Colour:* Maroon, green or blue *Market Value:* £100-£120/$150-$180

WAGON

Type 3 *Ref no:* 25a *Production Period:* 1946-1948 *Colour:* Grey, green or blue *Market Value:* £50-£80/$75-$120

WAGON

Type 4 *Ref no:* 25a *Production Period:* 1948-1950 *Colour:* Grey, green, light blue or cream *Market Value:* £50-£80/$75-$120

TV Related Models

This is not one of Dinky's major areas of production. They started in 1966 with items from some children's TV shows of the time, Captain Scarlet, Joe 90 and so on. These are good models but the follow up was minimal. A few SHADO models followed in the easrly 1970s and some more odd ones right up to the factory closure in 1979. A small range but those they did produce is generally well collected now.

'PRISONER' MINI-MOKE
Casting of 342 Austin Mini-Moke *Ref no: 106 Production Period:* 1967-1970 *Colour:* White with red & white striped canopy *Market Value:* £240-£300/$160-$200

ARMOURED COMMAND CAR
Gerry Anderson for pilot TV series 'The Investigator' 1973 *Ref no:* 602 *Production Period:* 1976-1977 *Colour:* Green, blue-green *Market Value:* £45-£60/$30-$40

AVENGERS GIFT SET
In 1979 catalogue but not issued *Ref no:* 307 *Production Period:* 1979-1979

CINDERELLA'S COACH
From film: 'The Slipper & the Rose' *Ref no:* 111 *Production Period:* 1976-1977 *Colour:* Pink & gold *Market Value:* £20-£30/$15-$20

EAGLE FREIGHTER
Casting as 359, from TV series 'Space 1999' *Ref no:* 360 *Production Period:* 1975-1979 *Colour:* White with red carrying frame *Market Value:* £60-£90/$40-$60

EAGLE TRANSPORTER
From TV series 'Space 1999' *Ref no:* 359 *Production Period:* 1975-1979 *Colour:* White & metallic green or blue & white *Market Value:* £60-£90/$40-$60

ED STRAKER'S CAR
From TV series 'SHADO' *Ref no:* 352 *Production Period:* 1971-1975 *Colour:* Red *Market Value:* £70-£100/$45-$70

ED STRAKER'S CAR
From TV series 'SHADO' *Ref no:* 352 *Production Period:* 1971-1975 *Colour:* Gold plated or yellow *Market Value:* £120-£140/$80-$90

GABRIEL MODEL T FORD
Casting as 475 Model T Ford *Ref no:* 109 *Production Period:* 1969-1971 *Colour:* Yellow & black *Market Value:* £90-£140/$60-$90

JOE'S CAR
From 'Joe 90' *Ref no:* 102 *Production Period:* 1969-1976 *Colour:* Green *Market Value:* £150-£200/$100-$130

KLINGON BATTLE CRUISER
From TV series 'Star Trek' *Ref no:* 357 *Production Period:* 1977-1979 *Colour:* Blue & white *Market Value:* £55-£75/$35-$45

KLINGON BATTLE CRUISER
Issued 1980, not in catalogue, marked (c) 1979 Paramount Pictures... & Dinky Toys *Ref no:* 372 *Reno:* to 802 *Production Period:* 1980-1980 *Colour:* Metallic blue *Market Value:* £15-£35/$20-$25

LADY PENELOPE'S FAB 1
From 'Thunderbirds'. Fires rocket, harpoons *Ref no:* 100 *Production Period:* 1966-1976 *Colour:* Shades of pink *Market Value:* £250-£360/$170-$240

MAXIMUM SECURITY VEHICLE
From 'Captain Scarlet & the Mysterons' *Ref no:* 105 *Production Period:* 1968-1974 *Colour:* White *Market Value:* £140-£180/$90-$120

MINI-KLINGON CRUISER
Ref no: 802 *Production Period:* —-

MINI-USS ENTERPRISE
Ref no: 801 *Reno:* of 371 *Production Period:* —-

PARAMEDIC TRUCK
From TV Series 'Emergency' with 2 figures *Ref no:* 267 *Production Period:* 1979-1979 *Colour:* Red, 'Emergency Rescue...' *Market Value:* £40-£45/$25-$30

PARSLEY'S CAR
From TV series 'The Adventures of Parsley', with cut-out card figures *Ref no:* 477 *Production Period:* 1970-1972 *Colour:* Green body *Market Value:* £90-£130/$60-$85

PINK PANTHER / PINK PANTHER'S JET CAR
Plastic, with gyrowheel, later without wheel, not marked Dinky Toys, unboxed stock released at factory closure in 1979 *Ref no:* 354 *Production Period:* 1972-1975 *Colour:* Pink *Market Value:* £50-£90/$35-$55

PURDEY'S TRIUMPH TR7
From TV 'The New Avengers', casting as 211 *Ref no:* 112 *Production Period:* 1978-1979 *Colour:* Yellow, silver stripes *Market Value:* £50-£90/$35-$60

SAM'S CAR
From 'Joe 90' *Ref no:* 108 *Production Period:* 1969-1974 *Colour:* Silver or gold *Market Value:* £100-£130/$70-$90

SAM'S CAR
From 'Joe 90' *Ref no:* 108 *Production Period:* 1969-1974 *Colour:* Red or light blue *Market Value:* £130-£180/$90-$120

SHADO 2 MOBILE
From TV series 'SHADO' *Ref no:* 353 *Production Period:* 1971-1979 *Colour:* Blue *Market Value:* £180-£220/$120-$150

SHADO 2 MOBILE
From TV series 'SHADO' *Ref no:* 353 *Production Period:* 1971-1979 *Colour:* Green *Market Value:* £90-£120/$60-$80

SPECTRUM PATROL CAR
From 'Captain Scarlet & the Mysterons' *Ref no:* 103
Production Period: 1968-1975 *Colour:* Metallic red
Market Value: £140-£180/$90-$120

SPECTRUM PURSUIT VEHICLE
From 'Captain Scarlet & the Mysterons' *Ref no:* 104
Production Period: 1968-1976 *Colour:* Metallic blue
Market Value: £140-£180/$90-$120

STAR TREK GIFT SET
357 klingon battle cruiser, 358 uss enterprise *Ref no:* 309
Production Period: 1978-1979 *Market Value:* £100-
£135/$70-$90

STEED'S JAGUAR
Not officially released because of Factory closure but
some made *Ref no:* 113 *Production Period:* 1979-1979
Colour: Green with gold line on sides *Market Value:* A

STRIPEY THE MAGIC MINI WITH CANDY, ANDY & THE BEARANDAS
Casting of 183 Morris Mini-Minor, 4 plastic figures *Ref no:*
107 *Production Period:* 1967-1969 *Colour:* White with
blue, red & yellow stripes *Market Value:* £270-£340/$180-
$225

THUNDERBIRDS II AND IV
Yellow plastic Thunderbird IV *Ref no:* 101 *Production
Period:* 1967-1973 *Colour:* Green or metallic dark green
Market Value: £300-£375/$200-$250

THUNDERBIRDS II AND IV
Larger version replacing 101 *Ref no:* 106 *Production
Period:* 1974-1979 *Colour:* Metallic blue *Market Value:*
£120-£165/$80-$110

TINY'S MINI-MOKE
From TV series 'The Enchanted House', casting of 342
Ref no: 350 *Production Period:* 1970-1972 *Colour:* Red,
white plastic canopy with yellow stripes *Market Value:*
£135-£165/$90-$110

UFO INTERCEPTOR
From TV series 'SHADO' *Ref no:* 351 *Production Period:*
1971-1979 *Colour:* Metallic green *Market Value:* £7-
£100/$45-$70

USS ENTERPRISE
From TV series 'Star Trek' *Ref no:* 358 *Production Period:*
1977-1979 *Colour:* White *Market Value:* £55-£75/$35-$45

USS ENTERPRISE
Issued 1980, not in catalogue, marked (c) 1979 Paramount
Pictures... *Ref no:* 371 *Reno:* to 801 *Production Period:*
1980-1980 *Colour:* White *Market Value:* £15-£35/$20-$25

Vans

Pre-War Vans

These are the most colourful models from Dinky Toys. The first van issued was 22d Delivery Van as part of the 22 Series which is covered in the CARS section. It received decals late in its life and lead directly to the most famous 28 Series of vans.

The 28 Series were produced with three different castings over the years from 1934 to 1941. The castings were as follows:

Type 1: a 2-piece lead model with a tinplate radiator surround, 1934-35

Type 2: a single piece mazak casting with an integral shield shaped radiator based on the 1934 Ford Y van, 1935-39

Type 3: a larger single piece mazak casting with an integral squared pattern radiator, based on the 1938 Bedford Delivery Van, 1939-41

The vans were sold initially in set boxes of six different liveries. The first sets, 28/1 and 28/1, appeared in 1934 using the type 1 castings. 1935 saw these replaced, on the same catalogue numbers, by the type 2 castings. A further set, 28/3, followed in 1936. A fourth set of type 2 vans, set 280, came in 1937. All four sets were changes to type 3 castings in 1939/40. Production ceased in 1940/41. The decals were spirit based and were in accurate colours and liveries for the companies advertising. The vans were sold in sets or loose from the boxes by the retailer. The later vans suffer particularly from fatigue.

A very small number of genuine factory made promotional vans were made for outside companies. These are listed as 28*1 to 28*4 in the tables.

In recent years there have been replacement decals of varying quality made, as well as replicas of these vehicles. The main give-away for the decals is the existence of a carrier film on the new decals which is barely noticeable on the originals.

The 31 Holland Coachcraft Van is on its own. The prototype was built on a Commer chassis and was used as a laundry van. The die was modified after only a year into the 29b Streamlined Bus.

ATCO VAN

'Atco lawnmowers sales and service'. Type 2 Ref no: 28n Production Period: 1935-1939/40 Colour: Green Market Value: £500-£900/$750-$1250

ATCO VAN

'Atco lawnmowers sales and service'. Type 3 Ref no: 28n Production Period: 1939/40-1941 Colour: Green Market Value: £500-£900/$750-$1250

BENTALLS VAN

'Bentalls Kingston-on-Thames. Phone KIN1001'. Type 2 Ref no: 28*1 Production Period: c.1937-c.1937 Colour: Green with cream roof & upper sides Market Value: A

BISTO VAN

'Ah! Bisto', then 'Bisto'. Type 2 Ref no: 280d Production Period: 1937-1939/40 Colour: Yellow Market Value: £500-£900/$750-$1250

BISTO VAN

'Bisto'. Type 3 Ref no: 280d Production Period: 1939/40-1940 Colour: Yellow Market Value: £500-£900/$750-$1250

CRAWFORD'S BISCUITS VAN

'Crawfords Biscuits', types 2 & 3 numbered 28p. Type 1 Ref no: 28l Production Period: 1934-1935 Colour: Red Market Value: £500-£900/$750-$1250

CRAWFORD'S BISCUITS VAN

'Crawford's Biscuits', type 1 was 28l. Type 2 Ref no: 28p Production Period: 1935-1939/40 Colour: Red Market Value: £500-£900/$750-$1250

CRAWFORD'S BISCUITS VAN

'Crawford's biscuits'. Type 3 Ref no: 28p Production Period: 1939/40-1941 Colour: Red Market Value: £500-£900/$750-$1250

DE BIJENKORF AMSTERDAM VAN

'De Bijenkorf Amsterdam, den Haag, Rotterdam'. Type 2 Ref no: 28*4 Production Period: c.1937-c.1937 Colour: Chocolate brown Market Value: A

DELIVERY VAN

Type 1 Ref no: 22d Production Period: 1933-1935 Colour: See 'CARS'

DELIVERY VAN (POSTWAR)

Ref no: 28 Reno: to 280

DUNLOP VAN

'Dunlop tyres'. Type 2 Ref no: 28h Production Period: 1935-1939/40 Colour: Red Market Value: £500-£900/$750-$1250

DUNLOP VAN

'Dunlop tyres'. Type 3 Ref no: 28h Production Period: 1939/40-1941 Colour: Red Market Value: £500-£900/$750-$1250

EKCO VAN

'Ekco radio'. Type 2 Ref no: 280e Production Period: 1937-1939 Colour: Green Market Value: £500-£900/$750-$1250

ENSIGN CAMERAS VAN

'Ensign Lukos Films' on right side, 'Ensign Cameras' on left. Type 1 Ref no: 28e Production Period: 1934-1935 Colour: Orange Market Value: £500-£900/$750-$1250

EXIDE AND DRYDEX VAN

'Exide Batteries' on right side, 'Drydex Batteries' on left. Type 2 *Ref no:* 28y *Production Period:* 1936-1939/40 *Colour:* Red *Market Value:* £500-£900/$750-$1250

EXIDE AND DRYDEX VAN

Exide Batteries' on right side, 'Drydex Batteries' on left. Type 3 *Ref no:* 28y *Production Period:* 1939/40-1941 *Colour:* Red *Market Value:* £500-£900/$750-$1250

FENWICKS VAN

'Fenwicks Newcastle-on-Tyne 2 Bond St.W'. Type 2 *Ref no:* 28*2 *Production Period:* c.1937-c.1937 *Colour:* Green with cream roof *Market Value:* A

FIRESTONE TYRES VAN

'Firestone tyres'. Type 1 *Ref no:* 28e *Production Period:* 1935-1935 *Colour:* White *Market Value:* £500-£900/$750-$1250

FIRESTONE TYRES VAN

'Firestone tyres'. Type 2 *Ref no:* 28e *Production Period:* 1935-1939/40 *Colour:* White, later blue *Market Value:* £500-£900/$750-$1250

FIRESTONE TYRES VAN

'Firestone tyres'. Type 2 *Ref no:* 28e *Production Period:* 1939/40-1941 *Colour:* Blue *Market Value:* £500-£900/$750-$1250

FRY'S VAN

'Fry's chocolate'. Type 2 *Ref no:* 28s *Production Period:* 1936-1939/40 *Colour:* Dark brown *Market Value:* £500-£900/$750-$1250

FRY'S VAN

'Fry's chocolate'. Type 2 *Ref no:* 28s *Production Period:* 1939/40-1941 *Colour:* Dark brown *Market Value:* £500-£900/$750-$1250

GOLDEN SHRED VAN

Silver Shred Marmalade' on right, 'Golden Shred Marmalade' on left side. Type 2 *Ref no:* 28a *Production Period:* 1936-1939/40 *Colour:* Cream *Market Value:* £500-£900/$750-$1250

GOLDEN SHRED VAN

Silver Shred Marmalade' on right, 'Golden Shred Marmalade' on left side. Type 3 *Ref no:* 28a *Production Period:* 1939/40-1941 *Colour:* Cream *Market Value:* £500-£900/$750-$1250

HARTLEY'S VAN

'Hartley's is Real Jam'. Type 3 *Ref no:* 280b *Production Period:* 1939-1939/40 *Colour:* Cream *Market Value:* £500-£900/$750-$1250

HARTLEY'S VAN

'Hartley's is Real Jam'. Type 3 *Ref no:* 280b *Production Period:* 1939/40-1940 *Colour:* Cream *Market Value:* £500-£900/$750-$1250

HOLLAND COACHCRAFT VAN

'Holland Coachcraft', die then modified to 29b Streamlined Motor Bus *Ref no:* 31 *Production Period:* 1935-1936 *Colour:* Red, green, dark blue, cream or orange with contrasting line *Market Value:* £380-£500/$550-$750

HORNBY TRAINS VAN

'Hornby Trains, British & Guaranteed'. Type 1 *Ref no:* 28a *Production Period:* 1934-1935 *Colour:* Yellow, some orange *Market Value:* £500-£900/$750-$1250

HORNBY TRAINS VAN

'Hornby Trains, British & Guaranteed'. Type 2 *Ref no:* 28a *Production Period:* 1935-1936 *Colour:* Yellow *Market Value:* £500-£900/$750-$1250

HOVIS VAN

'Hovis for tea'. Type 2 *Ref no:* 28x *Production Period:* 1936-1939/40 *Colour:* White *Market Value:* £500-£900/$750-$1250

HOVIS VAN

Type 3 *Ref no:* 28x *Production Period:* 1939/40-1941 *Colour:* White *Market Value:* £500-£900/$750-$1250

KODAK CAMERAS VAN

'Use kodak film to be sure'. Type 1 *Ref no:* 28g *Production Period:* 1934-1935 *Colour:* Yellow *Market Value:* £500-£900/$750-$1250

KODAK CAMERAS VAN

'Use kodak film to be sure'. Type 2 *Ref no:* 28g *Production Period:* 1935-1939/40 *Colour:* Yellow *Market Value:* £500-£900/$750-$1250

KODAK CAMERAS VAN

'Use kodak film to be sure'. Type 3 *Ref no:* 28g *Production Period:* 1939/40-1941 *Colour:* Yellow *Market Value:* £500-£900/$750-$1250

LYONS' VAN

'Lyons' tea always the best'. Type 2 *Ref no:* 280b *Production Period:* 1937-1939 *Colour:* Dark blue *Market Value:* £500-£900/$750-$1250

MACKINTOSH'S VAN

'Mackintosh's toffee'. Type 2 *Ref no:* 280f *Production Period:* 1937-1939/4 *Colour:* Red *Market Value:* £500-£900/$750-$1250

MACKINTOSH'S VAN

'Mackintosh's toffee'. Type 3 *Ref no:* 280f *Production Period:* 1939/40-1940 *Colour:* Red *Market Value:* £500-£900/$750-$1250

MAISON DE BONNETERIE VAN

'Maison de Bonneterie Leverancier van H.M. de Koningin'. Type 2 *Ref no:* 28*3 *Production Period:* c.1937-c.1937 *Colour:* Red *Market Value:* A

MANCHESTER GUARDIAN VAN

'Manchester guardian'. Type 1 *Ref no:* 28c *Production Period:* 1934-1935 *Colour:* Black with red back *Market Value:* £500-£900/$750-$1250

MANCHESTER GUARDIAN VAN

'Manchester guardian'. Type 2 *Ref no:* 28c *Production Period:* 1935-1939/40 *Colour:* Red *Market Value:* £500-£900/$750-$1250

MANCHESTER GUARDIAN VAN

'Manchester guardian'. Type 3 *Ref no:* 28c *Production Period:* 1939/40-1941 *Colour:* Red *Market Value:* £500-£900/$750-$1250

MARSH AND BAXTER'S SAUSAGES VAN
'Marsh's sausages'. Type 1 *Ref no: 28k Production Period:* 1934-1935 *Colour:* Green *Market Value:* £500-£900/$750-$1250

MARSH AND BAXTER'S SAUSAGES VAN
'Marsh's sausages'. Type 2 *Ref no: 28k Production Period:* 1935-1939/40 *Colour:* Green *Market Value:* £500-£900/$750-$1250

MARSH AND BAXTER'S SAUSAGES VAN
'Marsh's sausages'. Type 3 *Ref no: 28k Production Period:* 1939/40-1941 *Colour:* Green *Market Value:* £500-£900/$750-$1250

MECCANO VAN
'Meccano Engineering for Boys', originally no. 22d. Type 1 *Ref no: 28n Production Period:* 1934-1935 *Colour:* Yellow *Market Value:* £500-£900/$750-$1250

MECCANO VAN
'Meccano Engineering for Boys', originally no. 22d. Type 2 *Ref no: 28n Production Period:* 1935-1935 *Colour:* Yellow *Market Value:* £500-£900/$750-$1250

OSRAM VAN
'Osram lamps a g.e.c. product'. Type 2 *Ref no: 28w Production Period:* 1936-1939/40 *Colour:* Yellow *Market Value:* £500-£900/$750-$1250

OSRAM VAN
'Osram lamps a g.e.c. product'. Type 3 *Ref no: 28w Production Period:* 1939/40-1941 *Colour:* Yellow *Market Value:* £500-£900/$750-$1250

OVALTINE VAN
'Drink Ovaltine for Health'. Type 2 *Ref no: 28t Production Period:* 1936-1939/40 *Colour:* Red *Market Value:* £500-£900/$750-$1250

OVALTINE VAN
'Drink Ovaltine for Health'. Type 3 *Ref no: 28t Production Period:* 1939/40-1941 *Colour:* Red, *Market Value:* £500-£900/$750-$1250

OXO VAN
'Oxo Beef At Its Best' on right side, 'Oxo Beef In Brief' on left. Type 1 *Ref no: 28d Production Period:* 1934-1935 *Colour:* Blue *Market Value:* £500-£900/$750-$1250

OXO VAN
'Oxo Beef At Its Best' on right side, 'Oxo Beef In Brief' on left. Type 2 *Ref no: 28d Production Period:* 1935-1939/40 *Colour:* Blue *Market Value:* £500-£900/$750-$1250

OXO VAN
'Oxo Beef At Its Best' on right side, 'Oxo Beef In Brief' on left. Type 3 *Ref no: 28d Production Period:* 1949/40-1941 *Colour:* Blue *Market Value:* £500-£900/$750-$1250

PALETHORPE'S SAUSAGES VAN
'Palethorpe's royal cambridge'. Type 1 *Ref no: 28f Production Period:* 1934-1935 *Colour:* Grey *Market Value:* £500-£900/$750-$1250

PALETHORPE'S SAUSAGES VAN
'Palethorpe's royal cambridge'. Type 1 *Ref no: 28f Production Period:* 1935-1938 *Colour:* Grey *Market Value:* £500-£900/$750-$1250

PICKFORDS REMOVAL VAN
'Pickfords Removal & Storage Over 100 branches'. Type 1 *Ref no: 28b Production Period:* 1934-1935 *Colour:* Dark blue *Market Value:* £500-£900/$750-$1250

PICKFORDS REMOVAL VAN
'Pickfords Removal & Storage Over 100 branches'. Type 2 *Ref no: 28b Production Period:* 1935-1935 *Colour:* Dark blue *Market Value:* £500-£900/$750-$1250

SECCOTINE VAN
'Seccotine sticks everything'. Type 2 *Ref no: 28b Production Period:* 1935-1939/40 *Colour:* Light blue *Market Value:* £500-£900/$750-$1250

SECCOTINE VAN
'Seccotine sticks everything'. Type 3 *Ref no: 28b Production Period:* 1939/40-1941 *Colour:* Light blue *Market Value:* £500-£900/$750-$1250

SHARP'S TOFFEE VAN
'Sharp's toffee maidstone'. Type 1 *Ref no: 28h Production Period:* 1934-1935 *Colour:* Black cab, red back *Market Value:* £500-£900/$750-$1250

SHARP'S TOFFEE VAN
'Sharp's toffee maidstone'. Type 2 *Ref no: 28h Production Period:* 1935-1935 *Colour:* Red *Market Value:* £500-£900/$750-$1250

SHREDDED WHEAT VAN
'Shredded wheat welwyn garden city herts'. Type 2 *Ref no: 280c Production Period:* 1937-1939/40 *Colour:* Cream *Market Value:* £500-£900/$750-$1250

SHREDDED WHEAT VAN
'Shredded wheat welwyn garden city herts'. Type 3 *Ref no: 280c Production Period:* 1939/40-1940 *Colour:* Cream *Market Value:* £500-£900/$750-$1250

SWAN'S PENS VAN
'Swans pens'. Type 2 *Ref no: 28r Production Period:* 1936-1939/40 *Colour:* Black *Market Value:* £500-£900/$750-$1250

SWAN'S PENS VAN
'Swans pens'. Type 2 *Ref no: 28r Production Period:* 1939/40-1941 *Colour:* Black *Market Value:* £500-£900/$750-$1250

VIROL VAN
'Give your child a Virol constitution'. Type 2 *Ref no: 28f Production Period:* 1938-1939/40 *Colour:* Yellow *Market Value:* £500-£900/$750-$1250

VIROL VAN
'Give your child a Virol constitution'. Type 3 *Ref no: 28f Production Period:* 1934/40-1941 *Colour:* Yellow *Market Value:* £500-£900/$750-$1250

VIYELLA VAN
'Vyella For the Nursery'. Type 2 *Ref no: 280a Production Period:* 1937-1939/40 *Colour:* Light blue *Market Value:* £500-£900/$750-$1250

VIYELLA VAN
'Vyella For the Nursery'. Type 3 *Ref no: 280a Production Period:* 1939/40-1940 *Colour:* Light blue *Market Value:* £500-£900/$750-$1250

WAKEFIELD'S OIL VAN
'Wakefield castrol motor oil'. Type 1 *Ref no:* 28m *Production Period:* 1934-1935 *Colour:* Green *Market Value:* £500-£900/$750-$1250

WAKEFIELD'S OIL VAN
'Wakefield castrol motor oil'. Type 2 *Ref no:* 28m *Production Period:* 1935-1939/40 *Colour:* Green *Market Value:* £500-£900/$750-$1250

WAKEFIELD'S OIL VAN
'Wakefield castrol motor oil'. Type 2 *Ref no:* 28m *Production Period:* 1939/40-1941 *Colour:* Green *Market Value:* £500-£900/$750-$1250

YORKSHIRE EVENING POST VAN
'Yorkshire evening post the original buff'. Type 2 *Ref no:* 280e *Production Period:* 1939-1939/40 *Colour:* Cream *Market Value:* £500-£900/$750-$1250

YORKSHIRE EVENING POST VAN
'Yorkshire evening post the original buff'. Type 3 *Ref no:* 280e *Production Period:* 1939/40-1940 *Colour:* Cream *Market Value:* £500-£900/$750-$1250

Post-War Vans

The type 3 van reappeared after the war but without decals as no.280. It also appeared as 34b with a loudspeaker on the roof.

The first post-war design vans was the series of Trojans, 31a and following. The paint finish and decals on these were excellent and they are very much desired now. Austin A40 and Bedford CA vans followed, but the major event in the Dinky van world was the Guy vans. These were built on the same chassis as the Guy lorries (see TRUCKS) but with a diecast van body with opening rear doors. A total of 6 different liveries was produced on the early chassis with one on the later Guy Warrior chassis. These are very expensive now but they are absolutely beautiful.

Some later Ford Transit and Bedford CF vans completed the story. The Bedfords in particular had a tremendous number of variations in livery. The only ones listed here are those known to have been on general sale in toy shops and those made by Dinky for the companies whose livery appears on the van sides. Many others were done for clubs and individuals that had no connection with the name on the side of the model. These latter should be treated as interesting, but not as full factory production.

AUSTIN VAN
'Shell - BP' *Ref no:* 470 *Production Period:* 1954-1959 *Colour:* Green cab, red back *Market Value:* £100-£130/$150-$200

AUSTIN VAN
'Nestlés' *Ref no:* 471 *Production Period:* 1955-1960 *Colour:* Red *Market Value:* £100-£130/$150-$200

AUSTIN VAN
'Raleigh Cycles' *Ref no:* 472 *Production Period:* 1957-1961 *Colour:* Green *Market Value:* £120-£150/$160-$225

BEDFORD PALLET-JEKTA VAN
'Dinky Toys' *Ref no:* 930 *Production Period:* 1959-1964 *Colour:* Orange & cream *Market Value:* £140-£180/$210-$270

BEDFORD TK BOX VAN
'Castrol' *Ref no:* 450 *Production Period:* 1965-1969 *Colour:* Green with white panels *Market Value:* £120-£160/$180-$240

BEDFORD VAN
Simpsons. Sold by Simpsons (Canada) *Ref no:* 410* *Production Period:* 1972-1972 *Colour:* Red with black upper *Market Value:* £70-£90/$100-$135

BEDFORD VAN
John Menzies. Available only at branches of this store *Ref no:* 410* *Production Period:* 1974-1975 *Colour:* Dark blue *Market Value:* £30-£40/$45-$60

BEDFORD VAN
Belaco. Used as a promotion to customers of Belaco *Ref no:* 410* *Production Period:* 1974-1974 *Colour:* Bronze with black roof *Market Value:* £80-£100/$120-$150

BEDFORD VAN
Danish Post. Danish market only *Ref no:* 410* *Production Period:* 1974-1976 *Colour:* Yellow, circular Danish Post sign decals *Market Value:* £70-£85/$100-$120

BEDFORD VAN
Marley Tiles. Sold at branches of Marley *Ref no:* 410* *Production Period:* 1975-1975 *Colour:* Red, 'Marley Building Supplies' *Market Value:* £40-£50/$60-$75

BEDFORD VAN
MJ Hire. On general sale at instigation of MJ Hire, not in the catalogues *Ref no:* 410* *Production Period:* 1975-1976 *Colour:* White, 'MJ Hire + Service' *Market Value:* £35-£45/$50-$70

BEDFORD VAN
Modellers' World. Code 2: 200 only, sold to readers of Modellers' World magazine *Ref no:* 410* *Production Period:* 1976-1976 *Colour:* White,'Modellers' World' decals *Market Value:* £20-£30/$30-$45

BEDFORD VAN
'Kodak' *Ref no:* 480 *Production Period:* 1954-1956 *Colour:* Yellow *Market Value:* £100-£130/$150-$200

BEDFORD VAN
'Ovaltine' *Ref no:* 481 *Production Period:* 1955-1960 *Colour:* Blue *Market Value:* £100-£130/$150-$200

BEDFORD VAN
'Dinky Toys' *Ref no:* 482 *Production Period:* 1956-1960 *Colour:* Cream & orange *Market Value:* £100-£120/$150-$180

BIG BEDFORD VAN
'Heinz' baked bean can *Ref no:* 923 *Production Period:* 1955-1958 *Colour:* Red chassis/cab, yellow back *Market Value:* £250-£350/$375-$525

BIG BEDFORD VAN
'Heinz' ketchup bottle *Ref no:* 923 *Production Period:* 1958-1959 *Colour:* Red chassis/cab, yellow back *Market Value:* £900-£1200/$1350-$1800

CUSTOMISED TRANSIT VAN
Not available until after factory closure *Ref no:* 390 *Production Period:* 1979-1979 *Colour:* Blue *Market Value:* £25-£35/$35-$45

DELIVERY VAN
Casting of 28 type 3 but rear windows filled in *Ref no:* 280 *Reno:* of 28 *Production Period:* 1945-1951 *Colour:* Red or blue *Market Value:* £50-£75/$75-$110

ELECTION MINI VAN
Casting of 273 Mini Van with plastic frame & speakers on rear, figure & microphone *Ref no:* 492 *Production Period:* 1964-1964 *Colour:* White *Market Value:* £200-£250/$300-$375

FORD TRANSIT
'Kenwood' *Ref no:* 407 *Production Period:* 1966-1969 *Colour:* Blue with white roof *Market Value:* £100-£140/$150-$200

FORD TRANSIT
'Hertz' *Ref no:* 407 *Production Period:* 1970-1974 *Colour:* Yellow *Market Value:* £70-£90/$100-$135

FORD TRANSIT VAN
Colour TV. In 1970 catalogue but not issued *Ref no:* 407

FORD TRANSIT VAN
'Motorway services' *Ref no:* 416 *Production Period:* 1975-1978 *Colour:* Yellow *Market Value:* £35-£45/$50-$70

FORD TRANSIT VAN
Made for Ford (England) 1,000,000 Transits *Ref no:* 416* *Production Period:* 1976-1976 *Colour:* Yellow, stickers *Market Value:* £110-£150/$165-$230

FORD TRANSIT VAN
'Motorway services' *Ref no:* 417 *Production Period:* 1978-1979 *Colour:* Yellow *Market Value:* £35-£45/$50-$70

GUY VAN
'Slumberland' *Ref no:* 514 *Production Period:* 1949-1951 *Colour:* Red *Market Value:* £250-£350/$375-$525

GUY VAN
'Lyons Swiss Rolls' *Ref no:* 514 *Production Period:* 1951-1952 *Colour:* Dark blue *Market Value:* £750-£1000/$1100-$1500

GUY VAN
'Weetabix' *Ref no:* 514 *Production Period:* 1952-1953 *Colour:* Yellow *Market Value:* £1200-£1600/$1800-$2400

GUY VAN
'Spratts' *Ref no:* 514 *Reno:* to 917 *Production Period:* 1953-1955 *Colour:* Red & cream *Market Value:* £300-£450/$450-$675

GUY VAN
'Spratts' *Ref no:* 917 *Reno:* of 514

GUY VAN
'Ever-Ready Batteries' *Ref no:* 918 *Production Period:* 1955-1958 *Colour:* Blue *Market Value:* £190-£250/$290-$375

GUY VAN
'Golden Shred' *Ref no:* 919 *Production Period:* 1957-1958 *Colour:* Red *Market Value:* £500-£750/$800-$1100

GUY WARRIOR VAN
"Heinz' ketchup bottle *Ref no:* 920 *Production Period:* 1960-1960 *Colour:* Red chassis/cab, yellow body *Market Value:* £1200-£1500/$1800-$2200

LOUD-SPEAKER VAN
Casting of 280 (no base) with closed back window *Ref no:* 34c *Reno:* to 492 *Production Period:* 1948-1957 *Colour:* Blue or green with silver *Market Value:* £50-£80/$75-$120

LOUD-SPEAKER VAN
Casting of 280 (no base) with closed back window *Ref no:* 34c *Reno:* to 492 *Production Period:* 1948-1957 *Colour:* Fawn or brown with silver *Market Value:* £70-£100/$100-$150

LOUDSPEAKER VAN
Ref no: 492 *Reno:* of 34c

MORRIS VAN
'Capstan', casting of 260 *Ref no:* 465 *Production Period:* 1957-1959 *Colour:* Light blue with dark blue lower panel *Market Value:* £200-£250/$300-$380

TROJAN 15CWT
'Chivers jellies' *Ref no:* 31c *Reno:* to 452 *Production Period:* 1953-1957 *Colour:* Green *Market Value:* £110-£150/$165-$225

TROJAN 15CWT VAN
'Esso' *Ref no:* 31a *Reno:* to 450 *Production Period:* 1951-1957 *Colour:* Red *Market Value:* £110-£150/$165-$225

TROJAN 15CWT VAN
'Dunlop'. Dunlop the World's Master Tyre' *Ref no:* 31b *Reno:* to 451 *Production Period:* 1952-1957 *Colour:* Red *Market Value:* £110-£150/$165-$225

TROJAN 15CWT VAN
'Oxo' *Ref no:* 31d *Reno:* to 453 *Production Period:* 1953-1954 *Colour:* Blue *Market Value:* £220-£300/$300-$450

TROJAN VAN
'Esso' *Ref no:* 450 *Reno:* of 31a

TROJAN VAN
'Dunlop' *Ref no:* 451 *Reno:* of 31b

TROJAN VAN
'Chivers' *Ref no:* 452 *Reno:* of 31c

TROJAN VAN
'Oxo' *Ref no:* 453 *Reno:* of 31d

TROJAN VAN
'Cydrax' *Ref no:* 454 *Production Period:* 1957-1959 *Colour:* Light green *Market Value:* £110-£150/$165-$230

TROJAN VAN
'Brooke Bond Tea' *Ref no:* 455 *Production Period:* 1957-1960 *Colour:* Red *Market Value:* £110-£150/$165-$230

Van Sets

DELIVERY VANS
Contents :28a, 28b, 28c, 28d, 28e (Ensign or Firestone), 28f Ref no: 28/1 Reno: type 1 Production Period: 1934-1935 Market Value: A

DELIVERY VANS
Contents : 28a, 28b, 28c, 28e, 28f, 28n Ref no: 28/1 Reno: type 2 Production Period: 1935-1939/40 Market Value: A

DELIVERY VANS
Contents : 28a, 28b, 28c, 28e, 28f, 28n Ref no: 28/1 Reno: type 3 Production Period: 1939/40-1941 Market Value: A

DELIVERY VANS
Contents : 28g, 28h, 28k, 28l, 28m, 28n Ref no: 28/2 Reno: type 1 Production Period: 1934-1935 Market Value: A

DELIVERY VANS
Contents : 28d, 28g, 28h, 28k, 28m, 28n Ref no: 28/2 Reno: type 2 Production Period: 1935-1939/40 Market Value: A

DELIVERY VANS
Contents : 28d, 28g, 28h, 28k, 28m, 28p Ref no: 28/2 Reno: type 3 Production Period: 1940-1941 Market Value: A

DELIVERY VANS
Contents : 28r, 28s, 28t, 28w, 28x, 28y Ref no: 28/3 Reno: type 2 Production Period: 1936-1939/40 Market Value: A

DELIVERY VANS
Contents : 28r, 28s, 28t, 28w, 28x, 28y Ref no: 28/3 Reno: type 3 Production Period: 1939/40-1941 Market Value: A

DELIVERY VANS
Contents : 280a, 280b, 280c, 280d, 280e, 280f Ref no: 280 Reno: type 2 Production Period: 1937-1939/40 Market Value: A

DELIVERY VANS
Contents : 280a, 280b, 280c, 280d, 280e, 280f Ref no: 280 Reno: type 3 Production Period: 1939/40-1940 Market Value: A

1/25 Scale Cars

A trio of Ford Capris in the large scale of 1/25 was an attempt to extend the range. It was not well received and they were deleted after only a couple of years so not many were sold. Now people seem to want them!

FORD CAPRI
Ref no: 2162 *Production Period:* 1973-1976 *Colour:* Metallic blue & black *Market Value:* £70-£90/$100-$130

FORD CAPRI POLICE CAR
Ref no: 2253 *Production Period:* 1974-1976 *Colour:* White *Market Value:* £90-£110/$130-$160

FORD CAPRI RALLY CAR
Ref no: 2214 *Production Period:* 1974-1976 *Colour:* Red & black *Market Value:* £90-£110/$130-$160